Business History in Spain (19th and 20th centuries)

Mercedes Fernández-Paradas / Carlos Larrinaga (eds.)

Business History in Spain (19th and 20th centuries)

PETER LANG

Bibliographic Information published by the Deutsche Nationalbibliothek
The Deutsche Nationalbibliothek lists this publication in the Deutsche Nationalbibliografie; detailed bibliographic data is available online at http://dnb.d-nb.de.

Library of Congress Cataloging-in-Publication Data
A CIP catalog record for this book has been applied for at the Library of Congress.

This publication was printed with the support of The Ministry of Science, Innovation and Universities of the Spanish Government and ERDF funds and Company History Study Group SEJ-271 of Junta de Andalucía (Spain).

GOBIERNO DE ESPAÑA MINISTERIO DE CIENCIA, INNOVACIÓN Y UNIVERSIDADES

UNIÓN EUROPEA
Fondo Europeo de Desarrollo Regional

Junta de Andalucía

Cover illustration: © 25236 Paco Marín/kutxateka.eus

ISBN 978-3-631-84385-7 (Print)
E-ISBN 978-3-631-84617-9 (E-PDF)
E-ISBN 978-3-631-84618-6 (EPUB)
E-ISBN 978-3-631-84619-3 (MOBI)
DOI 10.3726/b17988

Peter Lang – Berlin · Bern · Bruxelles · New York · Oxford · Warszawa · Wien

This publication has been peer reviewed.

www.peterlang.com

Foreword

The businessman has become a relevant factor to explain the process of economic growth and development. The research on entrepreneurship has multiplied at university. This term includes a triple meaning: the figure of the entrepreneur, the business function and the creation of companies. This multipurpose needs to be supported by a consistent theory about the company and the entrepreneur. And that is why the Business History, within the area of History and Economic Institutions, has gained more importance in Spanish historiography. From such research the consideration of the employer as an economic agent and the company as the core of productive activities is necessarily assumed. Indeed, the study of the life of a company can help us to understand how these entrepreneurs got around difficulties or took advantage of them. In short, how they adapted to changing circumstances.

In Spain, in recent years, the Business History has had a great impact in the academic field. In fact, since the beginning of the nineties, scientific meetings and publications on companies and entrepreneurs have multiplied at least at the research level. To the point that we can say that today the Business History enjoys great vitality among Spanish economic historians. Therefore, despite the fact that the studies of Business History have been late, if we compare them with the United States or the United Kingdom. Today we find a whole heap of works on the issue. All this in spite of the difficulties that the historian must face, above all, due to the companies' own doubts about showing their documentation. The difficulties in finding primary sources in several places. Despite this, we insist, there are many investigations that have been carried out for almost three decades, thus making up for the initial lack that existed in this field.

This book is a good proof of what we are saying. As it is not a History of the Companies in Spain, but the study of entrepreneurship in Spain in the 19th and 20th centuries through various examples. We have not even attempted to address all sectors, but only some. In order to analyze certain well-studied business experiences. With which we can examine business decision making in different sectors, geographical areas and times. In many cases we would be talking about case studies. That had an important search, study and research for several years. Therefore, had been subjected to strict investigative, far from amateur or complacent views, as has been so many times in this field. In general, the cases we have selected describe a broad panorama and are the result of research carried out by their authors. The companies, entrepreneurs and sectors that we present here, without any desire to be exhaustive, reveal the variety of initiatives and the multiple activities present in Spain during these two centuries.

Starting from this concept and this methodology, the book is divided into two well differentiated and intentionally asymmetric parts. A first, much shorter one, in which it has been chosen to present more general aspects that have to do with the topics discussed here. Specifically, companies, entrepreneurs or entrepreneurship, for example. And a second, more extensive, where different case studies referring to different economic sectors are presented. Some very representative of the economy of Spain in the Contemporary Age. For example, public companies of services in the cities and towns, banking and insurance, transport, the wine industry, and tourism. Obviously, there would be many other sectors to be analyzed, but, as we have explained, the objective is not to study all sectors. Only certain companies and entrepreneurs and focus on a few case studies that provide learning tools for university students and professionals for the decision making in the business world. With this hope, a group of professors from different Spanish universities present our research in a book, subjected to a double blind evaluation, that we hope will be useful to colleagues, students and professionals.

Mercedes Fernández-Paradas & Carlos Larrinaga

Contents

Gregorio Núñez Romero-Balmas

1 The second level of Spanish capitalism during the Restoration period: The Escoriaza group, a family-owned conglomerate in the world of public works

Abstract The different businesses within the railway sector are closely interwoven. Three of these businesses are especially important: the actual construction of the works, the supply of material and project restructuring. One particular family of entrepreneurs, the "Escoriazas", operated efficiently in all three of these segments. Through a conglomerate of family-run companies, for decades the group was engaged in the complex and fluid world of the periphery of the large railway businesses. To do this, the "Escoriazas" drew from a broad network of national and international financial contacts and formed a large group of companies and contractors, becoming masters in the constitution, management and dissolution of these companies. The historiography reveals it to be a highly interesting differentiated segment. On the one hand were the large railway companies; and on the other, the small construction contractors which are almost opaque for historians. This business conglomerate of the Escoriaza family is fairly transparent and can be used to explain how these businesses operated.

1 Introduction

Many decades ago, back in the nineteenth century, the business world in Spain was polarised between a small number of large, monopolistic companies, many of which are well-known, and a wide variety of small or very small companies that were highly competitive and accounted for the rest of the Spanish business fabric and are practically unknown to historians (González Ruiz & Núñez Romero-Balmas, 2016). In the past, and also today, one of the main problems of the Spanish economy has been precisely the poor articulation of the enterprise system and specifically the low growth capacity of small companies. A lack of medium-sized companies may also be observed. This phenomenon is relevant and very striking when compared with, for example, the case of Germany. This is the case not because medium-sized firms, on the whole family-run, are not feasible in Spain, but because institutional aspects or simply historical factors have made it this way and it is a situation that is very difficult to correct.

With respect to family-run companies in the historiography, there is an abundance of publications (Rose, 1995; Colli, 2003; Puig Raposo & Fernández Pérez, 2009; Lubinski et al., 2013) Recently, the consultancy firm KPGM and the Family Enterprise Institute in Spain published their fifth barometer regarding the situation of family-run companies, a category that is very similar to our object of study. The Barometer includes a survey of 288 companies or groups of companies of this type and highlights the following features: the great majority are managed by members of the same family (79 %) but not by the generation of the founders but by the second or third generation (75 %), even 8 % are managed by the fourth generation or younger; of course the immense majority of the capital (74 %) is owned by the family and very few (3 %) have needed and/or wanted to be listed on the stock exchange. Despite the alleged archaisms that are usually attributed to this category of firms – traditionalism, endogamy, a lack of professionalism in management, difficulties to grow when not listed, etc. – the above-mentioned features have not impeded these companies from employing between fifty and a thousand workers (63 %), reaching annual turnovers of between ten and two hundred million euros or having a noteworthy organisational stability, most having operated for more than twenty years (93 %, of which 53 % have been operating for fifty years) (Instituto de la Empresa Familiar and KPGM 2016). It is clear, therefore, that the organisational peculiarities of these second level companies do not limit the growth or diversification of their activities. Rather, they take advantage of specific opportunities that favour the flexibility, stability and long-term planning of these types of firms and the entrepreneurs who founded them. Modern studies in the field of business economics refer to medium-sized family-run companies and the historiography has also addressed the topic with a select but not exhaustive bibliography (Colli, Fernández Perez & Rose, 2003; Fernández Perez & Puig, 2004; Fernández Pérez & Colli, 2013; Fernández Pérez, 2017). We could also study this family conglomerate with solid international contacts from the perspective of the free-standing companies (Wilkins & Schröter, 1998).

The afore-mentioned serves as an introduction to present a second-level family group operating in the large business world of the Restoration Period in Spain (1874–1931): the Escoriaza family, and more specifically its principal and most well-known member, Nicolás Escoriaza, Viscount of Escoriaza. The group was made up of a wide variety of companies, a flexible conglomerate of firms that successively appeared and disappeared, entering and leaving the family group. Some of them were limited companies, others even listed and others simply public works contractors. The group also incorporated other types of firms such as hotels, real estate companies, public works and rail management firms, among others. All of this was managed by three generations of men initially from the political and business worlds. The activities of the family started a little after the liberal Sexennial began in 1868 and lasted until the end of the Franco regime.

2 The "Escoriazas"; three generations of entrepreneurs between two industrial revolutions

The Escoriaza family and more specifically Nicolás Escoriaza y Fabro, have received much attention in the historiography (Fernández Clemente, 1977; Germán Zubero, 1980; Biescas Ferrer, 1985; Fernández Clemente, 1997; Cayón García & Muñoz Rubio, 1998; Mohedano Barceló, 1998; Núñez Romero-Balmas, 2008a, 2019). There is no exhaustive and definitive study on the business conglomerate or a biographical study of the viscount due to the inability to locate the family archive, which is believed to have been lost during the war or the immediate post-war period.

A brief description of its century-old history will reveal three generations of entrepreneurs who, although, displaying clear differences over the years, were also characterised by their decisive resolve to ensure the continuity of the family group. The figure at the very heart of the group was Nicolás, undoubtedly the member with the highest profile both socially and in the business world. He was also the central node of the financial contacts network in Spain and abroad which determined the group's competitive advantage.

The first generation of the "Escoriazas" was formed by José Pascasio and his brother Eurípides. The former was a progressive politician born in Puerto Rico. After studying in Zaragoza, Vergara, Madrid and Seville, he soon gained prominence as an anti-dynasty politician and as a journalist (*Enciclopedia Universal Ilustrada Espasa-Calpe*). He was the son of a military officer which is why the biography of his early years is characterised by intense mobility (Melgar, 2003). His Caribbean roots undoubtedly motivated him to join the anti-slavery movement at a young age as a representative for Puerto Rico in 1868. During the Sexennial, he held several high-ranking state government positions including the Director General of Public Works. He left politics after the Republic was proclaimed and emigrated to France where he brought up his children and where undoubtedly he was able to establish a network of political and business contacts who his children were subsequently able to draw from with very good results. During the first few years of the Restoration he laid the foundations of the future business group, starting out in the complicated but lucrative business of acquiring and reconverting railway companies that were experiencing difficulties.

The second generation members of the family to lead the group were the sons of José Pascasio, particularly Nicolás, Manuel and Virgilio. Together with their father, they ensured the consolidation, growth and diversification of the family group, driven by both the state policy of secondary railways and the wave of electrification of the trams in Spanish cities. In the diversification process, the constitution of the company Cardé and Escoriaza (1897) in Zaragoza for the construction of rolling stock for railways and tramways represents a fundamental milestone, which, together with Nicolás' social networks, formed one of the principal bases of the group's competitive advantage. This company, which soon dominated the activity of installing electric motors in a good part of the Spanish tramway networks, survived for many decades. It even sought to diversify its activities (for example, the manufacture of material for the army, including the assembly of aeroplanes) during the 1920s, operating under the name of Material Móvil y Construcciones (1920). In this way, from the end of the nineteenth century and until the Spanish civil war, the family group formed a conglomerate made up of two branches. One was engaged in the construction and installation of rolling stock for railways and tramways with its head office in Zaragoza and directed by Manuel. The other was formed by a complex and changing group of railway or tramway companies, some engaged in developing construction projects that had failed or were in serious difficulty and others in carrying out long-term management projects. This side of the business was directed by Nicolás. He changed his address several times to Granada, Madrid and San Sebastián and seemed willing to undertake any initiative that he deemed feasible, from directing the Spanish section of the International Exposition of Brussels (1910) (probably personally commissioned by King Alfonso XIII) to the construction of reservoirs and canals within the framework of the policy to increase the number of hydraulic constructions for energy and irrigation. Manuel however, settled definitively in Zaragoza. He also diversified but by intervening in several local businesses, from town planning to the construction of a hotel, including regional railway companies, the tramways of Zaragoza and local banks (Banco Aragonés de Crédito), even sitting on the local council of the Banco de España in which he was succeeded by his brother.

The third generation of "Escoriazas" was basically formed by the sons of Nicolás (the Escoriaza Averly) and those of Manuel (the Escoriaza Castillón). Given the preferences of the two brothers, the third generation seemed very biased with respect to the two main branches of the family group as they had been shaped by their fathers and had suffered a major setback with the civil war. The Escoriaza Castillón, firmly established in Zaragoza, became consolidated as managers of the rolling stock construction company and other local businesses that prospered after the war, including the tramways and bus networks of Zaragoza. The Escoriaza Averlys, however, established in Madrid and consolidated in the management of secondary railways and tramways (e.g. Ferrocarriles de Castilla, Tranvía de Cádiz a San Fernando y la Carraca) lost their father in 1936, who was murdered in San Sebastián, and suffered the vicissitudes of the sector. Specifically, the nationalisation of the main railway companies to construct RENFE and the decline of the small networks, together with the motorisation of road traffic forced the decline of the local railways for goods traffic.

The "Escoriazas" knew how to take advantage of operating in the periphery of Spanish and international capitalism and the same can be said of the regional distribution of their initiatives. Their group was based in Zaragoza, an important and dynamic city but not among the principal areas of national industry, which were basically those of Barcelona and its surrounding area, Madrid, Bilbao and Valencia. A wider group of secondary cities in this industrialisation process, such as Seville, Málaga, Granada, Valladolid and Santander constituted a second urban and business level among which Zaragoza was particularly prominent.

3 Zaragoza

Throughout his life, Nicolás Escoriaza changed his address several times. The first choice was Zaragoza in the 1880s. This was by no means a mistake, rather a very significant move. The reason why he settled there could be the early ties of the Escoriaza family with the MZA railway company and its first operations as works sub-contractors. These activities grew and diversified very quickly. Later, when the group was able to take direct control over the railway and tramway concessionaire companies, the benefits and opportunities of its location became evident, given the many pending railway initiatives in the region. It is worth mentioning the company Ferrocariles de Zaragoza al Mediterráneo as an example and the first known operation of the "Escoriazas" at this operational level of the group (Núñez Romero-Balmas, 2019). In this way, Zaragoza became consolidated as the centre of the Escoriaza conglomerate for the whole of its long history and was the only place where it diversified activities with an industrial branch (los Talleres Carde y Escoriaza, a metal and wood carpentry firm engaged in the construction of wagons for railways), in parallel and complementing the execution of public works and the management of railway and tramway companies.

The city enjoyed a central location and operated as the capital of a good part of the Ebro basin, from the Pyrenees to the Iberian mountain range, from Navarra to Tarragona, and it was practically in the centre of the triangle formed by the principal industrial cities of Spain. It therefore constituted the centre of the large railway system of which the main lines had just been completed by the Norte and MZA railway companies in north-east Spain. From then on, different initiatives seeking to complement them and give them greater density were implemented through a secondary railway network, with the support of the State.[1] Making the most of their central location, the "Escoriazas" intervened in different business initiatives in the region. The fact that Nicolás, over time, established his residence in Madrid and San Sebastián shows his connection with the highest level industrial and financial networks, which he could endorse with the industrial capacity of the family based in the Iberian capital city (Núñez Romero-Balmas, 2010). Furthermore, the closeness of France also helped these entrepreneurs to establish contacts with Bordeaux, Paris and Brussels. These contacts accounted for a good part of their competitive advantage. This was similar to what occurred with the Tudor company, which shared international and national networks with Escoriaza and also chose Zaragoza as the place to base its industrial activity (Biescas Ferrer & Germán Zubero, 1992; Moreno Fernández & Sancho Sora, 2013).

On the other hand, the economy of Zaragoza at the time was already complex and dynamic and highly promising for the long term.[2] The city had a diversified business fabric in which, for example, metallurgy was a major sector at a decisive moment in Spain's industrialisation process. But, most of all, the city and its region intensely benefited from the protectionist turn imposed in 1891 by the Cánovas Tariff, particularly due to its protection of mass agricultural products such as wheat and sugar and associated industries.[3] On the other hand, one of the principal centres of the civil and administrative movement

1 Some of them were very important and particularly complicated such as the railway from Zaragoza to France via Canfranc and the Ferrocarril Central de Aragón (Valencia to Calatayud and Zaragoza), the execution of which was delayed for decades. For the case in hand, the secondary railways plan is particularly significant (Ministerio de Fomento, 1907).

2 For a detailed and fairly optimistic description of the industrial future of the city at the end of the 1920s (see Consejo de Industria, 1930).

3 Later, the 1906 tariff reinforced protectionism and the secondary railways plan gave rise to many initiatives which the "Escoriazas" actively took advantage of in order to drive the growth of their company (Serrano Sanz, 1987; Sáez García, 2005).

in favour of a hydraulic policy based on the construction of large hydraulic works and the extension of irrigation to a large-scale format was also based in Zaragoza, reaching a unique milestone in the founding of the Confederación Sindical Hidrográfica del Ebro in 1926, the first of its kind. We could say that the city and its region constituted a paradigm of the opportunities to be had in Spain at the end of the nineteenth century, as it formed part of the interior, agricultural territory, basically oriented both in terms of agricultural production and the agrofood industry complementing this, to the domestic market, highly protected by the 1891 and 1906 tariffs. In addition to all of this we should also mention the great opportunity derived from the availability of waterfalls which had an energy potential that was actively developed through local initiatives (Germán Zubero, 1990).

The Aragonese business fabric was completed with the promotion of several banking and insurance initiatives, in several of which the Escoriaza brothers participated. All of this highlights the vigour and broad vision of the family group and the solvency of the local context.[4]

Therefore, it is not surprising that the Escoriaza group chose Zaragoza as the centre of its activities of at least three complementary branches. First, the aforementioned execution of public railway works. Second, metallurgy and the construction of rolling stock for railways and tramways for companies throughout the whole of Spain. This was probably the differential element of the group in which it became a pioneer in Spain. And, closely related to the construction of rolling stock was the promotion, in some cases, and the modernisation and electrification in many others, of urban tramway networks in Spanish cities, which were singularly important and long-lived, including the company Tranvias de Zaragoza.[5] The third and final branch of activities was the intervention in a variety of local initiatives from town planning to real estate promotion and the hotel trade. It was precisely the urban sector that provided a final opportunity to

4 With respect to the evolution of the economy and industry in Aragon and, more specifically, in Zaragoza, a highly interesting summary can be found in the series of publications by Germán Zubero (2001, 2007, 2009). This author and other collaborators have never stopped studying the "Escoriazas". Examples of a more recent publication are Germán Zubero, Pinilla and Sancho (2018) and Mohedano (1998).

5 They also played a significant role in secondary railway management companies of the Iberian region, such as the Haro to Ezcaray and the Gallur-Sábada, all branches of the main lines of MZA and Norte.

the third generation of the group when the railway works and the management of tram and secondary rail companies declined and terminated and the manufacture of rolling stock was incorporated into another industrial group (CAF). Zaragoza enabled the Escoriaza Group to enhance its dynamism as a large city immersed in a century-long vigorous growth and modernisation process. The local trams are, undoubtedly the best example but they also intervened in several investments related to local town planning, real estate promotion, the hotel trade and any other medium or large scale activity that required a great intensity of capital and specific management needs. After the civil war, when the other branches of activity of the group, the secondary railways and tramways in particular, were disposed of, stagnated and/or began their terminal decline, the Group concentrated on its activities in Zaragoza and was able to remain active precisely in this branch of activities, of a local but highly promising scale.

In this respect, the constitution of the company Cardé y Escoriaza in 1897 for the manufacture of rolling stock for railways and tramways represented a fundamental strategic turn. Thereafter, the "Escoriazas", with the support of the Bordeaux-based constructor Pablo Cardé, became the suppliers of rolling stock for the large Spanish railway companies and soon became a leading agent in the imminent boom in the electrification of the Spanish tramways. Belgian investors and the "Escoriazas" themselves played a highly prominent role in this strategy (Martínez-López, 1998). The contacts that the family had with the railway industrial circles and the French and Belgian electrotechnical companies (the Française Thomson-Houston electric company, in particular) played a decisive role for the future of the group. As well as the electrical tramways of a good part of Spain we should also add the promotion of regional rail initiatives within the framework of the strategic and secondary railway plans (Ministerio de Agricultura, Industria y Comercio de España, 1904).

4 Following national sugar? Granada, Castilla, ...

After his successful installation in Zaragoza and becoming a member of the small business elite able to intervene in his own name and in close cooperation with the major railway companies and leading groups involved in the electrification of the Spanish tramways, Nicolás Escoriaza set his sights on the city of Granada. There was a tramway project there that had been delayed for more than a decade and did not have the support of local promoters or the intervention of foreign investors. For this reason, Escoriaza moved to this city with the intention of undertaking the project, managing it directly and from the outset addressing the technical and financial difficulties involved in electrification.[6]

In many aspects, the economy of Granada at the time was similar to that of Zaragoza. As in the Aragonese case, the territory included important cities, Granada, of course, as well as Málaga and Almería and a large group of long-standing smaller towns. But, contrary to Aragon, we could describe this area as Andalusia's "far east" which had a peripheral and isolated location in the national territory and encountered serious transport problems which only the coastal towns could overcome thanks to sailing (Fernández Sánchez, González Ruiz & Núñez Romero-Balmas, 2019). All of this made it a failed candidate to becoming the regional capital, secondary to the more dynamic cities of the country. Like Zaragoza, Granada and its region formed part of mainly agricultural territories that intensely benefited from the nationalist involution from 1891.[7] Therefore, cereal farming and olive growing and consequently, the flour and olive oil industries, even wine production before the phylloxera crisis (Piqueras Haba, 2005; Molleví Bortoló & Serrano Giné, 2007), and other segments of the agrofood industry were profitably extended throughout the province and required significant investment in transport infrastructures in order to overcome the topographic limitations. We should also add the promising innovations of the second industrialisation, particularly the production of cane sugar (on the subtropical coast) and beetroot (on the plains of the interior of the region, across the whole of the Intrabetic Basin); an expansion which, for at least a decade, allowed Granada to be thought of as the national capital of the sugar industry. Activities derived from the sugar industry were also developed, such as the production of alcohols and other equally modern activities that were more or less related to the above-mentioned industries such as the production of fertilisers and cements, essential oils and a relatively broad range of industries that were small but covered a wide range of activities from the production of cured meats and cheeses to small-scale metallurgy activities (Jiménez Blanco, 1986; Malpica & Martín, 1992; González Ruiz & Núñez Romero-Balmas, 2007; Martínez Soto & Rosado Cubero, 2017; Germán Zubero, 2020).

---

6 The tramway project acquired by Escoriaza also included a waterfall close to the capital (Núñez Romero-Balmas, 1999, 2005; Piñar Samos & Giménez Yanguas, 2004; González Ruiz & Núñez Romero-Balmas, 2007).

7 For the Andalusian economy of the time: Díez de Castro (1995), Bernal and Parejo (2001) and Parejo Barranco (2011). And for Granada in particular: Piñar Samos (1984) and Titos Martínez (1998).

In this way, a new and promising export base was developed in the region whose market was not necessarily limited to the small domestic consumption. And, like Zaragoza and its surrounding area, there was a large number of waterfalls in Granada which could be exploited with low-complexity and low-cost plants, one of which was installed by Escoriaza and his local tramway company. As in the case of the sugar industry, Granada seemed to be destined to become a regionally significant hydroelectric centre with many local companies, but the scarce demand and lack of cooperation between the local capitalists frustrated this expectation in the life cycle of the first generation of electrical industrial installations (Núñez Romero-Balmas, 1994, 1998; Piñar Samos & Giménez Yanguas, 2019). With all of its advantages, the logic of protectionism, which constituted the institutional support of the expansion of the Spanish flour and sugar industries, imposed limitations. The production of sugar expanded to other regions (Zaragoza, Valladolid, Madrid, Navarra) and, with overly high prices and costs, the supply soon exceeded demand even though the per capita demand was growing vigorously. The constitution of a quasi sugar monopoly in 1903 (Sociedad General Azucarera) reorganised this industrial branch, but, although a group was formed of free sugar producing companies that were proliferating in the province of Granada, the sector suffered from a golden decline as a result of the high protection and the limited internal demand (Martínez Soto & Rosado Cubero, 2017).

We could consider the business conducted by the "Escoriazas" in Granada in the same way as the first phase of their operations in the tramways of Zaragoza. They adapted to the usual model of intervention of tramway and railway installing companies. They took on a project that was experiencing difficulties, resolved the pending problems using financial contacts even on a European scale, mediating between them, ensuring the execution of the project and, once concluded, transferred the management and capital to other interested groups. A considerable part of this capital had to remain in local hands, which was apparently well-equipped at that time financially speaking and in terms of complementary initiatives.

In the case of Granada the group transferred the control of Tranvías Eléctricos de Granada to the Tudor company – later than the Banco Hispano Suizo para las Empresas Eléctricas – making way for the Duke of San Pedro de Galatino[8] (representative of a group interested in the construction and management of

8 Galatino took on many initiatives in the region, including two hotels/casinos, a mountain tramway and a hydroelectric company as well as the management of his agricultural and industrial assets in the plains of Granada Vega de Granada (Corral López, 1980; Titos Martínez, 1999; Núñez Romero-Balmas, 2019).

casinos and recreational centres), and Escoriaza was able to withdraw his resources leaving at the helm of the still expanding tramway project Alfredo Velasco Sotillos, a military engineer in whom he trusted, with experience in the Cuban War (Núñez Romero-Balmas, 2005, 2008b). The tramway project in Granada was then developed vigorously, while Escoriaza, formally outside of the project, continued with his initiatives in the region.

We will refer to two well-known projects; the construction and ultimate management of the Tranvías de Cádiz a San Fernando y la Carraca and its connection with another problematic project in the province of Granada, the complicated railway link between Guadiz and Baza through the company Caminos de Hierro de Granada (1917) based in Zaragoza. As was usually the case in this type of project, Caminos de Hierro de Granada sought to substitute a pre-existing company, the Granada Railway Co. Ltd., which was legally English although the majority of its shareholders were Spanish, a result, in turn of the Great Southern of Spain Railway Co. Ltd. Besides Escoriaza, the company was managed by Caminos de Hierro del Sur de España, owner of the Linares to Almería and Granada line (Caminos de Hierro Granada, 1918). Like many other projects of its kind, it was long and complex. Through the new company Caminos de Hierro de Granada, Escoriaza constructed a long deviation to complete the line, avoiding a problematic bridge in the municipality of Gor. Later, he recycled the old iron bridge, which was unfeasible due to the fragility of the slopes on which it was built and gave it to the company Tranvías de Granada for the project known as "coastal railway", the line from Granada to Motril (Burgos Núñez, Sáez Pérez & Olmo García, 2020; Calvo Poyo & Oña López, 2020). Escoriaza would explore different opportunities in the area and intervened where possible in some of them. An example is his application, in the name of the railway company, for a waterfall with six thousand litres of water and a usable power of 2.475 CV in Zújar and Freila. The project had been initiated by the Granada-born engineer and industrialist Pedro Moreno Agrela (Ministerio de Fomento de España, Dirección General de Obras Públicas, 1920). We should note that the Guadix-Baza railway line was never electrified.

A similar case to Granada is Valladolid, with clear advantages with respect to its central location: urban dynamism, a low population density, an agriculture based on cereals and wine crops, agricultural and industrial protectionism and initiatives that took advantage of the successive investment plans of the government to modestly and precariously adapt the regional economy to the opportunities of the second industrialisation (Carasa Soto, 1997; Moreno Lázaro 2001; Calvo Caballero, 2003). Again, the opportunities generated by the flour industry, the wineries, the sugar and alcohol making companies, reinforced from the beginning of the twentieth century by public investments in railways and irrigation works, enabled the centre of Castilla to attract the attention of foreign administrators and investors, and also that of Nicolás Escoriaza. It was centrally located, both in geographical terms in general and also with respect to the distribution of the main railway networks, which, in our case, propelled Nicolás to the board of directors of Ferrocarriles del Oeste after its reorganisation.

Nicolás returned to Castilla again at the beginning of the twentieth century to intervene in his usual activity of urban tramways and local secondary railways.[9] In this case he operated through the company Ferrocarriles Secundarios de Castilla, constituted in 1909 to construct and exploit the Palencia to Villalón and Medina de Rioseco to Palanquinos (183 km) lines in the area known as Tierra de Campos in the provinces of Valladolid and Palencia. This company was an affiliate of the Española de Ferrocarriles Secundarios (1910) which, as well as the Secundarios de Castilla was interested in the Huelva to Ayamonte railway line, several lines along the Galicia coast, those of Toledo to Navahermosa and Estada to Balaguer. The shareholders of Española de Ferrocarriles Secundarios included a noteworthy range of high industrial and national and foreign railway financiers such as Banesto, Vizcaya, Paribas, Banque Française pour le Commerce et l'Industrie, Société de Travaux, Dyle et Bacalan, Credit Mobilier Français, Mr Cahen, de Amberes, Cía, Credit Mobilier de Belgique, Marseillaise de Crédit and Générale de Chemins de Fer Économiques Belges. In 1930, after it had been seized by the government, Escoriaza became the Vice President of the board of directors, presided by General Sanjurjo. Later he undoubtedly played a relevant role in the reconstitution of the company and the merger of the two to form, in 1932, Ferrocarriles de Castilla y Española de Ferrocarriles Secundarios, which was presided by Jesús Escoriaza y Averly for many years.

Nicolás and Manuel Escoriaza were always aware of the opportunities of their surroundings, and intervened in the new and promising field of hydraulic investments, undertaking the Bachende reservoir project, aimed at improving the supply of the Canal del Príncipe de Asturias, in the River Esla, a classic in Spanish hydrology (Ministerio de Fomento, 1927).

---

9 Española de Ferrocarriles Secundarios, 1911; Española de Ferrocarriles Secundarios, 1923; Ferrocarriles de Castilla y Española de Ferrocarriles Secundarios, 1932.

5 Conclusions

In this study we have summarised the historical formation and evolution of a family group of companies that principally operated in the field of Spanish railways and tramways and their auxiliary industries at the end of the nineteenth century and a good part of the twentieth century. It was a flexible conglomerate of civil works contractors that efficiently articulated a complex network of personal contacts around a unique axis, the Escoriaza family, principally based in Zaragoza. The resulting conglomerate operated in a good part of Aragon and in many other parts of Spain. For three successive generations, the Escoriaza family positioned itself on the second level of railway initiatives, under the shadow and protection of the large companies in the sector and the large financial groups that controlled them, with the specialised mission to undertake minor constructions, partial railway projects and, very frequently, the reconversion of failed or long delayed projects. Throughout the history of the sector, the reconversion of railway companies has been an important business segment, sometimes highly profitable for those who knew how to organise and manage it. A segment that was also largely unknown. The second level public works described constituted a powerful incentive in Spain. After the large networks with the "Iberian gauge" had been terminated, the state began to implement its strategic and secondary railway plans (normally with a metric gauge), and the installation and electrification of electric tramways also began. The "Escoriazas" fully participated in the two waves of investment and also took part in certain initiatives of the new emerging business opportunity; the construction of hydraulic works.

The group's activity was based on close ties with top-level Spanish and foreign railway financiers, and therefore, on the close cooperation and mutual trust networks that, without a doubt, enabled them to establish strong ties with both the government and private finance. They all operated in a framework characterised by industrial protectionism and public investment, often based on public-private cooperation. Nicolás Escoriaza, who soon earned an excellent reputation in this context, displayed a high capacity to coordinate the reconversions and mergers of second level companies. Particularly remarkable was the business of failed ventures, an area that had yet to be explored and an abundance of which were to be found in the railway sector at the end of the nineteenth century and beginning of the twentieth century.

We have reviewed the documented records of the construction history of the Escoriaza group within the framework of secondary railways. Unfortunately, these did not constitute all of their activities. Some of them have not been captured by the usual business historiography compilations drawn from limited companies (through their financial reports) and/or the state concessions (published in the *Gaceta de Madrid*). Therefore, we are standing at the edge of the "dark matter" of the business universe made up of mostly very short-lived small companies involved in small-scale initiatives but, just like in the world of physics, they could have a greater mass than the universe that has been visible until now.

The family conglomerate studied in this article provides a good example of the opportunities and strategies that can be found at this border between the large and small company. As we can see, the Escoriaza group followed a clear pattern. It operated in regions where there did not seem to be many competitors of the same scale. Rather, it seems that the group preferred locations where there was no competition or where these competitors had previously failed and often it did so with the collaboration of prominent representatives of the large railway groups. Other provinces such as Malaga, Murcia and Alicante also constituted fertile ground for many railway and hydroelectric initiatives, but these were addressed by local or foreign interests that were well-established in the area. We would have to compile a complete and systematic panorama of all of these initiatives in large geographical areas in order to conduct a more precise comparison.

6 Sources

Anuario Financiero que comprende el historial de Valores Públicos y Sociedades Anónimas de España (1947). Ferrocarriles de Castilla y Española de Ferrocarriles Secundarios (pp. 248–249). Madrid.

Anuario Financiero y de Sociedades Anónimas de España (1923). Española de Ferrocarriles Secundarios. Madrid.

Construcción Moderna (1911). Española de Ferrocarriles Secundarios. IX(18), Sep 30, 381.

Enciclopedia Universal Ilustrada, 1931, Escoriaza, José Pascasio. Madrid: Espasa-Calpe.

References

Bernal, A. M. & Parejo, A. (2001). La economía andaluza: atraso y frágil vertebración. In L. Germán Zubero, E. Llopis Agelán, J. Maluquer de Motes & S. Zapata Blanco (Eds.), *Historia económica regional de España, siglos XIX y XX* (pp. 298–330). Barcelona: Crítica.

Biescas Ferrer, J. A. (1985). *El proceso de industrialización en la región aragonesa en el periodo 1900–1920*. Zaragoza: CSIC.

Biescas Ferrer, J. A. & Germán Zubero, L. (1992). *Una aproximación a la historia de Tudor en Zaragoza*. Zaragoza: Sicione S.A.

Burgos Núñez, A., Sáez Pérez, M. P. & Olmo García, J. C. (2012). El puente ferroviario de Gor y Dúrcal, una experiencia singular de la ingeniería en España. http://www.docutren.com/HistoriaFerroviaria/Vitoria2012/pdf/6035.pdf. Accessed 2020 July 25

Calvo Caballero, P. (2003). *Asociacionismo y cultura patronales en Castilla y León durante la Restauración (1876–1923)*. Valladolid: Junta de Castilla y León.

Calvo Poyo, F. J. & Oña López, J. J. de. (2020). Historia el Ferrocarril. 1. El cable Dúrcal-Motril en la provincia de Granada. http://www.vialibre-ffe.com/revista/historia/historia.htm. Accessed 2020 July 25.

Carasa Soto, P. et al. (1997). *Las élites castellanas de la Restauración. Una aproximación al poder político en Castilla*. Salamanca: Junta de Castilla y León.

Cayón García, F. & Muñoz Rubio, M. (1998). *La industria de construcción de material ferroviario. Una aproximación histórica*. Madrid: Fundación Empresa Pública.

Colli, A. (2003). *The history of family business, 1850–2000*. Cambridge: Cambridge University Press.

Colli, A., Fernández Perez, P. & Rose, M. B. (2003). National determinants of family firm development? Family Firms in Britain, Spain, and Italy in the Nineteenth and Twentieth Centuries. *Enterprise & Society*, 4 (1), 28.

Compañía de Caminos de Hierro Granada (Baza-Guadix) (1918). *Memoria leída en la Junta General ordinaria de Accionistas celebrada el 22 de abril de 1918. Ejercicio de 1917.* Barcelona: Henrich y Cía.

Consejo de Industria. Ministerio de Economía Nacional (España) (1930). Zaragoza. In *Apuntes para el momento de la industria española en 1930. II.* Madrid: Sucs. de Rivadeneyra S.A.

Corral López, A. (1980). *El duque de San Pedro de Galatino: prócer de Granada*. Granada: Diputación provincial. Instituto Provincial de Estudios y Promoción Cultural.

Díez de Castro, E. P. (ed.) (1995). *La empresa en Andalucía*, Madrid: Editorial Civitas / Instituto de Fomento de Andalucía.

Fernández Clemente, E. (1977). Treinta empresarios aragoneses en el primer tercio del siglo XX. *Cuadernos Aragoneses de Economía*, 2, 127–141.

Fernández Clemente, E. (1997). *Gente de orden. Aragón durante la dictadura de Primo de Rivera, 1923–1930. Tomo 3: la economía*. Zaragoza: Ibercaja.

Fernández Pérez, P. (2017). *Empresas familiares de América, Europa y Asia: Una aproximación cuantitativa*. Bogotá: Universidad de los Andes.

Fernández Pérez, P. & Colli, A. (Eds.) (2013). *The endurance of family business: A global overview*. Cambridge, MA: Cambridge University Press.

Fernandez Perez, P. & Puig, N. (2004). Knowledge and training in family firms of the European periphery: Spain in the eighteenth to twentieth centuries. *Business History*, 46 (1), 79.

Fernández Sánchez, P., González Ruiz, L. & Núñez Romero-Balmas, G. (2019). Puertos y profesiones en el sur de España. Profesionales y comerciantes en el litoral andaluz en 1931. In L. López Molina, T. Pontón Aricha & M. Vázquez Fariñas (Eds.), *Cádiz: del Floreciente siglo XVIII al Port of the Future del siglo XXI* (pp. 155–172). Madrid: Dickinson.

Germán Zubero, L. (1980). Escoriaza y Fabro, Nicolás. In *Gran Enciclopedia Aragonesa*. Zaragoza.

Germán Zubero, L. (Ed.) (1990). *ERZ (1910–1990). El desarrollo del sector eléctrico en Aragón*. Zaragoza: Institución Fernando el Católico.

Germán Zubero, L. (2001). Del cereal al metal. La trayectoria de la economía aragonesa. In L. Germán Zubero, E. Llopis Agelán, J. Maluquer de Motes, & S. Zapata Blanco (Eds.), *Historia económica regional de España, siglos XIX y XX* (pp. 331–356). Barcelona: Critica.

Germán Zubero, L. (2007). De la implantación del metal a la consolidación de la automoción en Zaragoza (1850–2000). In P. Pascual Domenech & P. Fernández Pérez, Paloma (Eds.), *Del metal al motor: Innovación y atraso en la historia de la industria metal-metálica española*. Bilbao: Fundación BBVA.

Germán Zubero, L. (2009). *Grandes empresarios aragoneses*. Madrid: LID editorial empresarial.

Germán Zubero, L. (2020). *El azúcar en la España contemporánea*. Web Page. Accessed 2020 Jul 10. Available at https://mdc.ulpgc.es/utils/getfile/collection/coloquios/id/1557/filename/1585.pdf.

Germán Zubero, L., Pinilla, V. & Sancho, A. (2018). *El transporte público en Zaragoza. Desde 1885 hasta la actualidad*. Zaragoza: Prensas de la Universidad de Zaragoza.

González Ruiz, L. & Núñez Romero-Balmas, G. (2007). L'evoluzione di un servizio municipale all'epoca della seconda industrializzazione: le tranvie di Granada. *Ricerche Storiche*. 37(2), 357–392.

González Ruiz, L. & Núñez Romero-Balmas, G. (2016). Estadísticas para la historia: Uso estadístico de fuentes mercantiles. In J. M. Herrerías Velasco

& J. Callejón Cèspedes (Eds.). *Investigaciones en métodos cuantitativos para la economía y la empresa. Homenaje al profesor Rafael Herrerías Pleguezuelo* (pp. 319–334). Granada: Editorial Universidad de Granada. URI: http://hdl.handle.net/10481/43516. Accessed 2020 July 25.

González Ruiz, L., Núñez Romero-Balmas, G. & Piñar Samos, J. (2007). *La Empresa de nuestros abuelos. Territorio e iniciativa económica en la Granada del primer tercio del siglo XX*. Granada: Fundación Caja Rural de Granada.

Instituto de la Empresa Familiar and KPGM (2016). *Barómetro europeo de la empresa familiar*. Quinta edición; Accessed 2020 Jun 25. Available at: www.iefamiliar.com/estudios-y-publicaciones/.

Jiménez Blanco, J. I. (1986). La remolacha y los problemas de la industria azucarera en España. 1880–1914. In R. Garrabou, C. Barciela & J. I. Jiménez Blanco (Eds.), *Historia agraria de la España contemporánea. 3. El fin de la agricultura tradicional* (pp. 280–316). Barcelona: Crítica.

Lubinski, C., Fear, J. & Fernández Pérez, P. (2013). *Family Multinationals: Entrepreneurship, Governance, and Pathways to Internationalization*. New York: Routledge.

Malpica, A. & Martín, M. (1992). *El azúcar en el encuentro entre dos mundos*. Madrid: Asociación General de Fabricantes de Azúcar de España.

Martínez-López, A. (1998). Las inversiones belgas en los tranvías y ferrocarriles de cercanías. Una perspectiva internacional, 1892–1935. In *150 Años de historia ferroviaria*. Alicante: Universidad de Alicante.

Martínez Soto, A. P. & Rosado Cubero, A. (2017). El fracaso del cartel la Sociedad General Azucarera de España: Un análisis desde la legislación sobre este sector industrial (1899–1931). In *XII Congreso Internacional de la Asociación Española de Historia Económica (Salamanca)* Salamanca: AEHE. https://www.aehe.es/wp-content/uploads/2016/01/Ana-Pascual-Mart%C2%B0nez-Soto-y-Ana-Rosado-Cubero.pdf. Accessed 2020 July 22.

Melgar, J. M. (2003). *Entrevista personal realizada el 4 de febrero de 2003 sobre su abuelo, don Nicolás Escoriaza*.

Ministerio de Agricultura, Industria y Comercio (España) & Allendesalazar, Manuel, Ministro de Agricultura Industria y Comercio (1904). Ley de ferrocarriles secundarios. In *Gaceta de Madrid*. 1904-08-02; (215): 385–387.

Ministerio de Fomento (España) (1920). Autorizando a D. Nicolás Escoriaza, Vizconde de Escoriaza, Presidente de la Compañía de los Caminos de Hierro de Granada para derivar 6.000 litros de agua del río Guadiana menor. In *Gaceta de Madrid*. 1920 Oct 14; (288), 223–224.

Ministerio de Fomento (España) and Benjumea y Burín, Rafael, Ministro de Fomento (1927). Real decreto-ley disponiendo que los concesionarios del

Canal del Príncipe de Asturias, en el río Esta, presente en este Ministerio dentro del plazo de ocho meses, el proyecto de la presa de embalse de dicho rio en el estrecho de Valliendes [Bachende]. In *Gaceta de Madrid*. 1927 Apr 3; 74–78.

Ministerio de Fomento (España). Dirección general de Obras públicas. Ferrocarriles (1907). Plan de ferrocarriles secundarios. In *Gaceta de Madrid*, 262, de 19/09/1907, pp. 1.160 a 1.161.

Mohedano Barceló, J. (1998). *La formación del distrito de Zaragoza, 1890–1913. Un modelo de organización empresarial en la coyuntura finisecular*. Inédito.

Molleví Bortoló, G. & Serrano Giné, D. (2007). El impacto de la filoxera en Andalucía según la diplomacia francesa. *Cuadernos Geográficos*, 40 (1), 133–148.

Moreno Fernández, J. R. & Sancho Sora, A. (2013). Especialización flexible y tipos de organización empresarial en España: el valle medio del Ebro, 1880–1935 [Web Page]. Zaragoza: Universidad de Zaragoza. Accessed 2020 Jul 15. Available at https://www.aehe.es/wp-content/uploads/2001/10/ramonmoreno.pdf.

Moreno Lázaro, J. (2001). La precaria industrialización de Castilla y León. In L. Germán Zubero, E. Llopis Agelán, J. Maluquer de Motes & S. Zapata Blanco (Eds.), *Historia económica regional de España, siglos XIX y XX* (pp. 182–208). Barcelona: Crítica.

Núñez Romero-Balmas, G. (1994). Origen e integración de la industria eléctrica en Andalucía y Badajoz. In J. Alcaide et all., *Compañía Sevillana de Electricidad. Cien años de Historia*.

Núñez Romero-Balmas, G. (1998). La hidroelectricidad en pequeña escala. In M. Titos Martínez, (Ed.), *Historia económica de Granada* (pp. 267–282). Granada: Cámara de Comercio, Industria y Navegación.

Núñez Romero-Balmas, G. (1999). *Raíles en la Ciudad. Empresa y ciudad en torno a los tranvías de Granada*. Granada: Caja General de Ahorros de Granada / Ayuntamiento de Granada.

Núñez Romero-Balmas, G. (2005). *Tejiendo redes empresariales en Andalucía oriental: Vida y obra de Alfredo Velasco Sotillos (1872–1936)*. Granada: Grupo de Estudios Históricos sobre la Empresa. Http://www.ugr.es/~teoriahe/RePEc/gra/wpaper/thepapers05_05.pdf. Accessed 2020 July 25.

Núñez Romero-Balmas, G. (2008a). Nicolás de Escoriaza y Fabro, vizconde de Escoriaza (1869–1937). In A. Parejo (Ed.), *Cien empresarios andaluces* (pp. 463–470). Madrid: LID Editorial Empresarial.

Núñez Romero-Balmas, G. (2008b). Alfredo Velasco Sotillos (1872–1936). In A. Parejo (Ed.), *Cien empresarios andaluces* (pp. 476–488). Madrid: LID Editorial Empresarial.

Núñez Romero-Balmas, G. (2010). Geografía Financiera de España en 1914: Notas sobre la co-emergencia de la gran industria y las finanzas locales a principios del siglo XX. In J. Morilla, J. Hernández Andreu, J. L. García Ruiz & J. M. Ortiz Villajos (Eds.), *Homenaje a Gabriel Tortella* (pp. 607–634). Madrid: LID Editorial.

Núñez Romero-Balmas, G. (2019). Administración pública y ferrocarril: Nicolás Escoriaza y Fabro en la encrucijada de la Restauración. In R. Molina Recio (Ed.), *Pioneros. Empresas y empresarios en el primer tercio del siglo XX en España* (pp. 177–204). Granada: Comares.

Parejo Barranco, A. (2011). *Grandes empresarios andaluces.* Madrid: LID Editorial Empresarial.

Piñar Samos, J. (1984). *El Banco de España y Andalucía (1874–1962).* Granada.

Piñar Samos, J. & Giménez Yanguas, M. (Eds.) (2004). *Granada. El tiempo de los tranvías.* Granada: Caja Granada.

Piñar Samos, J. & Giménez Yanguas, M. (2019). *El siglo de la luz. Paisajes y patrimonio de la electricidad en Granada.* Granada: CajaGranada–Endesa.

Piqueras Haba, J. (2005). La filoxera en España y su difusión espacial: 1878–1926. *Cuadernos de Geografía*, 77, 101–136.

Puig Raposo, N. & Fernández Pérez, P. (2009). La internacionalización de la gran empresa familiar española. Una perspectiva histórica. *Información Comercial Española, ICE: Revista de Economía*, 849, 27–38.

Rose, M. B. (Ed.) (1995). *Family Business.* Aldershot, Hants Brookfield, Vt.: Elgar.

Sáez García, M. Á. (2005). Aranceles e industria: El arancel de 1891 y sus repercusiones sobre el desarrollo de la industria española. *VIII Congreso AEHE*, Santiago de Compostela. https://www.google.com/search?q=S%C3%A1ez+Garc%C3%ADa%2C+M.+%C3%81..+%C2%ABAranceles+e+industria%3A+El+arancel+de+1891+y+sus+repercusiones+sobre+el+desarrollo+de+la+industria+espa%C3%B1ola%C2%BB&rlz=1C1PRFI_enES853ES878&oq=S%C3%A1ez+Garc%C3%ADa%2C+M.+%C3%81..+%C2%ABAranceles+e+industria%3A+El+arancel+de+1891+y+sus+repercusiones+sobre+el+desarrollo+de+la+industria+espa%C3%B1ola%C2%BB+&aqs=chrome..69i57.372252j0j15&sourceid=chrome&ie=UTF-8. Accessed 2020 July 19.

Serrano Sanz, J. M. (1987). *El viraje proteccionista en la Restauración. La política comercial española, 1875–1895.* Madrid: Siglo XXI.

Titos Martínez, M. (Ed.) (1998). *Historia económica de Granada.* Granada: Cámara de Comercio, Industria y Navegación.

Titos Martínez, M. (1999). *El Duque de San Pedro de Galatino.* Granada: Comares.

Wilkins, M. & Schröter, H. (Eds.) (1998). *The free-standing company in the world economy, 1830–1996.* Oxford: Oxford University Press.

Mariano Castro-Valdivia

2 Foreign companies in Spain (1911–1920)

Abstract Knowing the degree of presence of foreign companies in a territory is important to know the level of development of its economy. This chapter analyses the number of foreign companies in Spain in the second decade of the 20th century. Based on official data from the Ministry of Finance, published in *Gaceta Madrid*, on affiliation and capital of foreign corporations, the evolution of foreign investment in Spain for this period is explained. In addition, information on the countries, which have invested in Spain during the aforementioned decade, is provided, indicating the productive sector and its location. Finally, the work analyses the state of sectoral and regional concentration of foreign companies in terms of the investor, as well as their strategies of increasing protectionism in Spain.

1 Introduction

The study of foreign investment in a country provides an insight into the level of economic development of that territory. At the beginning of the 20th century, Spain still was an eminently agricultural country; industrialisation was concentrated around the big cities: Barcelona, Bilbao and Madrid, among others. The lack of entrepreneurial capacity, capital and technology facilitated the entry of foreign companies into almost all the productive sectors between the end of the 19th century and the beginning of the 20th century (Castro-Valdivia & Matés-Barco, 2020, 223). This subject, which is so relevant to research Spanish economic history, has always drawn historians' attention (Tortella, 1997, 607), which has led to a large number of works referring to foreign investment in Spain in very diverse sectors.

This chapter, whose main objective is to study the foreign companies existing in Spain in the first decades of the 20th century, follows this line of research. The interest of this work lies in three aspects, which are outlined throughout the text. Firstly, the importance of foreign investment in the economic analysis; secondly, assessing the relevance which it had in Spain; and, finally, the role these companies have played in the country's modernisation process.

Worldwide, some recent calculations have placed foreign investment at 10 % of GDP, which equates it to the weight of tourism in economic activity. Although the importance of foreign capital in the capitalist system is not negligible, its prominence in national economies has generated multiple controversies. The interpretation has been diverse. On some occasions, academic literature has censored international loans. On the one hand, there is talk of "domination", "foreign control" and even "colonialism"; and some describe it as "loss of sovereignty in the face of foreign interference". Others quote David Landes (1999) when he states that "over the years I have come to understand better and better that capitalism means movements of capital". In this context, various theories have emerged that either applaud or disallow the investment of foreign capital in a given country. Direct investment from abroad is sometimes identified with multinational companies, and this relationship is not always accurate. And at other times, the positive or negative aspects are valued according to personal convictions, although in the most recent stages, a more objective view prevails which perceives foreign investment as an aid to growth (Tascón Fernández, 2008). It should be noted that this is an undeniable property which makes up for the shortage of capital in the least developed countries and allows projects to be carried out which would, otherwise, would be unfeasible. Moreover, this foreign capital tends to be accompanied by modern technology, often unattainable by its own means for the recipient host country.

Classical economics highlighted the similarity between international capital movements and those within the same country. However, more attention has been paid to the former than to the latter. Gabriel Tortella (2008) has pointed out several reasons. The first is the different legislative treatment they receive in different states, which complicates transactions between them. The second is based on the different currencies of each nation, which makes it difficult to gauge the value of products, exchange rates, etc. The third is related to the political dimension of this type of business, as in the case of a national company that is going to be acquired by a foreign one; especially if it is a strategic sector, since it is considered a loss of sovereignty. Lastly, the leading role played by states in this type of exchange, for example, with the loans that result in the famous Foreign Debt.

The second half of the 19th century, especially since 1870, saw the first globalisation of the economy. The changes generated by the application of steam to the means of transport –railways, ships, etc. – and those experienced in communications (telegraph), coincided with significant technological and institutional advances. This accumulation of actions facilitated the movement of capital and the emergence of the first multinational companies. It is worth asking what motivates a company or an individual entrepreneur to invest abroad. It seems clear that the advantages outweigh the difficulties and even their expectations may exceed those of local investors, but several causes can be listed. On the one hand, technological superiority; on the other hand, the organisational structure which may be more advanced or the financial possibilities. Some authors have pointed out that this pre-eminence is not enough to justify the desire to invest abroad. Others have based it on cultural ties and potential relations of trust (Broder, 1976; O'Rourke & Williamson, 1999; Comín, 2005; Castro Balaguer, 2007; Castro-Valdivia, 2019).

This chapter analyses the foreign companies existing in Spain in the second decade of the 20th century. It is based on official data from the Ministry of Finance, published in *Gaceta de Madrid*, on the membership and capital of foreign corporations set for the calculation of the tax liability of the third Rate of Contribution on Profits from Movable Wealth that they had to pay. This tax obligation has made it possible to ascertain the capital of foreign companies established in Spain between 1911 and 1920, the period in which this procedure was in force. The first data was published in *Gaceta de Madrid* on 15 December 1911 and the last one on 22 November 1924.

The work has been structured in three sections. Following this introduction, the development of foreign investment is examined in the second section. The third analyses foreign companies by sector: tramways, machinery, gas, water, mining, electricity, bank, wine, chemistry, wood, foreign trade, trade, coal for boats and others. Finally, some brief conclusions are presented together with the sources and references used.

2 Foreign investment in Spain

The most developed countries lead investment processes abroad. During the 19th century, England and France were the great exporters of capital to the rest of the world. In the case of Spain, French entrepreneurs led most of the foreign investment initiatives (Cameron, 1971; Costa Campi, 1983).

In the first decades of the 20th century, this Anglo-French duopoly gradually disappeared with the entry of Belgian, German, Italian, American, Canadian, Norwegian, Danish and Argentinean capital. The data published in *Gaceta de Madrid* by the Ministry of Finance on the capital of foreign companies in Spain between 1911 and 1924 corroborate this. The nationality of the 122 listed companies was as follows: French, 28 %; English, 26 %; Belgian, 19 %; German, 7 %; Italian, 3 %; American, 3 %; Norwegian, 2 %; Danish, 1 %; Argentinean, 1 %; unspecified, 10 %.

Tab. 1 shows the evolution of the capital of foreign companies in Spain aggregated by sector in the second decade of the 20th century. In 1911, according to information from the Contribution on Profits from Movable Wealth, there were seventy-three foreign companies, with a declared capital of almost 231 million *pesetas*. At the end of the period, 1920, there were seventy-seven with a patrimony close to 435 million *pesetas*. This represents an average annual increase in foreign investment in Spain of almost 9 % between 1911 and 1920. The average capitalisation value for this decade reached 415 million *pesetas*.

The behaviour of a country's foreign investment is very volatile and is conditioned by the political, economic and social situation, both national and international. There is an inverse relationship between this type of investment and the degree of uncertainty in the host country. The more security the socioeconomic model of that country has, the less risk there is and therefore the greater foreign investment it will attract. The second decade of the 20th century was marked by a tragic event, the First World War (1914–1918), which was a determining factor in the development of foreign investment in Spain. This grew significantly until the beginning of the war, with the invested capital doubled in just three years. During the war, and due to Spain's neutrality, the capitalisation of foreign companies continued to grow. In 1917, the maximum asset value of the period was reached, with 482 million *pesetas*, and the maximum number of registered foreign companies, ninety-seven. From that moment on, before the end of the war and a Spanish policy in favour of the nationalisation of the productive sectors, which promoted the acquisition of foreign corporations by native entrepreneurs, the number of these companies decreased as did their equity value (Castro Balaguer, 2007).

3 Foreign companies in Spain

This section analyses the disaggregated data on foreign investment by sector collected in Tab. 1. After ordering the census of companies obtained from the research, and establishing a minimum of three companies to establish a productive sector, the data have given rise to thirteen sectors plus one of others.

3.1 Tramways

It is the leader of the sector in 1911 by number of companies, twelve, and by capitalisation, with almost 60 million *pesetas*, 26 % of the total. The number of companies registered in the period analysed was sixteen, being the sector that contributes the most to the group of foreign companies, 13 % of the 122 registered. This sector was dominated by Belgian companies, 75 % (Núñez Romero-Balmas, 1991). The rest were of French or English origin. The evolution of the capitalisation of foreign tramway companies during the second decade of the

20th century was similar to other sectors. The patrimony of these companies increased until 1914, when it reached 67 million *pesetas*. From this moment on, companies in this sector began to decapitalise. There were slight upturns in 1917 and 1919, but they did not compensate for the accumulated loss of value since the beginning of the First World War. In 1920, the eleven foreign companies that continued in this sector had a capitalisation of almost 46 million *pesetas*, 10 % of total foreign investment. The weight of this sector in foreign investment as a whole was losing weight. In 1920, it was the fifth, while in 1911 it was the first, although it was still the sector that contributed the most to foreign companies. Finally, it should be noted that the Belgian company *Los Tranvías de Barcelona* was the leading company in this sector, reaching its maximum capitalisation of 28,752,639.80 *pesetas* in 1914.[1]

3.2 Machinery

It is the second sector in the ranking by number of companies in 1911, twelve, although the asset value of these is relatively low, almost 5 million *pesetas*, 2 % of the total. The number of companies registered in the period analysed was fifteen, 12 % of the total. In terms of the nationality of these companies, one third were French, followed by English, German and American companies, in that order. The First World War conditioned the evolution of the capitalisation of foreign machinery companies during the second decade of the 20th century. The assets of these companies increased until 1914, when they reached almost 7 million *pesetas*. During the war, capitalisation decreased by 30 %. Between 1918 and 1919, there was a strong recapitalisation of the sector. In 1919, the value of the eleven companies that made up the sector was slightly more than 9 million *pesetas*. In 1920, there were only six foreign companies left in this sector with assets of over 6 million *pesetas*. The disinvestment observed at the end of the period was very significant. The weight of the sector in total foreign investment was similar during the period. In 1920, it was the eighth, when in 1911 it was ninth in the capitalisation ranking. The importance of this sector by the number of companies it contributed to the whole decreased significantly. In 1911, it accounted for 16 % of the total, while in 1920 it was only 8 %. Finally, it should be noted that the American company, Singer Sewing

1 *Gaceta de Madrid*, 31 January 1918, no. 31.

Tab. 1: Foreign companies in Spain (1911–1920)

		YEARS			
		1911		1912	
		NUMBER OF COMPANIES	CAPITAL IN PESETAS	NUMBER OF COMPANIES	CAPITAL IN PESETAS
SECTORS	TRAMWAYS	12	54,987,762.51	13	59,581,015.28
	MACHINERY	12	4,782,710.91	14	6,356,229.05
	GAS	7	43,100,021.15	7	46,939,245.91
	WATER	6	39,478,919.92	6	39,401,176.11
	MINING	6	21,344,883.69	6	23,081,377.00
	ELECTRICITY	6	11,144,189.88	6	11,455,066.56
	BANK	5	21,676,739.82	5	24,969,912.76
	WINES	2	6,198,814.84	4	6,432,788.61
	CHEMISTRY	2	5,248,397.04	3	8,558,389.06
	WOOD	2	4,611,018.99	2	4,693,519.26
	FOREIGN TRADE	1	487,361.00	1	766,934.12
	TRADE	0	0.00	0	0.00
	COAL FOR BOATS	0	0.00	0	0.00
	OTHERS	12	17,813,981.02	12	19,970,708.03
TOTALS		73	230,874,800.77	79	252,206,361.75

Tab. 1: (Continued)

		YEARS			
		1913		1914	
		NUMBER OF COMPANIES	CAPITAL IN PESETAS	NUMBER OF COMPANIES	CAPITAL IN PESETAS
SECTORS	TRAMWAYS	11	57,630,297.74	12	67,061,190.22
	MACHINERY	13	6,432,824.59	13	6,745,158.37
	GAS	7	41,066,680.69	7	48,727,755.65
	WATER	6	39,674,427.20	7	46,911,483.25
	MINING	7	50,384,848.12	7	67,832,238.07
	ELECTRICITY	8	134,964,070.62	8	138,313,498.15
	BANK	5	27,543,893.30	5	32,673,997.87
	WINES	4	6,892,371.66	4	6,580,664.77
	CHEMISTRY	3	10,521,832.75	2	10,593,696.70
	WOOD	2	5,530,766.96	2	5,536,692.13
	FOREIGN TRADE	3	2,277,600.70	3	1,798,689.92
	TRADE	1	1,420,515.91	1	1,473,638.51
	COAL FOR BOATS	0	0.00	3	1,687,540.12
	OTHERS	14	23,733,884.20	13	24,952,861.15
TOTALS		84	405,632,906.06	87	460,889,104.88

Tab. 1: (Continued)

		YEARS			
		1915		1916	
		NUMBER OF COMPANIES	**CAPITAL IN PESETAS**	**NUMBER OF COMPANIES**	**CAPITAL IN PESETAS**
SECTORS	TRAMWAYS	12	64,540,609.70	11	59,139,422.80
	MACHINERY	13	6,269,104.81	12	5,505,938.70
	GAS	7	49,807,465.89	7	41,806,296.22
	WATER	7	49,260,177.91	7	46,584,591.38
	MINING	9	86,881,241.78	9	83,239,768.13
	ELECTRICITY	8	134,590,292.52	8	143,926,848.89
	BANK	5	34,026,307.36	5	36,710,975.79
	WINES	3	5,701,590.10	4	5,949,773.75
	CHEMISTRY	3	10,578,709.30	3	11,076,130.71
	WOOD	2	5,535,212.26	2	8,132,034.91
	FOREIGN TRADE	3	1,612,933.29	3	1,747,561.80
	TRADE	4	1,613,171.76	3	2,424,300.30
	COAL FOR BOATS	3	794,783.92	3	791,284.15
	OTHERS	15	25,975,737.76	17	29,307,163.22
TOTALS		94	477,187,338.36	94	476,342,090.75

Tab. 1: (Continued)

		YEARS			
		1917		1918	
		NUMBER OF COMPANIES	CAPITAL IN PESETAS	NUMBER OF COMPANIES	CAPITAL IN PESETAS
SECTORS	TRAMWAYS	14	61,748,196.09	13	48,886,960.99
	MACHINERY	12	4,894,297.64	12	6,956,251.19
	GAS	7	40,974,653.55	5	36,462,047.85
	WATER	7	44,033,446.84	6	42,362,060.49
	MINING	9	85,262,292.76	9	77,452,730.25
	ELECTRICITY	8	153,814,175.73	9	147,991,456.38
	BANK	6	38,143,463.38	7	49,918,116.86
	WINES	4	5,746,241.09	4	5,165,072.45
	CHEMISTRY	3	12,957,005.32	3	11,052,602.16
	WOOD	3	8,275,878.46	3	8,327,467.44
	FOREIGN TRADE	3	1,998,733.62	3	1,891,233.36
	TRADE	3	2,306,915.13	3	1,880,701.37
	COAL FOR BOATS	2	767,949.08	2	727,460.41
	OTHERS	16	21,459,766.53	12	12,157,169.79
TOTALS		97	482,383,015.22	91	451,231,330.99

Tab. 1: (Continued)

	YEARS			
	1919		1920	
SECTORS	NUMBER OF COMPANIES	CAPITAL IN PESETAS	NUMBER OF COMPANIES	CAPITAL IN PESETAS
TRAMWAYS	12	51,440,901.10	11	45,729,113.07
MACHINERY	11	9,293,064.37	6	6,296,462.47
GAS	5	35,196,607.44	3	33,761,215.66
WATER	6	42,347,193.52	6	47,606,652.71
MINING	9	86,393,727.13	7	65,977,018.86
ELECTRICITY	9	141,749,192.41	8	141,082,391.38
BANK	8	70,613,168.66	7	55,566,434.90
WINES	4	5,102,688.99	4	5,986,777.73
CHEMISTRY	3	12,881,844.54	2	4,538,150.81
WOOD	2	8,122,134.59	2	9,345,460.04
FOREIGN TRADE	3	1,907,361.18	3	1,874,235.72
TRADE	3	1,718,905.43	3	1,589,957.13
COAL FOR BOATS	2	778,284.47	2	737,587.78
OTHERS	13	10,840,621.50	13	14,525,073.20
TOTALS	90	478,385,695.33	77	434,616,531.46

Source: Own elaboration from the data extracted from the third Rate of Contribution on Profits from Movable Wealth published in the *Gaceta de Madrid* between 15 December 1911 and 22 November 1924.

Machinery Company, was the main company in this sector in terms of capitalisation, reaching its maximum value at the end of the period, 1920, with 1,482,696.10 *pesetas*.[2]

3.3 Gas

This sector was the third largest in terms of the number of companies in 1911, seven, and had a value of slightly more than 43 million *pesetas*, 19 % of the total. The number of companies registered in the period analysed was seven, 6 % of the total (Fernández-Paradas, 2015; Fábregas, 2017).This sector was dominated by French companies, 71 %. The rest were of English or Belgian origin. The evolution of the capitalisation of foreign gas companies during the second decade of the 20th century was similar to that of the other sectors. The assets of these companies increased until 1915, when they reached almost 50 million *pesetas*, with the exception of 1913, when there was a specific decrease. From this moment on, the companies in this sector were decapitalised. In 1920, the three foreign companies that continued in this sector had a capitalisation of almost 34 million *pesetas*, 8 % of the total foreign investment. The weight of the sector in the total of foreign investment was losing weight. In 1920, it was the sixth when in 1911 it was the second. Its importance in terms of the number of companies it contributed to the whole decreased. In 1911, it represented 10 % of the total, while in 1920 it went down to 4 %. Finally, it should be noted that the leading company in this sector was the French company *Lebón y Compañía*, which in 1915 reached its maximum capitalisation of 40,314,021.63 *pesetas*[3] (Castro-Valdivia; Fernández-Paradas & Matés-Barco, 2019).

3.4 Water

It is the fourth sector by number of companies in 1911, six, and a patrimonial value of more than 39 million *pesetas*, 17 % of the total. The number of companies registered in the period analysed was seven, 6 % of the total. English companies, 57 %, dominated this sector. The rest were of Belgian and French origin, in that order. The evolution of the capitalisation of foreign companies dedicated to water supply during the second decade of the 20th century showed a similar behaviour to the rest of the sectors. The assets of these companies increased until 1915, when they exceeded the maximum capitalisation of the

2 *Gaceta de Madrid*, 12 January 1921, no. 12.
3 *Gaceta de Madrid*, 10 October 1917, no. 283.

sector in this period of more than 49 million *pesetas*. During the First World War, these companies in this sector were gradually decapitalised. From 1919 onwards the equity value of these companies recovered, but did not compensate for the loss of value accumulated during the war. In 1920, the six foreign companies that continued in this sector had a capitalisation of almost 48 million *pesetas*, 11 % of the total foreign investment. The weight of this sector in the total foreign investment was gaining weight, at the end of the period, 1920, was the second when at the beginning, 1911, was the eighth. The importance of this sector in terms of the number of companies it contributes to the whole decreased. In 1911, it accounted for 10 % of the total, while in 1920 it rose to 8 %. On the other hand, it should be noted that the capitalisation of the sector was highly concentrated in the French company *Sociedad General de Aguas de Barcelona*, which in 1920 reached its maximum capitalisation of 33,746,156.10 *pesetas*[4] (Matés-Barco. 2019a, 2019b; Castro-Valdivia & Matés-Barco, 2020).

3.5 Mining

It is the fifth sector by number of companies in 1911, six, and a patrimonial value slightly superior to 21 million *pesetas*, 9 % of the total. The number of companies registered in the period analysed was eleven, 9 % of the 122. French companies, 50 %, dominated this sector. The rest were of English and Belgian origin, in that order. The evolution of the capitalisation of foreign companies dedicated to mining during the second decade of the 20th century showed a similar behaviour to that of the other sectors. The assets of these companies increased until 1915, when they reached around 87 million *pesetas*. From that moment on, the companies in this sector were gradually decapitalised. There were upturns in 1917 and 1919, but they did not compensate for the loss of value accumulated during the First World War. In 1920, the seven foreign companies that continued in this sector had a capitalisation of almost 66 million *pesetas*, 15 % of total foreign investment. The importance of this sector in the total of foreign investment was gaining weight. In 1920 it was the second when in 1911 it was the eighth. The number of companies contributing to the total increased slightly. In 1911, it accounted for 8 % of the total, while in 1920 it rose to 9 %. On the other hand, it should be noted that the capitalisation of the sector was highly concentrated in two companies: the French company *Minera*

4 *Gaceta de Madrid*, 5 October 1922, no. 278.

y Metalúrgica de Peñarroya and the English company *The Río Tinto C.º Ltd.* Specifically, the maximum equity value of the first company corresponds to the 1914 financial year with 50,488,620.13 *pesetas*.[5] In the case of the second, the maximum corresponds to the fiscal years 1919 and 1920, when the same value was set at 28,294,604.63 *pesetas*.[6]

3.6 Electricity

It is the sixth sector by number of companies in 1911, six, and a patrimonial value slightly superior to 11 million *pesetas*, 5 % of the total. The number of companies registered in the period analysed was nine, 7 % of the 122 (Fernández-Paradas, 2008). This sector included French (2), English (2), Belgian (2), German (2) and Canadian (1) companies. The evolution of the capitalisation of foreign electricity companies during the second decade of the 20th century is unique. On 14 December 1911, the Canadian company *Riegos y Fuerza del Ebro* was founded in Barcelona, which was the largest foreign investment made in Spain during this period. According to the first fiscal year of this company, 1913, its capital was 122,500,000.00 *pesetas*.[7] The incorporation of this company into the statistics of the sector meant a very significant increase in the sector with respect to the whole. In 1911, electricity companies only represented 5 % of total foreign investment; from 1913, their weight in this sector increased to 33 %. During the First World War, and until the end of the decade, the capitalisation of foreign companies dedicated to electricity decreased, except in 1916 and 1917 when it increased. The maximum capitalisation of this sector was reached in 1917 with almost 154 million *pesetas*. In 1920, the eight foreign companies that continued in this sector had a capitalisation of slightly more than 141 million *pesetas*, 32 % of total foreign investment. The weight of this sector in total foreign investment increased significantly at the end of the period. In 1920, it was the first in the ranking while in 1911 it was the sixth. The importance of this sector by the number of companies it contributed to the whole increased. In 1911, it accounted for 8 % of the total, while in 1920 it rose to 10 %. Finally, the Canadian company *Riegos y Fuerza del Ebro* was the leading company in the sector and in 1920 it had a net worth

5 *Gaceta de Madrid*, 6 November 1918, no. 310.

6 *Gaceta de Madrid*, 22 April 1921, no. 112, for 1919 y *Gaceta de Madrid*, 3 August 1921, no. 186, for 1920.

7 *Gaceta de Madrid*, 14 January 1917, no. 14.

of 130,519,016.42 *pesetas*,[8] although it was in 1917 when it reached its maximum capitalisation of 138,488,837.24 *pesetas*.[9]

3.7 Bank

It is the seventh sector by number of companies in 1911, five, and a patrimonial value of more than 22 million *pesetas*, 10 % of the total. The number of companies registered in the period analysed was nine, 7 % of the 122. English companies, 33 %, dominated this sector. The origin of the rest of the banks was as follows: German, French, Italian, North American, and Argentine. The evolution of the capitalisation of foreign banks during the second decade of the 20th century was unique. The assets of these companies increased throughout the period, except in 1920, when they fell by 21 %. The maximum asset value of the banking sector was in 1919 with almost 71 million *pesetas*. In 1920, the seven foreign banks, which continued to operate, had a capitalisation of almost 48 million *pesetas*, 11 % of total foreign investment. The weight of this sector in total foreign investment increased at the end of the period. In 1920, it was the third in the ranking while in 1911 it was the fourth. The importance of this sector by the number of companies that it contributes to the whole increased. In 1911, it accounted for 7 % of the total, while in 1920 it rose to 9 %. On the other hand, the French company *Crédit Lyonnais* led this sector from 1911 to 1919. In 1916, it reached its maximum asset value of 25,646,029.89 *pesetas*.[10] Finally, in 1920 the sector was led by the Argentine company *Banco Español de Río de la Plata* with a capital of 25,580,187.12 *pesetas*.[11]

3.8 Wines

It is the eighth sector by number of companies in 1911, two, and a patrimonial value slightly superior to 6 million *pesetas*, 3 % of the total. The number of companies registered in the period analysed was four, 3 % of the 122. All the companies in this sector were English. The evolution of the capitalisation of foreign wine companies during the second decade of the 20th century was similar to other sectors. The assets of these companies increased until the beginning of the First World War. The sector reached its maximum capitalisation in 1913

8 *Gaceta de Madrid*, 5 July 1921, no. 186.
9 *Gaceta de Madrid*, 12 January 1921, no. 12.
10 *Gaceta de Madrid*, 30 November 1916, no. 335.
11 *Gaceta de Madrid*, 21 October 1920, no. 295.

with almost 7 million *pesetas*. During the rest of the period, the patrimonial value of the sector decreased. There were upturns in 1916 and 1920, but they were not enough to recover the lost capitalisation. In 1920, the four foreign wine companies that continued to operate had a capitalisation of nearly 6 million pesetas, 1 % of total foreign investment. The weight of this sector in total foreign investment decreased at the end of the period. In 1920, it was ninth in the ranking while in 1911 it was seventh. The importance of this sector in terms of the number of companies it contributed to the whole increased. In 1911, it accounted for 3 % of the total, while in 1920 it rose to 5 %. Finally, the English company *González Byass C. º Limited* was the leading company in this sector and in 1920, it had a net worth of 4,795,446.96 *pesetas*,[12] although it was in 1917 when it reached its maximum capitalisation of 6,090,499.52 *pesetas*.[13]

3.9 Chemistry

It is the ninth sector by number of companies in 1911, two, and a value of assets slightly above 5 million *pesetas*, 2 % of the total. The number of companies registered in the period analysed was three, 2 % of the 122. Two companies were French and another without specifying its nationality. The evolution of the capitalisation of foreign chemical companies during the second decade of the 20th century was unique. The assets of these companies increased until the beginning of the First World War. Between 1911 and 1914, the value of the assets of this sector grew by 87 %. During the war, 1914–1918, the behaviour of the sector was uneven. The sector increased its capitalisation in 1916 and 1917, while it decreased in 1915 and 1918. Nevertheless, the capitalisation of the sector was maintained during the period and was not affected as in other sectors. The foreign chemical sector reached its maximum capitalisation in 1919 with almost 13 million *pesetas*. In 1920, there were only two companies registered in this sector. The French company *Union Española de Fábricas de Abonos de Productos Químicos y de Superfosfatos* was the leading company in the sector until it disappeared from the statistics consulted. The last data from this company corresponds to the 1919 financial year when it had a value of 8,409,446.38 *pesetas*.[14] This generates a bias in the comments on the evolution of this sector in this decade, which must be taken into account. In 1920, the capitalisation of foreign companies, which continued to operate, was less than

12 *Gaceta de Madrid*, 29 January 1922, no. 39.
13 *Gaceta de Madrid*, 5 September 1917, no. 195.
14 *Gaceta de Madrid*, 22 April 1921, no. 112.

5 million pesetas, 1 % of total foreign investment. The weight of this sector in total foreign investment decreased at the end of the period. In 1920, it was the tenth in the ranking while in 1911 it was the eighth. The importance of this sector by number of companies contributing to the whole remained at 3 %.

3.10 Wood

It is the tenth sector by number of companies in 1911, two, and a value of assets slightly less than 5 million *pesetas*, 2 % of the total. The number of companies registered in the period analysed was three, 2 % of the 122. Two of them were of Norwegian origin, while the third was Belgian. The evolution of the capitalisation of foreign timber companies during the second decade of the 20th century was unique. The assets of these companies increased during the decade. With significant increases in 1913 (18 %), 1916 (47 %) and 1920 (15 %). The patrimonial value of these only fell slightly in 1919, when the disappearance of the Norwegian Company *Compañía Escandinava de las Canarias* from the sector statistics and a slight contraction in the capitalisation of the leading company in the sector, Norwegian company *Compañía de Maderas*, explain this atypical data of this historical series. In 1920, the two companies that continued to operate had a capitalisation of over 9 million *pesetas*, 2 % of total foreign investment. The weight of this sector in the total foreign investment increased at the end of the period. In 1920, it was seventh in the ranking while in 1911 it was tenth. The importance of this sector by number of companies contributing to the whole remained at 3 %. Finally, in 1920, the Norwegian Company *Compañía de Maderas* had an equity value of 8,448,780.60 *pesetas*.[15]

3.11 Foreign trade

It is the eleventh sector by number of companies in 1911 with one company, the English company *Fyffes Limited*, with a capitalisation of 487,361.00 *pesetas*[16] and an insignificant weight over the total. The number of companies registered in the period analysed was three, 2 % of the 122. All the companies in this sector were British and located in the Canary Islands. Their business was import and export maritime trade. The evolution of the capitalisation of foreign trade companies during the second decade of the 20th century was similar to that of other sectors, with increases in capitalisation until the beginning of the First World

15 *Gaceta de Madrid*, 17 September 1913, no. 318.
16 *Gaceta de Madrid*, 1 December 1920, no. 336.

War and a subsequent decapitalisation until the end of the period. Until 1913 the sector expanded, with the incorporation of two new companies: English company *Elder Dempster (Grand Canary) Limited* and English company *Elder Dempster Tenerife Limited*. These, together with the existing one, made the capitalisation of the sector reach the maximum value of the series in that year, when it exceeded 2 million *pesetas*. In 1920, the three companies that continued to operate had a capitalisation of less than 2 million *pesetas*, less than 1 % of the total foreign investment. The weight of this sector in total foreign investment did not change at the end of the period. Finally, in 1920, the company with the largest capitalisation was the English company *Elder Dempster Tenerife Limited*, which had a net worth of 854,235.72 *pesetas*.[17]

3.12 Trade

It is the twelfth sector by number of companies. No companies were registered in this sector until the 1913 tax year. The French company, *Établissements Debray*, which traded in coffee, is the only one listed for this year. It had a capitalisation of 1,420,515.91 *pesetas*[18] and weighed less than 1 % of the total. The number of companies registered in the period analysed was four, 3 % of the 122. Two of them were of French origin, one English and one Belgian. The evolution of the capitalisation of foreign trading companies during the second decade of the 20th century was similar to that of other sectors, with increases in capitalisation in the first half of the decade and a decrease in the second. The maximum asset value of companies in this sector was in 1916, when it exceeded 2 million *pesetas*. In 1920, the three companies that continued to operate had a capitalisation of less than 2 million *pesetas*, less than 1 % of total foreign investment. The weight of this sector in total foreign investment did not change at the end of the period. Finally, in 1920, the company with the largest capitalisation was the French company *Établissements Debray*, with a capitalisation of 1,420,515.91 *pesetas*.[19]

3.13 Coal for boats

It is the thirteenth sector by number of companies. No company was registered in this sector until the 1914 tax year, when all the companies in this sector were

17 *Gaceta de Madrid*, 23 December 1921, no. 357.
18 *Gaceta de Madrid*, 1 December 1920, no. 336.
19 *Gaceta de Madrid*, 22 April 1921, no. 112.

set up. The number of companies registered in the period analysed was three, 3 % of the total. All the companies in this sector were English and were located in the Canary Islands. Like many of the sectors mentioned above, this sector was conditioned by the First World War, with increases in capitalisation in the first half of the decade and a decrease in the second. In this case, the maximum value of the companies in this sector was in 1914, with almost 2 million *pesetas* of capitalisation. In 1920, only two companies continued to operate and had a capitalisation of less than one million *pesetas*, less than 1 % of total foreign investment. The weight of this sector in total foreign investment did not change at the end of the period. Finally, in 1920, the company with the largest capitalisation was the English company *Gran Canary Coaling C.º Limited*, with a capitalisation of 500,000.00 *pesetas*.[20]

3.14 Others

Finally, we have grouped in the sector of others the rest of the companies that have not been able to be associated. In this category of miscellany, there are twenty-eight companies that attend to very different activities: automotive, cement, cork, glass, hotel & catering, lamps, metal packaging, oil, photography, polishes, publicity, textiles, tobacco and tyres. Of these, nine were French, four were English, three were Belgian, three were Italian, two were American, one was German, one was Danish and five were unspecified. In 1911, twelve corporations appeared in this category with a capitalisation of almost 18 million *pesetas*. The evolution of the capitalisation of this category has followed the trend of the remains of the sectors analysed. In 1916, the maximum equity value of this category was reached with more than 29 million *pesetas* and sixteen companies. In 1920, only thirteen corporations remained and their capitalisation was almost 15 million *pesetas*. Finally, the Italian company *Metalgraf*, which manufactured metal packaging, is the company with the largest assets in this category with 2,856,400.00 *pesetas*.[21]

4 Conclusions

Knowing the evolution of a country's foreign investment allows us to explain how its economic and social development has been. Economic historians search through archives and libraries to obtain data that can explain it. In this case,

20 *Gaceta de Madrid*, 14 August 1920, no. 227.
21 *Gaceta de Madrid*, 24 August 1923, no. 236.

Spanish tax legislation from the beginning of the 20th century has made it possible to obtain information on the evolution of the capitalisation of foreign companies in the second decade of the 20th century by determining their capital in order to calculate the tax liability of the third Rate of the Contribution on Profits from Movable Wealth that they had to pay. These data were published in *Gaceta de Madrid* between 1911 and 1924. Following the research, 122 foreign companies were listed, which we have grouped by productive sector and analysed throughout this chapter.

The data indicate that 80 % of the foreign companies registered correspond to investors from four countries: France, England, Belgium, Germany, in that order. However, the most significant investment was the incorporation of the Canadian company *Riegos y Fuerza del Ebro* at the end of 1911, which contributed more than 122 million *pesetas* of direct foreign investment to the Spanish economy.

The evolution of the global capitalisation of these companies during the second decade of the 20th century (Tab. 1) shows a trend behaviour, both at a sectoral and aggregate level, correlated with two aspects which affected the Spanish economy during this decade. On the one hand, Spain's neutrality during the First World War (1914–1918) allowed it to increase the growth of its economy and facilitate foreign investment. On the other hand, at the end of the war, there was a desire to nationalise the productive sectors that were in foreign hands. Therefore, foreign investment in Spain had a generalised growth phase in all productive sectors between 1911 and 1914. During the war, in general, there was a decrease in capitalisation, although sectors with an increase in capitalisation were observed: banking, electricity, machinery, mining, wood and chemistry, among others. This may explain why the maximum value of foreign investment is in the fiscal year 1917 (482 million *pesetas*) and not in 1914. After the end of the war and the entry into force of the policy in favour of the nationalisation of foreign companies. The volume of companies and capital decreased in the last years of that decade, being very significant in some productive sectors, such as gas.

Finally, it should be noted that much of the foreign investment in this period was concentrated in the provision of network services: water, electricity, gas and tramways. In addition to these productive sectors, important investments were made in mining and banking.

5 Sources

Gaceta de Madrid, various issues between 1911 and 1924.

References

Broder, A. (1976). "Les investissements étrangers en Espagne au XIXe siècle: Méthodologie et Quantification". *Revue d'Histoire Economique et Sociale*, 54(1), 29–63.

Cameron, R. E. (1971). *Francia y el desarrollo económico de Europa, 1800–1914. Conquistas de la paz y semillas de guerra*. Madrid: Tecnos.

Castro Balaguer, R. (2007). "Historia de una reconversión silenciosa. El capital francés en España, c.1800–1936". *Revista de Historia Industrial*, 33, 81–82.

Castro-Valdivia, M. (2019). "La figura del empresario y el avance historiográfico de la Historia de la Empresa". In J. M. Matés-Barco, (coord.): *Empresas y empresarios en España. De mercaderes a industriales* (pp. 19–36). Madrid: Pirámide.

Castro-Valdivia, M. & Matés-Barco, J. M. (2020). "Los servicios públicos y la inversión extranjera en España (1850–1936): las empresas de agua y gas". *Historia Unisinos,* 24(2), 221–239. https://doi.org/10.413/hist.2020.242.05. 2 July 2020.

Castro-Valdivia, M., Fernández-Paradas, M. & Matés-Barco, J. M. (2019). "Las empresas extranjeras de agua y gas en España (circa 1900–1921)". In J. M. Matés-Barco y A. Torres-Rodríguez (coords.): *Los servicios públicos en España y México* (pp. 51–71). Madrid: Silex.

Comín, F. (2005). "La segunda Industrialización en el marco de la primera Globalización". In F. Comín; M. Hernández Benítez y E. Llopís Agelán (Eds.): *Historia Económica Mundial, Siglos X-XX* (pp. 239–286). Barcelona: Editorial Crítica.

Costa Campi, M. T. (1983). *Financiación Exterior del Capitalismo Español en el siglo XIX*. Barcelona: Universidad de Barcelona.

Fábregas, P. (2017). "La estrategia de la implantación de la industria del gas en España (1826–2010)". In I. Bartolomé Rodríguez; M. Fernández-Paradas y J. Mirás Araujo (Eds.): *Globalización, nacionalización y liberalización de la industria del gas en la Europa latina (siglos XIX–XXI)* (pp. 21–44). Madrid: Marcial Pons.

Fernández-Paradas, M. (2008). "La industria eléctrica y su actividad en el negocio del alumbrado en España (1901–1935)". *Ayer*, 71, 245–265.

Fernández-Paradas, M. (2015). "La regulación del suministro de gas en España (1841–1936)". *Revista de Historia Industrial*, 61, 49–78.

Landes, D. (1999). *La riqueza y la pobreza de las naciones: por qué algunas son tan ricas y otras son tan pobres.* Barcelona: Crítica.

Matés-Barco, J. M. (2019a). "El abastecimiento de agua a Barcelona (1850–1939): Origen y desarrollo de las compañías privadas" *Historia Contemporánea*, 59–1, 165–194. https://doi.org/10.1387/hc.19434. 2 July 2020.

Matés-Barco, J. M. (2019b). "Estrategia empresarial y control del mercado: la gestión del abastecimiento de agua potable". In J. M. Matés-Barco, (coord.): *Empresas y empresarios en España. De mercaderes a industriales* (pp. 223–240). Madrid: Pirámide.

Núñez Romero-Balmas, G. (1991). "Fuentes belgas sobre la electrificación de los tranvías españoles. El "Recueil Financier" de Bruselas". *Revista de Historia Económica*, IX (3), 561–574.

O'Rourke, K. H. & Williamson, J. G. (1999): *Globalization and history: The evolution of a nineteenth-century Atlantic economy.* Cambridge: MIT Press.

Tascón Fernández, J. (2008). "Los últimos cien años de inversión extranjera en España. Volviendo la vista atrás... Europa". In J. Tascón Fernández (Coord.): *La inversión extranjera en España* (pp. 75–87). Madrid: Minerva.

Tortella, G. (2008). "El capital extranjero en la formación del capitalismo español". In J. Tascón Fernández (Coord.): *La inversión extranjera en España* (pp. 31–48). Madrid: Minerva.

Tortella Casares, T. (1997). "Una guía de fuentes sobre las inversiones extranjeras en España entre 1780 y 1914". *Revista de Historia Económica – Journal of Iberian and Latin American Economic History*, 153, 607–623.

Jorge Lafuente del Cano

3 Entrepreneurial profiles in the Transition to democracy in Spain

Abstract The Transition to democracy was an event of the first magnitude in the political and economic history of Spain in the 20th century. There were various protagonists of these events who, at least in part, continue to have an influence in the country nowadays. Among them, worthy of note was the participation of professionals from different areas who dedicated some years of their career to public life at a moment of change, uncertainty and hope after the end of the dictatorship. In this chapter, the role of some entrepreneurs who played a notable part in Spanish politics at that time is studied. The influence of their professional career, their ideas concerning enterprises and the public sector, and their management capabilities are worthy of special attention in this analysis.

1 Introduction

Leopoldo Calvo-Sotelo, the last entrepreneur to become President of the Government in Spain, was sworn in on February 25, 1981. The role of the entrepreneurs as a collective has acquired an ever increasing importance in the analysis of the Transition to democracy in Spain, possibly the most studied event in Spain's contemporary history, alongside the Spanish Civil War.[1] The turbulent and up to a point violent history of Spain in the 19th and 20th centuries helps to explain why a peaceful and fairly successful event—passing from a dictatorship to democracy—has on occasions been presented as exemplary. Although it is true that, over the last few years, new approaches have also arisen that are more critical from the political and economic point of view concerning those decisive events.

The unforeseen swiftness with which the institutional changes occurred, with scarcely two years passing between the demise of the dictator in November 1975 and the celebration of the first democratic elections in June 1977, as well as the weight of some personalities—in both the Government and the opposition—determined that the political question should be the great

---

1 The web page of the *Fundación Transición Española* (*Spanish Transition Foundation*) offers an ample selection of titles: http://www.transicion.org/Bibliografia_FTE_2020.pdf.

protagonist in the first studies of the period. Later, the economic consequences of the change also took up their place in the analysis, demonstrating elements of both change and continuity between the previous regime and the new democratic system (Fuentes Quintana, 1983; García Delgado, 1990; Betrán et al., 2009). Over time, other actors have also acquired a prominent role in the literature. A good example is the economic representatives, such as the trade unions and the entrepreneurs. The role of the entrepreneurs and their influence on the political changes demonstrates how the very opening up of the system itself enabled the appearance of new actors on the public stage. While some works have pointed to the characteristics of continuity and discontinuity in the economic hierarchy of the Franco regime and the first years of democracy (González Fernández, 2012), others have stressed the new role that the employers played in the political and economic spheres (Cabrera, 2003; Cabrera & Del Rey, 2011; García Crespo, 2019).

This chapter analyzes a series of entrepreneurs who had a singular political role in the Governments of the Transition to democracy: persons linked to the center who had carved out an important career path in the private sector, in several different enterprises in the country, and who, at the start of the political change, decided to enter politics. Such questions as the prestige of their entrepreneurial curriculum, the way in which their training in the private sector influenced the political decisions they took, as well as the similarities and differences between their profiles, are all the subject of particular attention.

2 Professionals in politics: The case of the center

The Franco regime lasted for almost 40 years. The prohibition of political parties—except for a brief attempt to create associations towards the end of the regime—meant that, following the death of Franco, numerous projects and new formations emerged (Juliá, 2017, p. 14). On the one hand, there were some traditional parties in exile linked in general terms to the political left or to some nationalist positions. In the center, however, almost everything remained to be done. Thus there were numerous initiatives to articulate a political space in which the presence of reformist personalities with links to the regime was evident (Palomares, 2006). In this setting, the electoral coalition was created that, in the end, would obtain the victory in the first two elections (1977 and 1979). It is relevant here to look at the origins of the Central Democratic Union (Unión de Centro Democrático—UCD) of Adolfo Suárez, as it clearly showed the phenomenon of professionals with consolidated prestige who dedicated some years of their lives to public activity.

Paradoxically, the least representative case was that of president Suárez himself since, despite having spent some years working as a lawyer, he did not have a brilliant professional curriculum; he did, however, have a long political career within the Franco regime as a solicitor, a civil governor and director general of the public television (Fuentes, 2011). It was actually a surprise when he became president of the Government in July 1976 precisely because of that prolonged link with the old regime (Powell, 2007, p. 75). In any case, from the very beginning of his term of office, he showed a desire to transform the system to make it a democracy, through reforms but using the Franco regime's own laws. Thus, after passing some important laws (essentially the "Law for Political Reform" in January 1977) and legalizing political parties, it was then possible to call a free election. Faced with this perspective, several ministers of his Government, as well as other personalities, coincided in the necessity to create a new formation that would serve as an electoral platform for the president of the Government. Thus, the UCD was born, first as an electoral coalition and later as a party.

The UCD was never a normal formation, since it was founded from the top down and was conditioned by the presence of several personalities who claimed their personal share in the power (Alonso Castrillo, 1996). Some of these personalities led small parties with very few members, while others had various groups of followers who joined the centrist project. Neither was the ideology clearly defined beyond a very basic idea: the need to contribute, from a moderate stance, to the political transformation in Spain, which would be enshrined in a new constitutional text. Thus, several different and heterogeneous groups formed the centrist coalition: reformers from the Franco regime, liberals, Christian democrats, social democrats (Figuero, 1981; Hopkin, 2000).

In this motley political group a series of professionals, of notable prestige, stood out. They had taken up positions in the final days of the old regime with a view to the future process of democratizing the country. Some of them, in addition, had held office during the dictatorship. Thus, the reach of the sociological change that was to come later can be appreciated: if the role of a series of professionals who decided to dedicate some years of their lives to politics became significant in the Transition (many of them returning to their professions after completing their public stint); over time, the figure of the political professional was to become consolidated which, in the opinion of some, is one of the contributing factors towards the current political deterioration in Spain (Uriarte, 1997, pp. 266–270).

The UCD and its ministers are a case in point in that respect, since its creation from nothing and the absence of a dogmatic program meant that many professionals of a moderate disposition approached the formation towards the end of the 1970s. Of course, there were still civil servants and those high political positions, but the professionals also made up an important group. They were essentially liberal professionals: including lawyers, engineers, teachers and professors.

There were also entrepreneurs. The numbers were smaller than for the professional categories, yet they were always present. As an example, we could mention the following politicians from the centrist formation who developed at least a part of their career in the private sector: Iñigo Cavero (Minister for Education, Culture & Justice), Joaquín Garrigues Walker (Minister of Public Works & City Planning), José Lladó (Minister of Commerce and Transport), Alberto Oliart (Minister of Industry, Energy & Health), Manuel Clavero Arévalo (Minister of Culture & Regions), or Landelino Lavilla (president of the parliament). In this chapter, the figures of four entrepreneurs have been selected; entrepreneurs who achieved success in their enterprises as well as notable responsibilities in the Government of Spain. Despite certain differences, some common traits can also be appreciated in their various careers.

3 Engineers and entrepreneurs

The first examples of politicians of the UCD who actively worked in the private sector are the engineers Juan Miguel Villar Mir, Salvador Sánchez-Terán and Leopoldo Calvo-Sotelo (who will be discussed in detail below). Their careers have common elements but also notable differences. The first parallel characteristic is, logically, their common training as civil engineers. This is a clear factor of great influence in the public life of Spain in the 19th and 20th centuries. Engineers made up a select collective of great prestige with a series of shared values that came to identify them (Martykánova, 2007).

After the Civil War, when the three were studying (Calvo-Sotelo was born in 1923, Villar Mir in 1931 and Sánchez-Terán in 1934), the need for technicians and managers had brought about a reinforcement of the professional prestige and technical competence associated with engineers (Lafuente del Cano & Ortúñez Goicolea, 2020, p. 136). In those days, and until 1957, the School of Civil Engineering (Escuela de Caminos) was organically dependent upon the Ministry of Public Works, which meant that, upon completing their studies, the graduates became civil servants in the Administration. A good number of the School's graduates thus developed their professional careers in the public sector, although others preferred to join the private sector or to combine both options.

First of all, we shall look at Juan Miguel Villar Mir, who can be characterized as a man of industry. After completing his degree in Engineering, he went on to further his studies in both Spain and the USA, obtaining a Degree in Law and various Diplomas in Economics and Business Management (VVAA, 2010, p. 83).

Villar Mir entered the School of Civil Engineering at 18 years of age, in 1949. He graduated as number 1 of his promotion and years later he obtained his PhD (Villar Mir, 2008). His career, to a large extent, exemplifies the flexible relations between the public and private sectors that characterized engineers at that time, in the midst of the full process of Spain's economic expansion (Cabrera & Del Rey, 2011, p. 267). In the case of Villar Mir, his link to the public sector was twofold. He first of all gained the position, by way of an exam, of Professor in Accounting & Legislation in the Technical School of Engineering of Public Works in the Polytechnic of Madrid, while some years later he also became the Professor of Company Organization in the Higher Technical School of Civil Engineering in the same university. His second link was serving in the Administration, where he took on several different responsibilities beginning at the end of the 1950s: auxiliary engineer in the port of Cádiz, deputy director general of Ports and Maritime Signals, director general of Employment and, finally, president of the National Work Protection Fund between 1967 and 1968 (BOE, n. 253, 11/12/1967).

Simultaneously, from 1955 onwards, he began an intensive business activity that would turn out to be highly useful in both his short political career and, later on, when creating his own entrepreneurial group. That year of 1955, he began to work in the construction company *Dragados y Construcciones* (Torres Villanueva, 2017). However, his entrepreneurial career really took off in 1968. At that time he became president of *Hidro Nitro*, a company that produced electrochemical products and also electrical energy; this was followed by a brief stint as president of the *Empresa Nacional Carbonífera del Sur, S.A.* and of the *Empresa Nacional de Celulosas, S.A.* His good management (Fernández Moya, 2017) led him to become, in 1970, the managing director of one of the principal industrial groups in Spain: the *Altos Hornos de Vizcaya*, a steel works. He carried out a renovation and modernized the company, thus catapulting him to the first and only political position he held: Minister of Finance and third Vice-president of the Government in December 1975. In that Cabinet, the first under the new monarchy, he coincided with Leopoldo Calvo-Sotelo. Villar Mir has said that both of them had received previous offers to enter the Government, but that they had refused to be ministers under Franco (Villar Mir, 2008, p. 95).

In any case, it would seem that his trajectory as a teacher and especially as a company director allowed him to enter the government at a decisive moment, but one also replete with uncertainties: Arias Navarro, the last president with Franco, stayed at the head of the government and showed a very limited desire for reform in comparison to some of his principal ministers (Palomares, 2006, pp. 236–237). In addition, the economic situation seemed to be particularly complicated: the last Governments of Franco had not taken any measures to deal with the petroleum crisis that had begun quite suddenly in October 1973 (Comín & Hernández, 2013, p. 307), so the first Governments of the new regime found themselves immersed in a situation that was deteriorating day by day. Between 1974 and 1977 the Governments carried out a very relaxed, compensatory policy (Pelet, 2002, p. 275).

In this context, the Finance Minister Villar Mir decided to devalue the peseta in February 1976, fixing a level of exchange with the dollar of 66.54 pesetas for buyers and 66.60 for sellers. This was the third devaluation of the peseta since 1959, the year that the Stabilization Plan started to function, the first plan to substantially modify Spain's economic development since the Civil War. On the other hand, during his term of office, he tried to develop the much debated White Paper on the Reform of Spain's Tax System (Fernández Moya, 2017).

Nevertheless, he did not have enough time to do more and his political career ended after six months, when Adolfo Suárez became president of the Government. Although some reports talked of Villar Mir possibly reinstatement the Cabinet (Fuentes, 2011, p. 246), he was first of all replaced by Eduardo Carriles and, shortly afterwards by Francisco Fernández Ordóñez. Despite his brief passage through politics, this engineer had an important influence on that first Government following the death of Franco. However, he did not repeat his political vocation. From 1976 onwards, he dedicated his work to the entrepreneurial world, becoming one of the most important businessmen in the country, especially after the Foundation of his own Group in 1987.

Secondly, we have Salvador Sánchez-Terán, who was a very particular case. He became a civil engineer in 1958. His career began in a private company the following year, but shortly after that he joined the Administration, where he took on several responsibilities in the Housing Ministry, the Directorate General of Highways and as president of *RENFE* (the national railway company), between 1970 and 1973 (González Martínez, 2017).

At the same time as he was studying to become an engineer, another decisive element in his career was his relation to the National Catholic Association of Propagandists, who allowed him to work as the president of Catholic Action from 1959, establishing a series of important contacts for his future professional and political career. It was precisely the serious internal crisis that this association suffered, and that would provoke his resignation, was what catapulted Sánchez-Terán towards his major entrepreneurial project, the foundation of *PROLESA* in 1968, which has been defined as the first political enterprise (González Martínez, 2017, p. 57). In fact, this entrepreneurial initiative, that the engineer promoted and presided over until 1973, was established in the editorial sector, but its background was political: a place for dialog and discreet meetings of various people who were looking for a reformist solution for after the Franco regime.

His relations through Catholic Action and his entrepreneurial initiatives allowed him to exercise some principles which he could make use of later on during his political career. In 1976, following the death of Franco, he was chosen as Civil Governor of Catalonia, from which position he acted as the patient negotiator for Adolfo Suárez with Josep Tarradellas—president of the Government of Catalonia in exile—in order to reestablish that regional government. He was successful in his mission and achieved his objective before the new Constitution was passed.

His management of the situation in Catalonia led him to enter the Cabinet. He was chosen as Minister for Transport between February 1978 and May 1980, and later Minister for Employment between May and September of 1980. Despite the brevity of this second period, he was able to put into practice some of the knowledge he acquired in the entrepreneurial world. In fact, his main objective was one of great significance (Cosgaya, González & Lafuente del Cano, 2016), as it supposed recognizing that the situation of the economic crisis would last a long time and the problem of unemployment in Spain could become structural, at the time being around 10 %. He thus decided to try to get the support of all the institutional social forces, both public and private, in order to try to change the labor model. However, he did not have time to develop such an ambitious project and nor did Spain's political situation allow him to achieve any great consensus: in May 1980, the socialist party (PSOE) presented a motion of no confidence—though unsuccessful—against the Government of Suárez.

After leaving the Government, and during the remainder of the term of office of the UCD, he was president of Telefónica, the public telephone company, and with the victory of the socialists in 1982 he definitively abandoned politics to dedicate himself full time to the entrepreneurial world.

4 President of the government

The surname Calvo-Sotelo had already been involved in events during Spain's recent history. José Calvo-Sotelo, Leopoldo's uncle, a minister in the dictatorship of Primo de Rivera and a member of parliament during the Second Republic, was assassinated on July 13th 1936, just before the start of the Civil War. The contacts that the Calvo-Sotelo family had favored the insertion into the world of work for the young Leopoldo Calvo-Sotelo who, nevertheless, had a successful academic career, finishing as number one of his promotion in civil engineering (Lafuente del Cano & Ortúñez Goicolea, 2020, p. 131).

His professional career in the world of business began the year before he finished his degree, which is one more example of the professional prestige associated with engineers, as mentioned above. Thus, in 1949, he received a call from the Banco Urquijo, a financial group. This was to be the start of a long and fruitful relationship. The bank had developed a varied industrial portfolio and, from the mid-1940s onwards, had introduced a series of innovations linked to the figure of Juan Lladó (Puig & Torres, 2008, p. 107). Lladó had become the CEO of the *Banco Urquijo* in 1944 and was later elected as president. His desire to participate in the reindustrialization of the country led him to create a Study Service to analyze different projects for their possible funding by the bank. It was this Society that Calvo-Sotelo joined. Once he completed his studies, and after deciding upon a job in the private sector (renouncing his place as a civil servant), Calvo-Sotelo began to work officially for the *Banco Urquijo.* A short time later he became the head of one of the companies that had been analyzed in the Study Service. The company was *Perlofil*, the first company to commercialize nylon in Spain. This material had recently been created and had a great importance during the Second World War. Calvo-Sotelo thus became one of the youngest managing directors in the country.

This entrepreneurial experience was important for two reasons: first of all for his management ability and secondly for his ability to form teams. Both these skills would come in particularly useful in his later political career. His management expertise was demonstrated with the achievement of financial stability so as to thus ensure the future of the company: in 1963, he reached an agreement with the Dutch industrial group *AKU*, which merged with *Perlofil* (Nogueira, 2015). This agreement led to his promotion in the *Banco Urquijo.* On the one hand, he became an advisor of the bank, while on the other, he took up the position as the head of the *UEE*, Spain's explosives company, one of the great Spanish companies that had, until 1917, enjoyed a monopoly in the production and distribution of explosives in Spain.

The situation of the *UEE* in the 1960s was, however, somewhat complicated, as the company was losing money: Calvo-Sotelo proposed a strategy based on expansion and diversification, a strategy that proved to be right. Some years later, in 1970, the company merged with the *Spanish Minas Río Tinto Company*, giving rise to the *Unión Explosivos Río Tinto*, whose results in the years immediately following the merger demonstrated the success of Calvo-Sotelo's management (Lafuente del Cano & Ortúñez Goicolea, 2020, p. 137). He thus cemented his position in the bank until 1975, when he was chosen as a minister in the first Government of the Monarchy after the death of Franco.

Calvo-Sotelo thus began a brief but intense political career that culminated in 1981 when he became President of the Government. His consolidated entrepreneurial career was partly responsible for his entry into politics. Parallel to his business work he had maintained a series of contacts, within the limited formation of associations allowed by the dictatorship, with some personalities who defended a democratic solution to the end of the Franco era. He was thus in a perfect position to take the leap into the public arena. What is more, between 1967 and 1968, he had taken up his first public office as the president of the railways company, *RENFE*.

He was chosen as Minister for Commerce in December 1975 and, some months later, he became Minister of Public Works, then in the first cabinet of Adolfo Suárez. His relationship with the president from Ávila was decisive in his political career. He became one of the founders of the electoral platform, the UCD, which the president of the Government joined and led to victory in the first democratic elections following Franco's demise, in June 1977.

After some months as spokesperson of the parliamentary group of his party, he returned to the Cabinet in 1978 to take charge of the new Ministry for Relations with the European Communities. This position was decisive in his political career as it allowed him to make the jump to the top spot a short time later. Furthermore, it clearly reflected some elements of management that he had developed during his time in business.

The reason for the creation of this new Ministry lies within Spain's desire to be able to join the European Economic Community (EEC). Although there had been a certain rapprochement during the Franco regime—even signing a preferential economic agreement in 1970—entry had been vetoed due to the lack of any kind of democracy in the country (Bassols, 1995, p. 123). The regime change that was taking place in Spain following Franco's death provided some hope, for the first time, that there may be a real possibility of Spain joining, something that was considered of vital importance, both politically and economically.

The first mission that Calvo-Sotelo had as minister was something he had learnt in business: the formation of teams. This was essential, as the new Ministry had been created from scratch and did not have its own staff. As in the case of *Perlofil*, the ex-entrepreneur decided on the creation of a small, well-knit working team—20–30 persons—in both the origin of its members—in general from other economically minded ministries—and the technical profile (Lafuente del Cano, 2017, pp. 62ss). It is necessary to point out that a part of this Ministry team would accompany him throughout the rest of his political career, including his time as president of the Government, which would seem to indicate merits of his choice.

The second mission involved starting up the negotiation. Here, he had to bring into play his management ability, since there were three different fronts open, two exterior and one interior. The interior front involved setting up a pedagogical campaign throughout the national territory concerning the significance of the EEC and the results that the country could obtain by joining. In his opinion, this was necessary because the country's general, but diffuse European feeling was not focused on clear and precise knowledge of the European institutions and this could lead to a certain amount of frustration in the future. The exterior front involved talking with both the EEC authorities in order to be able to initiate, as soon as possible, the real negotiations (that began in February 1979) and the member states themselves individually, as they would determine the rhythm and the contents of the negotiating table.

During his term of office as Minister for Relations with the European Communities, the negotiations with Spain began and advanced in some of the issues. However, the Spanish expectations of a rapid entry to the EEC came up against a problem in June 1980. The president of the French Republic, Valery Giscard d´Estaing, gave a speech defending a pause in the negotiations. In his opinion, the internal problems of the EEC (among other issues, the British claim over their "check", the consequences of the economic crises of 1973 and 1979) should be resolved first before any expansion could be contemplated. The French fear of Spain's agricultural competition may well have been part of the reason for this intervention by the French president (Lafuente del Cano, 2019, p. 359). Although the negotiations did not formally stop, in practice some of the most important issues, such as agriculture, were vetoed and could not be negotiated, despite the wishes of Spain.

In any case, it would seem that the delay should not be attributed to Calvo-Sotelo and that, on the contrary, his handling of the negotiations was rewarded. In September 1980 he was named Finance Minister and second vice-president of the Government. A few months later, in February 1981, he became president of the Government following the resignation of Adolfo Suárez, beset by the economic crisis and the internal division within his own party (Fuentes, 2011, pp. 392ss.). The ex-entrepreneur came to the Moncloa (the residence of the president) at a critical moment of Spain's Transition: on top of the problems inherited from his predecessor, he now had to deal with the attempted coup in the very session of parliament dedicated to his investiture as president, February 23, 1981. Thus, Calvo-Sotelo's term of office began with the imperious need to restore constitutional normality following the failed coup attempt.

As in his earlier posts, his management abilities were tested and he had to choose his priorities, since the internal crisis of his party was ongoing and he had only a minority government in parliament that needed continuous external support.

The economic question was one of his priorities, where he looked for an agreed solution to the crisis (through the National Employment Agreement of 1981 as his flagship) and a failed industrial reconversion project that would finally be developed in a future legislature and with another party. Furthermore, from the point of view of domestic policy, laws concerning divorce and education were passed, not without some strong dissent in his own party. In addition, a law was set in motion to harmonize regional development, although some of its articles were later declared unconstitutional.

As for foreign policy, the priorities were clear: to accelerate Spain's entry to the international institutions. This was not achieved in the case of the EEC, as the French position meant progress was very slow, but entry to NATO was achieved, in May 1982.

Assuming his successes and failures, Calvo-Sotelo decided to throw in the towel. The situation in his party was unsustainable, with a constant trickle of MPs abandoning the party and joining the opposition; so he decided to bring forward the general elections to October 1982. This time the PSOE of Felipe González obtained a comfortable absolute majority and the UCD practically disappeared. Following the end of his political career, and after some problems narrated by Calvo-Sotelo himself with a certain sense of humor (Calvo-Sotelo, 2003, pp. 203–208), the ex-president returned to the *Banco Urquijo*, where he had developed his entrepreneurial career and where he remained until his retirement in 1998.

5 A representative of the employers

The figure of Agustín Rodríguez Sahagún has remained inextricably linked in the collective memory of the Transition to Adolfo Suárez, not only because of their common origin (both were from Ávila), but also because of their close friendship and tight collaboration, both in the UCD and in the new centrist formation that the ex-president founded in 1982 and over which he presided until 1991: the Democratic & Social Center (Centro Democrático y Social—CDS). Nevertheless, the profile of Sahagún is rich in nuances and presents multiple characteristics: entrepreneur, representative of the employers, Minister for Industry, Minister for Defense, President of the UCD, top of the list member of parliament for Madrid.

Agustín Rodríguez Sahagún belonged to the same generation as Villar Mir and Sánchez-Terán, since he was born in 1932. Although he also considered studying Engineering, he finally chose a degree in Economic Sciences at the University of Deusto, later completed with a degree in Law at the University of Valladolid in Spain and, abroad, with—among other qualifications—a degree in Political Sciences at the University of Caen and another in Company Management at the *Instituto per l'Addestramento nell'Industria* of Milán.

His professional career was first of all focused on teaching, and he was a lecturer at the University of Deusto, in the National Enterprise Institute in Bilbao (Cosgaya, J. & Lafuente del Cano, J., http://www.transicion.org/80bios/Rodriguez.pdf).

He later turned towards a career in the State Administration, as he wished to obtain a position as a state civil servant, that of Trade Specialist. Nevertheless, political circumstances got in his way: the requirement of being a member of the National Movement of Franco, and which Rodríguez Sahagún had never wanted to join due to the republican past of his family (Del Río, 1991, p. 56).

Due to this unsuspected detail, his professional activity turned towards the private sector. He worked in *Echeverría S.A.*, a steel works of Bilbao, where he reached the position of managing director in 1959; in the *Banco de Bilbao* and in an advisory capacity for several entities. Some of his own projects began to appear in a similar way: the first, related to distance learning and correspondence courses; the second, in the editorial world, *Ediciones Deusto,* founded in 1960. His jump to the large companies came some time later, around 1967. Some of his main initiatives were *International Altex*, *Procex* and, above all, the *Compañía Petrolera Latino-Americana*, with which he took on several trips abroad, got to know the entrepreneurial structure of Spain and other countries, as well as obtaining generous profits (Del Río, 1991, pp. 97–98).

At the start of the process of democratization, several political and economic sectors began to look for their place in Spain's new public space. Just as numerous political parties were created, entrepreneurial association also took its first steps with the appearance of numerous entities: sectorial, regional and, progressively, national (Flores, 2000, p. 696). Rodríguez Sahagún played an important role in some of these organizations: from 1976 to 1977 he was the co-founder of the Spanish Confederation of Entrepreneurs (CEE: Confederación Empresarial Española), the Spanish Confederation of Small & Medium-sized Businesses (CEPYME: Confederación Española de la Pequeña y Mediana Empresa), of which he was president for a time, and the Spanish Confederation of Business Organizations (CEOE: Confederación Española de Organizaciones Empresariales) which, in the end, became the representative organization of Spanish employers and of which he was the vice-president.

His experience as an entrepreneur and an employer, added to his good relations with Adolfo Suárez, persuaded him to become a member of the UCD, becoming the Minister for Industry from 1978 on. He knew the economic situation of the country well, as well as the large companies; so the centrist party tried to carry through a law of industrial reconversion, which finally did not succeed. In addition, he was also the negotiator with the principal trade unions and his ex-colleagues the employers in order to put into practice the economic and social Pacts signed in the Moncloa Palace at the end of 1977. Nevertheless, his term of office lasted barely a year, as he was named Minister of Defense following the elections of 1979. This was a post further away from his own interests, but he agreed upon the express request of the president of the Government (Del Río 1991, p. 109). It was a highly delicate position since the Armed Forces were a frequent target of the terrorist band ETA and some members of the Army considered the government's response too weak. It should not be forgotten that the attempted coup of the 23-F 1981 occurred precisely during the term of office of Rodríguez Sahagún. His next post was just as complicated: president of UCD, after the resignation of Suárez in 1981. Once more, he had to put into practice knowledge acquired from his professional experience: the delicate situation of Spain's economy; the ability to negotiate with all the tendencies in the party that was quickly breaking up; as well as with the employers. The CEOE, led by the Catalonian entrepreneur Carlos Ferrer Salat, maintained constant disputes with the centrist Governments, accusing them of carrying out excessively social democratic policies (Calvo-Sotelo, 1990, p. 157ss.). Rodríguez Sahagún, ex-employer, did not manage to improve relations with the employers in the end.

In 1982, following the electoral debacle, a good part of the leaders of the UCD abandoned politics. Rodríguez Sahagún, however, faced another challenge with the new centrist formation that Adolfo Suárez had created that same year (Díez Miguel, 2017). Sahagún became a member of parliament for Vizcaya, a city councilor for Madrid and finally mayor of the capital city, from 1989 to 1991. He renounced reelection a few months before his death in November of the same year in Paris, where he had gone for a cardiovascular operation. He was the only one of the four subjects of this chapter who did not return to a career in the private sector, but this was because of his political loyalty to and friendship with the ex-president, Adolfo Suárez, whom he accompanied throughout his political career.

6 Conclusions

The Transition to democracy was a decisive period in the recent history of Spain in which a series of singular characteristics occurred and with which the entrepreneurs were closely involved.

The existence of a prolonged authoritarian regime that impeded democratic political life resulted in the creation of diverse channels through which to direct political concerns. Many of them turned into coalitions and parties once the democratic process began. It is thus not surprising that one of these new formations, the UCD, created around the figure of the president of the Government, should attract numerous personalities with a political vocation. Some of them were from the old regime itself, others had not dedicated themselves to public life at all, but they had had a prolonged professional career. There were also cases of professionals linked to both the public and private sectors. In fact, such a connection between the Administration and enterprises was a characteristic of part of the economic history of the Franco era.

Among the members of the centrist party were several examples of persons with links to the entrepreneurial world. The four cases analyzed in this chapter are a good reflection of the position of the center, of the UCD and a part of Spanish society in the face of political change following the death of Franco.

Differences and similarities can be found in all of them.

Three of them, Calvo-Sotelo, Villar Mir and Sánchez-Terán were trained as engineers and began their professional careers at a time when the country's economic progress demanded young people with a technical formation. The traditional prestige that engineers enjoyed in Spain increased even more in the period in question here, if such a thing is possible. What is certain is that many of them ended up working for the State Administration, while others found a professional opening in enterprises or by combining both sectors.

Calvo-Sotelo had a long professional career in the private sector until he was chosen as a minister in 1975. In his role as a man of industry, he acquired a series of skills, such as teamwork and management, which turned out to be particularly useful in his later years in politics, in the various ministerial positions he occupied and as president of the Government.

As for Villar Mir, he combined his work in the enterprise with that in the public sector, as well as with teaching in a university. Although his political career was brief, it would seem clear that his previous experience was decisive in helping him reach the third vice-presidency of the Government.

Finally, the last engineer, Sánchez-Terán, had a peculiar career in which he also combined the public and private sectors and also founded a company in which political projects that did not fit any public forum were hidden. His contacts of those years and his negotiating skills would seem to have been the key to his joining the UCD and his later political responsibilities.

Rodríguez Sahagún was not an engineer, but an economist. This was perhaps why his career was more purely entrepreneurial. Not only did he have success in business, but he also played a relevant role in the creation of the first employers' organizations at the start of the Transition. Paradoxically, this did not serve to smooth things over and improve the difficult relationships between his party—that he even at one time led—and the organization that, over time, would become consolidated as the representative of the employers, the CEOE.

After their time in politics, three of them returned to the private sector with notable success. Villar Mir founded his own company with which he has obtained very good economic results; Calvo-Sotelo continued to be linked to the *Banco Urquijo*; while Sánchez-Terán occupied several management positions: in *Telefónica*, the national telephone company, the *COPE*, a radio station, and the car company *TATA Motors*. The case of Rodríguez Sahagún was quite different, as he was involved in politics until his early death in 1991: following the debacle of the UCD, he joined the new party of Adolfo Suárez, the CDS.

In spite of the differences in their careers, their passage through private enterprises had a singular influence in their political lives, due both to the accumulated prestige and the contacts they achieved and which situated them with a good position on the starting blocks during the final days of the Franco era and the start of the process of change in the country that occurred following Franco's death.

References

Alonso Castrillo, S. (1996). *La apuesta del centro: historia de la UCD*. Alianza: Madrid.

Bassols, R. (1995). *España en Europa*. Madrid: Política International.

Betrán, C., Cubel, A., Pons, M. A. & Sanchís, T. (2009). *La España democrática (1975–2000). Economía.* Madrid: Síntesis.

Cabrera, M. (2003). Empresarios y políticos en la democracia. De la crisis económica a las incertidumbres de la Transición. *Economía Industrial*, 349–350, 51–62. https://www.mincotur.gob.es/Publicaciones/Publicacionesperiodicas/EconomiaIndustrial/RevistaEconomiaIndustrial/349/06%20MERCEDES%20CABRERA.pdf. Accessed on September 14, 2020.

Cabrera, M. & Del Rey, F. (2011). *El poder de los empresarios. Política y economía en la España contemporánea (1875–2010).* Barcelona: RBA.

Calvo-Sotelo, L. (1990). *Memoria viva de la Transición*. Barcelona: Plaza & Janés/Cambio16.

Calvo-Sotelo, L. (2003). *Pláticas de familia (1878–2003).* Madrid: La esfera de los libros.

Cosgaya, J., González Martínez, C. & Lafuente del Cano, J. (2016). Mercado laboral y cambio de modelo económico: la breve ejecutoria de Sánchez-Terán en el Ministerio de Trabajo. *Trabajo: Revista iberoamericana de relaciones laborales*, 34, 3–12.

Comín, F. & Hernández, M. (2013). *Crisis económicas en España, 1300–2012: lecciones de la historia*. Madrid: Alianza.

Del Río, A. (1991). *Agustín Rodríguez Sahagún*. Madrid: Grupo Libro.

Díez Miguel, D. (2017). *Adolfo Suárez y el Centro Democrático y Social (1982–1991). Tesis doctoral.* Valladolid: Universidad de Valladolid. http://uvadoc.uva.es/bitstream/handle/10324/26491/TESIS1300-171019.pdf?sequence=1&isAllowed=y

Fernández Moya, M. (2017). Juan Miguel Villar Mir. In E. Torres Villanueva (dir.), *Cien empresarios madrileños* (pp. 668–675). Madrid: LID.

Flores, A. (2000). Los empresarios y la transición a la democracia en España. *Estudios Sociológicos*, 18 (54), 695–726.

Figuero, J. (1981). *UCD, la empresa que creó Adolfo Suárez*. Madrid: Grijalbo.

Fuentes, J. F. (2011). *Adolfo Suárez. Biografía política*. Barcelona: Planeta.

Fuentes Quintana, E. (1983). La prioridad política de la economía en la transición española. *Pensamiento iberoamericano*, 3, 118–127.

García Crespo, G. (2019). La democracia del libre mercado. La intervención patronal en el sistema política de la Transición. *Historia y Política*, 42, 297–330. https://revistas.ucm.es/index.php/HPOL/article/view/67724/4564456552974. Accessed on September 14, 2020.

García Delgado, J. L. (1990). *Economía española de la Transición y la democracia*. Madrid: CIS.

González Fernández, A. (2012). Los empresarios y la huelga entre la estabilización y la democracia. *Historia y Política*, 27, 281–307.

González Martínez, C. (2017). *Salvador Sánchez-Terán, un político de la Transición*. Madrid: ACCI.

Hopkin, J. (2000). *El partido de la Transición: ascenso y caída de la UCD*. Madrid: Acento.

Juliá, S. (2017). *Transición: Historia de una política española (1937–2017)*. Barcelona: Galaxia Gutenberg.

Lafuente del Cano, J. (2017). *Leopoldo Calvo-Sotelo y Europa*. Madrid: Sílex.

Lafuente del Cano, J. (2019). Los empresarios españoles ante el cambio: retos, dificultades y esperanzas. In J. M. Matés-Barco (coord.), *Empresas y empresarios en España De mercaderes a industriales* (pp. 353–368). Madrid: Pirámide.

Lafuente del Cano, J. & Ortúñez Goicolea, P. P. (2020). Leopoldo Calvo-Sotelo: ingeniero, empresario y político frente a la integración europea. *Historia y Política*, 43, 121–155. https://revistas.ucm.es/index.php/HPOL/article/view/69745/4564456553524. Accessed on September 4, 2020.

Martykánová, D. (2007). Por los caminos del progreso. El universo ideológico de los ingenieros de caminos españoles a través de la Revista de Obras Públicas (1853–1899). *Ayer*, 68, 193–219. http://revistaayer.com/sites/default/files/articulos/68-8-ayer68_CrisisDescomposicionFranquismo_Sanz.pdf. Accessed on September 2, 2020.

Nogueira, A. (2015). Leopoldo Calvo-Sotelo, el presidente que fue empresario: una visión entre el mercado y el Estado. *Revista Empresa y Humanismo*, 23 (1), 87–111. https://revistas.unav.edu/index.php/empresa-y-humanismo/article/view/38213/33942. Accessed on September 4, 2020.

Palomares, C. (2006). *Sobrevivir después de Franco. Evolución y triunfo del reformismo, 1964–1977*. Madrid: Alianza.

Pelet, C. (2002). Los últimos cuarenta años de la peseta: De Bretton Woods a la Unión Monetaria. *Acciones e Investigaciones Sociales*, 15, 265–282.

Powell, Ch. (2007). El reformismo centrista y la Transición democrática: retos y respuestas. *Historia y Política*, 18, 49–82.

Puig, N. & Torres, E. (2008). *Banco Urquijo. Un banco con historia*. Madrid: Turner.

Uriarte, E. (1997). El análisis de las élites políticas en las democracias. *Revista de Estudios Políticos*, 97, 249–275.

Villar Mir, J. M. (2008). Leopoldo Calvo-Sotelo y Bustelo: el ingeniero humanista. *Cuenta y Razón*, 5, 93–96.

VVAA. (2010). Juan Miguel Villar Mir. Presidente de OHL y Grupo Villar Mir. *Cuenta y Razón*, 15, 81–88.

Juan Manuel Matés-Barco

4 Water supply companies in the Spanish Levante (1840–1939)

Abstract The goal of this chapter is to present the group of private drinking water supply companies that emerged in the Levante region of Spain during the final decades of the 19th century and the first decades of the 20th century. Additionally, the work analyses the role these entities played in the urban modernisation process and describes some of their characteristics. The company *Aguas Potables y Mejoras de Valencia*, which over the years became part of the *Aguas de Barcelona* group, was especially important. A variety of factors explain the range of enterprises that operated in this region. Firstly, the Water Laws of 1866 and 1879 ratified the powers of municipal councils and spurred the granting of concessions to private companies for the supply of water to population centres. Secondly, local and foreign developers were attracted to an economic activity that was very innovative at that time.

1 Introduction

The goal of this chapter is to present the group of private drinking water supply companies that emerged in the Levante region of Spain during the final decades of the 19th century and the first decades of the 20th century. Additionally, the work analyses the role these entities played in the urban modernisation process and describes some of their characteristics. The company *Aguas Potables y Mejoras de Valencia*, which over the years became part of the *Aguas de Barcelona* group, was especially important. A variety of factors explain the range of enterprises that operated in this region. Firstly, the Water Laws of 1866 and 1879 ratified the powers of municipal councils and spurred the granting of concessions to private companies for the supply of water to population centres. Secondly, local and foreign developers were attracted to an economic activity that was very innovative at that time (Matés-Barco, 2014, 2016).

2 The geographical and demographic context

The region of Spain known as the Levante includes the current Communities of Valencia and Murcia, and occupies a large strip along the eastern coast of the Iberian Peninsula. This chapter, for reasons of space, focuses on the study of the former. The Valencian Community comprises three provinces: Castellón,

Valencia and Alicante. Castellón, a city of the Levante with a typical Mediterranean climate, can be described as an agricultural, commercial and political-administrative city. The city of Valencia, the centre of the fertile region, is surrounded by a halo of medium-sized cities that form with it the true metropolitan area and the real industrial heart of the region. The existence of such an important consumer nucleus and the ease of communication with other towns were factors that triggered its industrialisation process. Alicante is mainly a port city, operating not only for the region that surrounds it but also for an extensive hinterland that greatly exceeds the boundaries of the province. The defining feature of the Old Kingdom of Valencia were the orchards and cultivated areas developed by the Muslims in the Middle Ages. Orange trees, vegetable rows and rice fields alternated in the variegated Valencian agricultural landscape. In the drier regions of the Levante, typical crops of the Mediterranean triad continued to be cultivated: vines, olives and cereals.

In the city of Valencia, population growth rates were much lower than those in the northern regions and in Catalonia. It can be said that the Turia River capital was immersed in a slow urbanisation process in which the percentage of the population living in the city went from 32 % in 1860 to 46.4 % in 1900. During the first third of the 20th century, a fundamental change in the dynamics of urbanisation in the Levante region took place. Some cities even lost population between 1900 and 1930, a fact that contrasts with the regions around the city of Valencia, where towns expanded at an accelerated pace (Piñón and Roselló, 1994, pp. 168–172).

Valencia, in the second half of the 19th century, represented the model of a city that, without being a focus of industrial development, went through a process of urban modernisation closely linked to a specific form of growth. It was not an enclave exclusively dependent on agriculture, nor was its growth based only on its administrative function as the capital of the province, nor could it be defined only as a commercial centre. It embodied the interrelationship of all these factors, which made it a city that was growing demographically and urbanistically, despite not having large factories (Pons and Serra, 1992, p. 101).

In the Valencian Community, two patterns or models of spatial development stand out: that of the Centre and North of the region and that of Alicante. In the former, a sort of macrocephaly imposed itself on this dual space in which much of the wealth and population was concentrated in the coastal plains, contrasted with a less populated and poorer interior. The success of the coastal region was based on a rich agricultural tradition that generated strong demand, leading to the growth of an industrial base that boosted the population. In the province of Alicante, a multi-nuclear model predominated, based on tradition and the continuation of that pattern in the modern industrialisation; an interior with numerous medium-sized towns with diverse industries and the intensive use of labour; and, finally, a coastal strip with traditional agriculture.

Historically, municipal and county densities have only partially reflected the actual location of the population. For example, in the Region of Murcia, the three largest municipalities – Murcia, Cartagena and Lorca – have traditionally accounted for more than 50 % of the population. However, in these and other municipalities, there has been a great concentration in the vicinity of irrigated or coastal areas, with the dry and mountainous sectors being sparsely populated.

3 The establishment of water supply companies in the region

The Spanish Mediterranean coast, from the French border to Murcia, contained the largest number of water supply companies: 136 of the 273 documented enterprises, a figure that represents 49.8 % of the total. The importance of this large area is underlined by the early appearance of water companies that, to a large extent, have continued up to the present day. There are several reasons for this situation: the deep-rooted and ancient urban tradition, the high population density, the centuries-long attention paid to hydraulic works designed for irrigation, and the strength of these regions in the Spanish economy as a whole (Villar, Castro and Matés, 2019).

The primacy of the Mediterranean coast was evident in the second half of the 19th century in the establishment of drinking water supply companies. The early progress of Catalonia is evident through the figures, since it represented 34.1 % of the companies established; the Valencian region was in similar conditions with 18.8 %. This advantage manifested itself in a logical slowdown in the creation of companies in the 20th century; Catalonia accounted for 29.7 % and the Valencian region for 8.4 % of those incorporated at that time (Matés-Barco, 2013, 2019a).

The provincial distribution of water supply companies was uneven. Valencia with 15 and Alicante with 19 were the pioneers, while Castellon with five companies had the least number of enterprises in the region. In the period 1840–1900, 16 companies were established (18.8 % of the national total), unevenly distributed, and the large number of companies that emerged in the province of Alicante is noteworthy. During this period, 11 companies were created in the province of Alicante, compared to three in Valencia and two in Castellón de la Plana. These figures represent 12.9 %, 3.5 % and 2.3 %, respectively, of the total number of companies founded at this stage at the national level (Matés-Barco, 2004).

Between 1901 and 1939, there were 23 companies in the Valencian region (13.8 % of the national total), distributed by province as follows: Alicante, eight; Castellón, three; and Valencia, 12. Everything indicates that the same momentum existing in the previous stage was maintained, since the small decrease with respect to the national total is a symptom of the survival of some enterprises that emerged in the previous stage.

In the province of Alicante, water supply companies were established outside the capital: Denia, with two, and Aspe, Crevillente, Elda, Orihuela and Rafol de Almunia, with one enterprise each. This number represented 4.8 % of the companies founded during this period in the whole country. It can be seen that they were not established in large cities, but rather in small or medium-sized towns, regional capitals in some cases or nuclei noted for their industrial activity, such as Crevillente. But in all the towns, the agricultural factor stands out above any other activity. This panorama resulted in small companies, where the investment required was not too high. To a large extent, the familiarity of the agricultural sector with water and its distribution facilitated the formation of small water supply companies.

The urban system of the province of Alicante shows one almost generalised characteristic: the enterprises were mostly based in municipalities that exceeded 7,000 inhabitants in 1860. The appearance of the companies occurs above all in the first decades of the 20th century, a period of maximum expansion of the sector due to their establishment in medium-sized cities. In general terms, between 1860 and 1930, these communities had an annual population growth rate of less than 1 %.

In Castellón, we only have information regarding three companies in the province (1.8 % of the national total), one in the capital and the other two in the towns of Segorbe and Villafamés. On this occasion the model is repeated; these are small towns with a prominently agricultural nature, which are the starting point for a type of enterprise that is also of limited size.

Valencia was the province with the highest number of water supply enterprises in this region with 12, representing 7.2 % of the national total. Together with the five that appeared in the capital, the rest were distributed among various towns in the Valencian countryside: Alcira, Aldaya, Buñol, Torrente, Sagunto, Alcácer and Tabernes de Valldigna. Most of these towns are close to the capital, in the fertile region surrounding Valencia itself; some are a little further away, in the countryside of Sagunto, in the Ribera Alta or in the foothills of the mountains near the province of Alicante. And all of them have the common denominator of being located in a strip near the coast. That is to say, this is a set of medium-sized cities that formed a halo around the capital. If we exclude some important enterprises based in the capital, the rest formed part of the typical group of small companies established in the first decades of the 20th century and anchored in lightly industrialised towns (Matés-Barco, 2017, 2018).

4 The attraction of the Levante coast: Valencia and Alicante

Alicante and Valencia, with 18 and 14 companies, respectively, are provinces that confirm the importance of the Mediterranean area as a development nucleus for water supply companies. In the capital of Alicante, the first projects date back to 1879 when the *Canal de Alicante* company was established (1879) with the aim of exploiting the existing underground aquifers in the municipalities of Sax and Villena. The water was extracted through two wells that provided 35 litres per second, but this was still insufficient. The construction of the aqueduct generated multiple problems, in particular a dispute over the concession of the supply. The litigants were the Town Hall and the Marquis of Benalúa, the latter being the owner of the Alcoraya waters and the Sax wells.[1] This situation delayed the work, until in 1907 a new company was formed, *Sociedad del Canal de la Huerta*, which was in charge of building the pipeline, enabling the water to reach the city in 1909. Consumption for a population of around 50,000 inhabitants was calculated at about 3,000 cubic metres per day – 60 litres per inhabitant per day – objectives that were not achieved because they far exceeded the actual capacity. The initial capital was set at two million pesetas, represented by 4,000 shares worth 500 pesetas each[2] (Morales and Vera, 1989, pp. 31–32). Alicante temporarily solved its water problem with the arrival in 1909 of water from 15 wells in Zarzalejos, located in the municipality of Villena, which were supplied by a 68-kilometre-long aqueduct with a capacity of one cubic metre per second.

In 1883, British interests in the area were already evident with the establishment of the *Alicante Water Work* company, which was dissolved shortly thereafter in 1898. In the same year, *Aguas de Alicante* was established as a result of Belgian interests in the area, with a nominal capital of three million francs; in

1 In the centre of the city, in the Plaza de Isabel II, was the fountain that served to officially inaugurate the water supply of Sax in 1898. The water cisterns were built at one end of the city. Universal Illustrated Encyclopaedia (1929–1930), I, pp. 386–387

2 Anuario Financiero de Valores Mobiliarios (1916), p. 25. Anuario Financiero y de Sociedades Anónimas de España (1918), p. 631.

1919 this was increased to four million and in 1921 to five million (Castro and Matés, 2020). The capital was divided into 12,000 shares of 250 francs each, of which 11,200 were delivered, fully paid up, to the *Compagnie Générale des Conduites d'Eau* in payment for the contribution of plans, concessions, lands, artesian wells and the distribution network of the town of Alicante. With the 1919 increase, 4,000 new shares of 250 francs each were created for this purpose, of which 1,200 were issued at the rate of 275 francs, and the rest were for the acquisition of the Sax pipeline to Novelda, its capital thus being represented by 16,000 shares of 250 francs. The concession for the supply of water to Alicante expired in 1958 and the installations were returned to the municipality free of charge[3] (Vidal Olivares, 1986, p. 162). The company's aspiration to expand should be noted, since it included among its objectives "the obtaining, execution and exploitation of water supply concessions in Spain, especially in Alicante"; in other words, it did not want to confine itself solely to the east coast. The Belgian company sold its shares to the company *Aguas Potables y Mejoras de Valencia* in 1926 (Matés-Barco, 2002).

In Valencia, after more than seventy years of studies that never managed to get off the ground, various projects were undertaken in the final years of the 18th century and the first years of the 19th century. The commissions made up of members of the *Sociedad Económica de Amigos del País* followed one after another, but the lack of financial means delayed decision making. In 1844, like in other cities such as Cadiz, a rich merchant named Tomás Liñán bequeathed a large portion of his estate to pipe waters from the Turia River in accordance with the design presented by the *Sociedad Económica*. Liñán's will required that the work be started within a year. As the capital budgeted for the works was much higher than that received by the bequest, it was decided to create a company to cover the rest with the contributions of the shareholders (Aguilar, 1990, pp. 117–118).

In this way, a limited company called *Sociedad Valenciana* was formed to carry out the work (1846). Once the company was set up and until the 3,000 issued shares were sold, a mixed commission appointed by the city council and the *Sociedad Económica de Amigos del País* was in charge of carrying out the project. On 6 June 1846, various taxes were imposed on imported and consumer goods

3 Anuario Financiero y de Sociedades Anónimas de España (1921), p. 46; Id. (1922), p. 46; Id. (1927), pp. 512–515; Anuario Financiero de Bilbao que comprende el historial de los Valores Públicos y de Sociedades Anónimas de España (1948), p. 408. Anuario Financiero y de Empresas de España (1983), p. 65.

to help fund the piping of drinking water into the city. Ildefonso Cerdá worked as engineer-director of the works, assisted by Leodegario Marchessaux (Aguilar, 1990, pp. 114–115). The official inauguration took place on 19 November 1850 in the fountain in the Plaza de Calatrava. Between that year and 1880 various fountains were installed throughout the city.

Everything seems to indicate that this company was not focused on the household supply of water until the final years of the 19th century, and that its main purpose was to convey water for its use in public fountains. Furthermore, the supply of water was understood not only from a perspective anchored in the old drinking water system, but also that the undertaking was promoted by the Valencia city council and the members of the *Sociedad Económica de Amigos del País* – in practice both institutions were run by virtually the same people – who saw in the development of this type of project excellent opportunities to further their business interests (Pons and Serra, 1992, p. 82).

The need to carry out a series of improvements, especially for new filters to curb water losses and the construction of new cisterns, led to the appearance of various projects and the interest of a variety of private entrepreneurs in intervening in the water supply service. One of the most important of these projects was presented by Fernando de Vicente Charpentier in 1883, in which he asked the city council to lease the drinking water service to him in exchange for which he was obliged to carry out certain improvements to the system. In 1885, by means of a public auction, he was awarded the construction of a new cistern, designed by the architect Joaquín M. Belda, which doubled the capacity of the existing one (Aguilar, 1990, p. 117). In 1886, Charpentier agreed, by means of a contract with the city council, to carry out works to improve the drinking water service, including the construction of the new cistern, a pavilion, a monumental fountain, a filtration station and a sedimentation pond, as well as the distribution of fountains and hydrants and the carrying out of improvements to the distribution network by establishing an independent service in the northern area, on the other side of the river. In return, he would enjoy a 40-year concession for the drinking water service. However, the transfer of the service was granted on 31 January 1889 to the *Sociedad de Aguas Potables* under the name of Pérez y Cía, which came to replace the concessionaire Fernando de Vicente Charpentier. It was a provisional handover because the sedimentation basin was not yet completed (Aguilar, 1990, pp. 117–118).

The repeated problems with the supply led to the creation of a new company, *Aguas Potables y Mejoras de Valencia* (1890), which was to supply Valencia, Alcira, Carcagente, Gandía, Masarrochos and Godella. The initial capital was set at one million pesetas. In 1917, an issuance of 2,000 bonds was made, worth

1,000 pesetas each, with an annual interest rate of 5 %. In the following years – 1924, 1926, 1929 and 1930 – significant bond issuances were made.[4] In 1924, the company was listed on the Barcelona Stock Exchange and since 1927 it has been listed on the Colegio de Corredores de Valencia (Aguilar, 1990, pp. 107–118). Issuances of shares, bonds and debentures were fairly continuous from its foundation until 1936, with the aim of increasing its capital. The significant capital increases made in the 1920s led to its participation in other water companies such as *Aguas de Alicante* (1898) and *Omnium Ibérico* in 1930. The latter company had been set up in Barcelona to operate the drinking water supply concessions for the towns of Alcira and Gandía. The share capital was set at 1.2 million pesetas, which was increased in 1905 to 3.2 million pesetas; it was divided into 6,400 shares of 500 pesetas each and distributed a dividend of 5 % per year. It later became a subsidiary of *Aguas Potables y Mejoras de Valencia.* In 1960 it changed its corporate purpose and became a technical equipment company within its business group, more specifically dedicated to "agricultural and urban operations, mining operations, metre rental and water supply installations". Since 1970 it has had its registered office in Madrid, with offices in Valencia.[5]

Aguas Potables y Mejoras de Valencia got involved in businesses related to the electricity sector in the province of Castellón and even the company *Fuerzas Eléctricas.* In 1949 it leased the business of *Omnium Ibérico,* and extended the water supply to other towns in the area: Algemesí, Rocafort, Benimámet, Manises, Burjasot, etc. The increase in the number of subscribers was very significant from 1945 onwards, which shows the expansionary phase that was taking place at that time.[6]

In the first decades of the 20th century, other companies linked to the domestic water supply were set up. For example, *Española de Abastecimientos*

4 Anuario Financiero de Valores Mobiliarios (1916), p. 295. Anuario Financiero y de Sociedades Anónimas de España (1918), p. 637; Id. (1927), pp. 371–372. Anuario Financiero de Bilbao que comprende el historial de los valores públicos y de Sociedades Anónimas de España (1950), p. 406; Id. (1950), p. 406; Id. (1950), p. 406. Id. (1950), p. 406.

5 Anuario Financiero de Valores Mobiliarios (1916), p. 295. Anuario Financiero y de Sociedades Anónimas de España (1922), p. 55. Anuario Financiero de Bilbao que comprende el historial de los valores públicos y de Sociedades Anónimas de España (1970), p. 112. Anuario Financiero y de Empresas en España (1983), p. 68.

6 Anuario Financiero de Bilbao que comprende el historial de los valores públicos y de Sociedades Anónimas de España (1950), p. 409; Id. (1960), p. 171; Id. (1970), p. 112.

(1918) fits the profile of a company focused on the study, execution and operation of services and installations that led to an improvement for the people or areas where this service was implemented. The share capital was set at 1.1 million pesetas, represented by 2,216 shares of 500 pesetas each.[7] A second example was the establishment of *Aguas Potables y Riegos* (1923), for the exploitation of springs and with the aim of covering domestic consumption and irrigation. The initial capital was set at 300,000 pesetas, represented by 600 shares worth 500 pesetas each.[8] From the same period is *Citi, Aguas Subterráneas* (1927), an example of a company focused on lighting and the supply of water for all types of consumption.[9]

5 The importance of rural populations

In addition to the above-mentioned companies, which are well known due to their better documentation and for their achievements in the Valencian capital, the Levante region and the Mediterranean area in general stood out for the founding of a significant number of companies based in rural towns. Of these companies, hardly any data is recorded in the *Financial Yearbooks*, although one of the pioneering companies in Spain, *Aguas de Bufilla* (1848), should be highlighted. The nominal capital of this company was established at 178,750 pesetas, a not insignificant amount for a rural nucleus.[10]

We also know about the existence of other companies established in the final decades of the 19th century. For example, *La Exploradora* (1880), which set its share capital at 250,000 pesetas, divided into 500 shares of 500 pesetas each. The aim of this company, based in Alicante, was to search for groundwater for irrigation and to use surface water for the supply of drinking water.[11] A second case was the company *La Constante* (1884), which established its share capital at 500,000 pesetas, divided into 1,000 shares of 500 pesetas each. The objective

---

7 Anuario Financiero y de Sociedades Anónimas de España (1930), p. 221. Anuario Financiero de Bilbao que comprende el historial de los valores públicos y de Sociedades Anónimas de España (1970), p. 121.

8 Anuario Financiero y de Sociedades Anónimas de España (1927), p. 514. Anuario Financiero de Bilbao que comprende el historial de los valores públicos y de Sociedades Anónimas de España (1950), p. 409.

9 Anuario Financiero y de Sociedades Anónimas de España (1930), p. 223. Anuario Financiero de Bilbao que comprende el historial de los valores públicos y de Sociedades Anónimas de España (1948), p. 409.

10 Anuario Financiero y de Sociedades Anónimas de España (1922), p. 80.

11 Reseña Geográfica de España (1888), p. 914.

of this company was to bring drinking water from Torremanzanas to supply Alicante.[12] Other similar entities were *El Carranchalet* (1894), with an initial capital of 1,000 pesetas,[13] and *Jaime Macnaughtan* (1894), which obtained authorisation for the construction and supply of water to the municipality of Gandía in the province of Valencia.[14]

Some towns in the province such as Alcoy, Aspe and Denia also had early enterprises. The first of the municipalities, Alcoy, had a considerable population, 22,716 inhabitants in 1860 and 28,889 in 1900. Although its growth rate was not particularly high, 0.60 % and 0.64 % in the periods mentioned, it had good prospects due to its industrial potential, based on the paper and textile industries (Nadal, 1990, p. 302). The year 1884 saw the appearance of the *Nuevo Neptuno* company dedicated to water supply. At the time of its constitution, its nominal capital was set at 67,500 pesetas, divided into 270 shares of 250 pesetas each. The company's activity consisted of drilling artesian wells and using the water for domestic supply.[15]

The company *La Unión* was established in Aspe in 1871, a very early date for a rural community which at that time had around 7,000 inhabitants, and whose annual population growth rate was quite low, 0.25 % between 1860 and 1900, and even lower, 0.04 %, if we extend the period to 1930. The share capital was set at 42,240 pesetas, divided into 2,112 shares of 20 pesetas each, which received a dividend of 12 % per year, a relatively high figure compared to other contemporary companies that were larger and had greater financial capacity.[16] In 1927, in the same city, *Aguas Potables de Aspe* was established. The established share capital of 25,000 pesetas was represented by 500 shares of 50 pesetas each.[17]

Denia, with a population of below 5,000 inhabitants in 1860, which in 1900 exceeded 7,000 inhabitants, and a slow growth rate, saw the appearance of some water companies, of which *Aguas de Denia* (1870) was the first. Its corporate purpose was to collect and supply water for irrigation and to supply the population. As we have seen previously, this dual aspect was logical given the peculiarity

---

12 Reseña Geográfica de España (1888), p. 914.

13 Anuario Financiero y de Sociedades Anónimas de España (1922), p. 48.

14 Estadística de Obras Públicas (1898), p. 25. Reseña Geográfica de España (1888), p. 914. Anuario Financiero y de Sociedades Anónimas de España (1921), p. 45–77.

15 Reseña Geográfica de España (1888), p. 914.

16 Anuario Financiero y de Sociedades Anónimas de España (1921), p. 47.

17 Anuario Financiero y de Sociedades Anónimas de España (1930), p. 200; Id. (1935), p. 290. Anuario Financiero de Bilbao que comprende el historial de los valores públicos y de Sociedades Anónimas de España (1950), p. 408; Id. (1970), p. 94.

of the environment and the importance of irrigation in the Valencian countryside. The initial capital was set at 200,000 pesetas and the 800 shares that were issued were sold at 250 pesetas each. In 1931, 200 bonds were issued at 500 pesetas each with an annual interest rate of 5 %.[18] On the other hand, *Aguas y Riegos de Denia* (1906), with a share capital of 174,250 pesetas, made household supply compatible with supplying water for irrigation.[19]

Elche, another important municipality in the province, had a population of 17,554 inhabitants in 1787, but suffered a significant drop to 9,753 in 1860. By 1900 it had recovered somewhat to 14,218 inhabitants and in 1930, once the growth rate had returned, it reached 23,159 inhabitants. The annual growth rate for the period was 1.24 %. Despite the crisis suffered in the first decades of the 19th century, it managed to recover and saw the presence of national companies such as *La Antisequía* (1894), which had a share capital of 30,000 pesetas, represented by 120 shares of 250 pesetas each. Only 20,250 pesetas were subscribed.[20] Foreign companies also settled in Elche, such as *Elche Water Works* (1900), which established its share capital at 932,000 pesetas (Castro, Fernández and Matés, 2019; Costa, 1981, p. 59).

The city of Orihuela followed a similar trajectory to Elche with respect to the evolution of the population. In 1787 it had 22,913 inhabitants, falling to 9,039 in 1860, recovering in 1900 to 10,231 inhabitants and reaching 11,148 in 1930. The rate of growth, with an annual rate of 0.3 %, was considerably slower. In this municipality, the existence of the company *La Catalana* is known, although little information is available about its activities.

Likewise, Crevillente was a small industrial town with a population of 7,551 inhabitants in 1860, 10,031 in 1900 and 10,330 in 1930. The annual growth rate was 0.45 %. *La Crevillentina* was established in this enclave (1903), with a capital of 100,000 pesetas. The company's corporate purpose specified the supply and piping of water to homes.[21]

Somewhat later, a series of companies were set up to supply neighbourhoods in the city itself, as well as in small towns in the Valencian countryside and in municipalities in Alicante. Many of these towns had less than 5,000 inhabitants.

---

18 Anuario Financiero y de Sociedades Anónimas de España (1921), p. 48. Anuario Financiero de Bilbao que comprende el historial de los valores públicos y de Sociedades Anónimas de España (1948), p. 408.

19 Anuario Financiero de Bilbao que comprende el historial de los valores públicos y de Sociedades Anónimas de España (1948), p. 409.

20 Anuario Financiero y de Sociedades Anónimas de España (1922), p. 48.

21 Anuario Financiero y de Sociedades Anónimas de España (1922), p. 48.

Below is a brief description of the companies established in these towns, ordered by their year of foundation. Firstly, *Riegos y Canalización Agraria* (1917) was founded in Barcelona to deliver water to the city of Sagunto, with the aim of supplying the population and for irrigation. Its share capital was set at 10,000 pesetas. Sagunto had 6,685 inhabitants in 1860, which grew to 7,081 in 1900 and 10,260 in 1930. The annual growth rate of 0.61 % was within the normal rates for the region, except for the more developed urban centres.[22]

In 1918 *Aguas de Aldaya* and *Aguas de Buñol* were established with the aim of supplying the towns of their respective names. The former set its nominal capital at 190,000 pesetas and issued 250 shares worth 760 pesetas each. In 1920 it paid a dividend of 25 pesetas per share.[23] The latter company had a nominal capital of 67,500 pesetas at the time of its constitution, which was increased to 135,000 pesetas in 1930.[24] One year later, *Aguas de Baladrán* was established (1919) with a nominal capital of 100,000 pesetas.[25]

The Valencian town of Torrente had a population of 6,480 inhabitants in 1860. From an early date it became an important centre for emigration from the surrounding areas and experienced considerable growth, reaching 10,154 inhabitants in 1930. In this context of rapid urban growth, the company *Aguas de Torrente* (1920) emerged with a share capital of 60,000 pesetas.[26]

The population of Elda in Alicante was below 5,000 inhabitants in 1900; however, by 1930 it already had 12,562 people, evidencing a very high annual growth rate. As in other similar towns, the rapid increase in population often led to the creation of water supply companies. In this case, *Aguas del Canto* (1923) emerged with a nominal capital of 100,000 pesetas at the time of its foundation, which rose to 225,000 pesetas in 1924. Its share capital was made up of 4,500 shares of 50 pesetas each.[27] *Aguas de Alcácer* (1928) was established in

22 Anuario Financiero y de Sociedades Anónimas de España (1922), p. 56.

23 Anuario Financiero y de Sociedades Anónimas de España (1921), pp. 45–77; Id. (1922), p. 82; Anuario Financiero de Bilbao que comprende el historial de los valores públicos y de Sociedades Anónimas de España (1970), p. 121.

24 Anuario Financiero y de Sociedades Anónimas de España (1921), pp. 45–77; Id. (1922), p. 82; Anuario Financiero de Bilbao que comprende el historial de los valores públicos y de Sociedades Anónimas de España (1950), p. 409.

25 Anuario Financiero y de Sociedades Anónimas de España (1927), pp. 45–77.

26 Anuario Financiero y de Sociedades Anónimas de España (1922), p. 82.

27 Anuario Financiero y de Sociedades Anónimas de España (1927), p. 514. Anuario Financiero de Bilbao que comprende el historial de los valores públicos y de Sociedades Anónimas de España (1970), p. 94.

a nearby area. The share capital was set at 250,000 pesetas, divided into 500 shares of 500 pesetas each.[28]

The appearance of new companies continued into the 1930s. An example is *Aguas de Rafol* (1932), which established its initial capital at 500,000 pesetas, issuing a total of 2,000 shares worth 250 pesetas each. Subsequently, due to the expansion of *Aguas Potables y Mejoras de Valencia*, it ceased to supply water to homes and by 1970 had become a company dedicated to providing water for irrigation.[29] A second case occurred in the Valencian town of Tabernes de Valldigna. This town had 5,728 inhabitants in 1860, which increased to 7,840 in 1900 and reached 10,029 inhabitants by 1930. This momentum led to the foundation of *Riegos y Aguas Potables de Tabernes* (1932), a company which established its share capital at 650,000 pesetas.[30] Documentary sources show the existence of other small companies, but which had little presence in the market for the supply of drinking water.[31]

As can be seen, rural areas became very important for the water supply sector. In a region where obtaining water was challenging, the companies found a solution by bringing together two essential objectives: providing water for household supply and for irrigation, which was the other critical issue in the area. This dynamic enabled many companies to establish themselves in small rural towns, as they had a fairly secure market with both types of customers. Thus they needed to make the two activities compatible.

In Castellón, the third province of the Valencian region, the most important enterprises were directly related to the construction of reservoirs dedicated essentially to the storage of water for irrigation. The first significant initiative was the creation of *Fomento Agrícola Castellonense* (1888), for the exploitation

28 Anuario Financiero y de Sociedades Anónimas de España (1930), p. 225.

29 Anuario Financiero y de Sociedades Anónimas de España (1933), p. 365. Anuario Financiero de Bilbao que comprende el historial de los valores públicos y de Sociedades Anónimas de España (1970), p. 94.

30 Anuario Financiero y de Sociedades Anónimas de España (1935), p. 300. Anuario Financiero de Bilbao que comprende el historial de los valores públicos y de Sociedades Anónimas de España (1948), p. 409.

31 Anuario Financiero y de Sociedades Anónimas de España (1921), pp. 45–77; Id. (1922), pp. 80–82; Id. (1927), p. 485; Id. (1930–1935). Anuario Financiero de Bilbao que comprende el historial de los valores públicos y de Sociedades Anónimas de España (1948), 408; Id. (1950), pp. 408–409; Id. (1960), pp. 167–172; Id. (1970), pp. 94 y 121.

of the concession it held in perpetuity for the supply of irrigation water in Castellón. The share capital was set at 1,400,000 pesetas, composed of 2,800 shares of 500 pesetas each. The second initiative was the foundation of *General de Riegos* (1905), constituted in Barcelona for the construction and exploitation of the María Cristina reservoir (Castellón), with a share capital of 1.5 million pesetas and 30,000 shares at 50 pesetas.[32] Private enterprise had little presence in the drinking water supply sector, and only isolated references to small towns in Castellon can be found.

In the town of Segorbe in Castellón, the company *La Esperanza* (1913) was set up. The share capital was set at 100,000 pesetas. This small town dedicated essentially to agricultural work had 7,261 inhabitants in 1860, 6,428 in 1900 and 6,084 in 1930, which shows a continuous decline in population.[33] In Onda, the company *La Ondense* was established (1882) to provide water for the city. The share capital was fixed at 350,000 pesetas, divided into 3,500 shares with a value of 100 pesetas each. Onda had fewer than 5,000 inhabitants before 1900, when a population of 5,716 was recorded, and by 1930 there were 6,715 residents.[34] Finally, in the small municipality of Villafamés, whose population did not exceed 5,000 inhabitants during the period in question, Riegos de Moró was set up (1926) with the aim of tapping groundwater for irrigation, domestic and industrial use. The initial capital was set at 50,000 pesetas, divided into 1,000 shares of 50 pesetas each, of which only 15,000 pesetas were subscribed. The concession was obtained for 25 years.[35]

6 Conclusions

The importance of private water supply companies should be highlighted, especially if we look at the great expansion of the sector between 1900 and 1936. The regional distribution of water supply companies in the early stages of the sector essentially corresponds to the Spanish industrial and urban map. In other words, there was a clear relationship between regions with a strong urban or industrial growth rate and companies focused on domestic supply (Ruiz Villaverde, 2013).

32 Anuario Financiero y de Sociedades Anónimas de España (1922), pp. 44 y 49.
33 Anuario Financiero y de Sociedades Anónimas de España (1922), p. 59.
34 Reseña Geográfica de España (1888), p. 914.
35 Anuario Financiero y de Sociedades Anónimas de España (1930), p. 223.

The business geography of the sector was essentially centred on three areas: Barcelona, Alicante and Valencia, which were the focal points of these companies, while in Andalusia, due to its urban structure, diversification was much greater. Valencia is one of the regions with the greatest concentration of business in the water supply sector, both in terms of the number of companies and the capital invested. To a large extent, the region benefited from the importance of the agricultural cities, without forgetting that in the second half of the 19th century Valencia was the third most industrialised region in the country, as Nadal indicated (1990, pp. 297–300). Likewise, the pairing of household water supply with the search for water for irrigation played an important role in the development of this sector in this Mediterranean region.

The significant number of companies that began to emerge in the first decades of the 20th century is a clear indication of the importance of the sector. The existing legislation of this stage was another far-reaching factor, prompting city councils to look to private companies to solve the water supply problem (Núñez, 2004). Nor can we forget the knowledge gained in observing the business strategies carried out by Britain and French companies (Matés-Barco, 2019b, 2021b, 2021a). As the century progressed, foreign investment began to withdraw due to the global conflict of 1914 and the subsequent nationalistic legislation that appeared in Spain, leaving much of the water sector in the hands of Spanish capital. These were the years that saw the greatest expansion, in which Spanish entrepreneurs took advantage of the occasion to establish many of these companies.

7 Sources

Anuario Financiero de Bilbao que comprende el historial de los valores públicos y de Sociedades Anónimas de España (AFB) (1915–1972). *Aguas*. Bilbao: Banco de Vizcaya.

Anuario Financiero de Valores Mobiliarios (AFVM) (1916–1918). Madrid.

Anuario Financiero y de Empresas en España (AFEE) (1983–1985). *Aguas y Balnearios*. Madrid.

Anuario Financiero y de Sociedades Anónimas de España (AFSAE) (1916–1977). *Sociedades de Aguas Potables y de Riegos*. Madrid.

Estadística de Obras Públicas (1895–1900). *Compañías concesionarias de abastecimientos de aguas*. Madrid: Ministerio de Fomento.

Reseña Geográfica y Estadística de España (1888). *Obras de abastecimiento*. Madrid.

References

Aguilar Civera, I. (1990). *El orden industrial en la ciudad. Valencia en la segunda mitad del siglo XIX*. Valencia: Diputación.

Castro-Valdivia, M., Fernández-Paradas, M. & Matés-Barco, J. M. (2019). Las empresas extranjeras de agua y gas en España (circa 1900–1923). In J. M. Matés-Barco & A. Torres-Rodríguez (coords.), *Los servicios públicos en España y México* (pp. 51–74). Madrid: Silex.

Castro-Valdivia, M. & Matés-Barco, J. M. (2020). Los servicios púbicos y la inversión extranjera en España (1850–1936): Las empresas de agua y gas. *História Unisinos*, 24(2), 221–239. Doi: 10.413/his.2020.242.05.

Costa Campi, M. T. (1981). Iniciativas empresariales y capitales extranjeros en el sector servicios de la economía española durante la segunda mitad del siglo XIX, *Investigaciones Económicas*, 14, 45–83.

Enciclopedia Universal Ilustrada (1929). *Valencia* (I, pp. 386–387). Madrid: Espasa-Calpe.

Matés-Barco, J. M. (2002). Strategies of foreign firms in the sector of water supply in Spain (1850–1990). In H. Bonin (coord.), *Transnational companies, 19th–20th centuries* (pp. 301–316). París: Plage.

Matés-Barco, J. M. (2004). The development of water supplies in Spain: 19th and 20th centuries. In A. Giuntini, P. Hertner & G. Núñez (Eds.), *Urban growth on two continents in the 19th and 20th centuries: Technology, networks, finance and public regulation* (pp. 165–178). Granada: Comares.

Matés-Barco, J. M. (2013). La conquista del agua en Europa: los modelos de gestión (siglos XIX y XX). *Agua y Territorio*, 1, 21–29. DOI: https://doi.org/10.17561/at.v1i1.1030.

Matés-Barco, J. M. (2014). Las empresas concesionarias de servicios de abastecimiento de aguas potables en España (1840–1940). *Transportes, Servicios y Telecomunicaciones*, 26, 58–89. http://www.tstrevista.com/sumarios/sum26/sumario_26_002_es.asp. Access 2020 December 17.

Matés-Barco, J. M. (2016). La regulación del suministro de agua en España, siglos XIX y XX. *Revista de Historia Industrial*, 61, 17–49.

Matés-Barco, J. M. (2017). El servicio público de abastecimiento de agua en España (siglos XIX y XX): El proceso de acumulación de competencias de los ayuntamientos. *Revista Brasileira de História & Ciências Sociais – RBHCS*, 9–18, 36–57. DOI: 10.14295/rbhcs.v9i18.448.

Matés-Barco, J. M. (2018). La distribution de l'eau dans les villes d'Espagne (1840–1936): Le rôle des compagnies privées. *Histoire, Économie & Société*, 3, 14–29.

Matés-Barco, J. M. (2019a). El abastecimiento de agua a Barcelona (1850–1939): Origen y desarrollo de las compañías privadas. *Historia Contemporánea*, 59–1, 165–194. https://doi.org/10.1387/hc.19434. Accessed 2020 December 17.

Matés-Barco, J. M. (2019b). Estrategia empresarial y control del mercado: la gestión del abastecimiento de agua potable. In J. M. Matés-Barco (coord.), *Empresas y empresarios en España. De mercaderes a industrials* (pp. 223–240). Madrid, Pirámide.

Matés-Barco, J. M. (2021a). Public services in Spain: The role of water supply companies. In M. Vázquez-Fariñas, P. P. Ortúñez-Goicolea & M. Castro-Valdivia (Eds.), *Companies and entrepreneurs in the history of Spain. Centuries long evolution in business since the 15th century.* London: Palgrave.

Matés-Barco, J. M. (2021b). Small, medium and large companies in the supply of water in Spain (1840–1940). In J. M. Matés-Barco & L. Caruana (Eds.), *Entrepreneurship in Spain: A history.* London: Routledge. (in press).

Morales Gil, A. & Vera Rebollo, F. (1989). *La mancomunidad de los Canales del Taibilla.* Alicante: Instituto Universitario de Geografía, Academia Alfonso X El Sabio.

Nadal, J. (1990). El desarrollo de la economía valenciana en la segunda mitad del siglo XIX: ¿una vía exclusivamente agraria?. In J. Nadal & A. Carreras (dir.), *Pautas regionales de la industrialización española, siglos XIX y XX* (pp. 296–314). Barcelona: Ariel.

Núñez, G. (2004). La municipalisation des services locaux et les entreprises municipales en Espagne dans la première moitié du XXe siècle. In Ch. Bouneau & A. Fernández (Eds.), *L'entreprise publique en France et en Espagne* (pp. 209–223). Pessac Cedex: Centre Aquitain d'Histoire Moderne et Contemporaine, Maison des Sciences de L'homme d'Aquitaine.

Piñón, J. L. & Roselló, V. M. (1994). Valencia. In M. Guardia, F. J. Monclús & J. L. Oyón (Eds.), *Atlas histórico de ciudades europeas* (pp. 155–181). Barcelona: Salvat.

Pons, A. & Serna, J. (1992). *La ciudad extensa. La burguesía comercial-financiera en la Valencia de mediados del XIX.* Valencia: Diputació.

Ruiz-Villaverde, A. 2013. Reflexiones sobre la gestión de los servicios urbanos del agua: un recorrido histórico del caso español. *Agua y Territorio*, 1, 31–39. https://doi.org/10.17561/at.v1i1.1031.

Vidal Olivares, J. (1986). Burguesía y negocios: la especulación en el sector servicios de la ciudad de Alicante a fines del siglo XIX (1880–1900). Anales de la Universidad de Alicante. Historia contemporánea, 2, 159–181.

Villar-Chamorro, F., Castro-Valdivia, M. & Matés-Barco, J. M. (2019). Crecimiento urbano y abastecimiento de agua potable en España: el protagonismo de las empresas privadas (1840–1950). Posición, 1, 1–21. https://716132a6-9cf5-45de-baee-6a15e46210f7.filesusr.com/ugd/df634b_947ca999aea740a9b61a2f4fd04be233.pdf. Accessed 2020 June 30.

Nuria Rodríguez-Martín

5 The gas industry in Madrid during the period following the Spanish Civil War: *Gas Madrid, S. A.*[1]

Abstract The misguided policies of autarky imposed by the Francoist authorities at the end of the Spanish Civil War, which aimed at economic self-sufficiency, were disastrous for the Spanish gas sector, since they prevented the supply of coal suitable for the manufacture of gas – which the country lacked – and the technological equipment essential to renovate the outdated factories. Likewise, the strong state interventionism in the national coal market affected gas companies in a very negative way. By studying the case of Madrid's gas sector and the story of *Gas Madrid S.A.* during the 1940s, this essay focuses on the problems faced by the gas industry during the period following the Spanish Civil War. Using the data available, this work examines both the production and consumption of gas in the capital, besides the run of the Madrid Gas Factory and the state of its facilities, and the relationship of the company with its customers.

1 Introduction

After the end of the Spanish Civil War (1936–1939), the authorities of the Franco regime imposed an autarchic policy that was devastating for the Spanish gas sector as it prevented the supply both of coal for the manufacture of gas (of which there was a shortage in Spain) and the technological equipment necessary to renew the obsolete factories. In addition, the strong state interventionism in the national coal market had a highly negative effect on the gas companies. This research studies the problems faced by the Spanish gas industry in the post-war period based on the analysis of the events in Madrid and the evolution of the company *Gas Madrid, S.A.* between 1939 and 1946. Using the available documentation, a reconstruction of the production and consumption of gas in

1 This work was supported by the R&D Excellence Project "La industria del gas en España: desarrollo y trayectorias regionales (1842–2008)" HAR2017-82112-P, funded by the Spanish Ministry of Science, Innovation and Universities and ERDF funds, and by a Postdoctoral Grant from the First Research and Knowledge Transfer Plan of the University of Malaga. The author would like to express her gratitude to Professor Mercedes Fernández-Paradas for her comments on previous versions of this essay.

the Spanish capital has been made. The study also analyses the functioning of the company's factory in Madrid, the state of its facilities and its customer relationships.

The trajectory of this company, a fundamental piece of Madrid's business fabric in the twentieth century, is inextricably linked to the political occurrences and social changes taking place in Spain during the first half of the last century. Its very creation cannot be understood without contemplating the socio-political situation prevailing in the country during the years of the First World War and the impact that this conflict had on the country even though it was neutral. This chapter analyses the situation of *Gas Madrid* during the years following the Spanish Civil War. It is a particularly interesting subject, given that, on the one hand, there is hardly any research on the topic and, on the other hand, the period of study was critical for the Spanish economy in general and for certain large companies in particular, including the gas companies, making their analysis especially attractive.

In order to carry out this research, as many available documentary sources as possible have been used, which, unfortunately are few. These sources include the official statistics of the period 1940–1949 drawn from different documents issued by the Vertical Trade Union of Water, Gas and Electricity.[2] Similarly, the economic *Memorias* (annual reports) of *Gas Madrid* and the 1946 *Memoria de los servicios técnicos* (Report of technical services) which compiles data from the preceding years have also been used. This document provides very rich and varied information about the company, the state and operation of its factory, its suppliers and clients. Although this publication indicates that this report is published annually, it has only been possible to locate the one for 1946.[3]

In addition to this introduction and a brief conclusion, the chapter is divided into three sections. The first section examines the trajectory of *Gas Madrid* from its creation in 1922 to the end of the Spanish Civil War, in order to gain a better understanding of the scale of this company and its importance in the history

2 The Vertical Trade Union of Water, Gas and Electricity was one of the 24 national syndicates created in 1941 by the Franco dictatorship (*Law of 23 June 1941 on the classification of Trade Unions*). The unions in the Franco regime were not class-based unions. Like the political parties, they were banned. Entrepreneurs and workers, who the regime called "producers", were legally obliged to join one of these "unions" forming part of the Spanish Syndical Organisation (OSE), commonly known as the Vertical Union.

3 The document is type written, not printed, and we assume that very few copies of it were made.

and transformation of the city of Madrid during the first third of the twentieth century. The second section addresses the evolution of the gas industry in Madrid based on the reconstruction of the data on production and consumption, within the framework of a strangled national economy. The conclusions confirm the difficulties experienced by the gas industry in Spain during the 1940s, the sector in which *Gas Madrid, S.A.* operated. These conclusions are even more relevant in the case of this firm as it was the only company of its kind operating in one of the largest cities in Spain which was also its political capital.

2 *Gas Madrid*: From its creation to the Spanish Civil War

The company *Gas Madrid* was established in December 1921. We should consider its creation within the context of the energy crisis suffered by Spain as a result of the development of the First World War. The scarcity and shortage of coal experienced by the country had an extraordinary effect on the gas companies operating in Spain (Fernández-Paradas, 2019a). In Madrid, the *Compañía Madrileña de Alumbrado y Calefacción por Gas* effectively operated as a monopoly, as it was the owner of the only gas factory in the city. Its main client was the City Council of Madrid, thanks to the capital's public service contract for street lighting, which consumed at that time seven million m^3 of gas per year (Ayuntamiento de Madrid, 1915). It also supplied gas to companies, retail outlets, public establishments and private homes that used gas for power, heating and fundamentally cooking. In 1917, amidst the energy crisis, the City Council of Madrid, which at the end of the day was the principal client of the company in the city, claimed that the firm had been failing to fulfil several essential clauses of the capital's public street lighting contract and proceeded to cancel the contract and seize the factory (Fernández-Paradas and Rodríguez-Martín, 2019).

The company went to court, initiating a lawsuit which was not resolved until 1922 after difficult negotiations between the City Council and the gas company which gave rise to a series of rules for the transaction of all the pending litigation between the two parties and with which a complicated process was finalised. The final agreement contemplated the possible transfer of the business to the Compañía de Gas or to "another entity" that it designated which was, precisely, *Gas Madrid, S.A.* founded on 24 December 1921 (Magaldi and Rodríguez Martín, 2020). The new company was subrogated to all the rights and obligations of the Compañía del Gas, including the entire service contract for gas street lighting and electricity for the city of Madrid, becoming the owner of its capital assets (*Contrato de cesión y suministro de alumbrado. . .*, 1922).

With respect to the creation of *Gas Madrid*, it should be noted that it was established thanks to the agreement between the former Compañía de Gas and the four electrical companies making up Madrid's electrical sector.[4] In order to form its social capital, the former contributed its industrial assets valued at 10 million pesetas[5] and the electrical companies contributed 6,300,000 pesetas. The board of directors was made up of representatives from the four electrical companies (*Hidroeléctrica Santillana, Unión Eléctrica Madrileña, Cooperativa Electra Madrid* and *Hidroeléctrica Española*), the banks that had financially backed the operation (*Banco de Vizcaya, Banco Urquijo, Banca Central* and *Banco Español de Crédito*) and the *Compañía Madrileña de Alumbrado y Calefacción por Gas*.

From this moment, *Gas Madrid, S.A.* operated without any significant setbacks until the outbreak of the Spanish Civil War in July 1936, when it was the country's third largest company in the gas sector, after only *Catalana de Gas y Electricidad* and *Gas Lebon*. On the eve of the war, *Gas Madrid* continued operating with the transferred factory, a complex located in the south of Madrid which covered an area of a street block. In addition to the buildings and constructions necessary to manufacture gas (laboratories, gasometers, workshops…) and to manage the business (offices, housing for workers…), the factory had its own railway siding on the Madrid rail beltway. In this way, the wagons transporting the coal and other materials accessed the factory via a tunnel. The factory had an annual production capacity of 36,500,000 m^3 of gas and was able to store up to 45,000 m^3 in its facilities. The gas was distributed throughout the city through one normal pressure network and another high pressure network with a length of 425 kilometres, which served its 16,000 clients and the network of public street lights, made up of 21,000 light points in 1929 (Ayuntamiento de Madrid, 1929).

The outbreak of the Spanish Civil War put the company's survival to the test. First, its business was affected by the division of the country into two areas after the coup of 18 July 1936. Its factories in Jerez de la Frontera and Valladolid were in the territory under the control of the rebel army and the factory in Madrid fell into the hands of the legal Republican authorities. Through a Decree dated

4 *Hidroeléctrica Española, Unión Eléctrica Madrileña, Cooperativa Electra Madrid* and *Hidráulica Santillana*.

5 Including the gas factories of Burgos, Jerez, Logroño and Valladolid. But shortly after its constitution, *Gas Madrid* disposed of its businesses in Burgos and Logroño.

30 August 1936, the government of the Republic intervened in all companies engaged in credit, production or consumption operations, including *Gas Madrid*, which came under the control of a Worker's Control Committee, at the heart of which bitter disputes raged between the socialist and anarchist members.

During the Civil War, the gas production of the Madrid factory plummeted. In 1935, the last year of peace, production was close to 37 million m^3, falling by 11,491,740 in 1937 and almost 14 million the following year. The production of sub-products such as coke also decreased spectacularly (Fernández-Paradas, 2019b). The three-year siege suffered by the Spanish capital, the last city to be occupied by Franco's army, prevented the entrance of the necessary coal. As a result, the consumption of gas also plummeted and the number of clients of the company fell sharply. They dropped from 26,816 in 1935 to only 8,199 in 1937. In 1940, *Gas Madrid* calculated a loss of 6 million pesetas caused by the drop in sales and clients during the Civil War.

We should also consider the damage caused to the infrastructures of the company by the air raids on the city. And, of course, the loss of human life, as more than one hundred of its employees perished in the war. After three years of resistance of the people, at the end of March 1939, the rebel troops began to occupy Madrid and on 1st April the victorious side officially declared the end of the war. A new stage then began plagued with difficulties for the gas companies and *Gas Madrid* and also for the country's economy in general, which suffered a severe depression lasting for more than a decade. The majority of authors agree that while the Civil War had negative effects on the Spanish economy, what was even more damaging was the immediate adoption by the new Franco authorities of a completely irrational autarchic economic policy which ignored the country's limited resources, delaying the recovery of the Spanish economy during the post-war period (González Enciso and Matés Barco, Coord., 2006).

3 *Gas Madrid* during the post-war period after the Spanish Civil War: Crisis in the production and consumption of gas

The gas companies, including *Gas Madrid*, were among the worst affected by the economic policy guidelines of the early years of the Franco regime. The main problem resided in the difficulties to obtain coal with which to manufacture the gas in the factories. The objective of self-sufficiency did not take into account the reality of the country's lack of resources. Spain had coal mines, but the coal extracted did not have the sufficient quality to manufacture gas through distillation.[6] Furthermore, national coal production did not cover the needs and growing demand of industry and the state interventionism mean that there was tight control of both production and also of the distribution and prices of coal. Not only was the production of coal insufficient in Spain, it was also more expensive as its price increased significantly. In 1940, the price of a tonne of coal at the mine was 21 % higher than that of 1935 and in 1949 it was 340 % higher (Fernández-Paradas and Martykánová, 2017). To these increases we would have to add the costs of its transport to the factories.

The official publications acknowledged the enormous difficulties with which the gas factories were operating due to the scarcity of fuel: "[. . .] the gas industry has not be favoured in the distribution of national coal [. . .] To compensate this deficit, the factories have been obliged to distil different substances [. . .] products which, as well has producing a much inferior gas, both in quantity and quality, have a limited use [. . .]" (Sindicato Vertical de Agua, Gas y Electricidad, 1947, p. 9). These "substances" were raw materials such as lignites, gasified coke, woods and lumber, marcs. . . According to Fernández-Paradas and Martykánová (2017), the use of materials other than coal in the Spanish gas factories was not only high in the 1940s but at the end of the decade their levels were still much higher than in 1939.

The scarcity of coal also drove the factory of Madrid, and those in the rest of Spain, to resort to other raw materials to produce gas, in this case, diesel. Even so, *Gas Madrid* benefited from the ties that it had with the Asturian coal company Duro Felguera, which supplied the majority of the coal consumed. Madrid Gas was also the owner of 145 hopper wagons for the transport of its quotas of coal. In this respect, we should consider the problems in rail transport caused by the mass destruction of the infrastructure and rolling stock during the Civil War.

However, the enormous increase in coal prices, previously mentioned, was a problem for *Gas Madrid* and the rest of the Spanish gas companies. In 1946, for example, the average price paid for a tonne of coal ex works increased by approximately 28 %, from 154.25 pesetas in January to 214.10 pesetas.

The gas factory in Madrid, the principal industrial asset of gas Madrid, was one of the 51 factories of this kind existing in Spain in the 1940s, sixteen of

6 Manufactured gas could be obtained through two procedures; distillation or gasification. The former was used in all of the gas factories in Spain in this period, with the only exception of the gas factory of Córdoba (Sindicato Vertical de Agua, Gas y Electricidad, 1944).

which came to a standstill in 1944 as they had no coal in order to operate. The state and activity of the factory in Madrid during the first half of the decade illustrates the difficulties encountered by the sector in general and for the company in particular. It was a century-old factory with modernised facilities. It had two oven batteries, one was a DIDIER continuous distillation oven and the other was a discontinuous distillation KOPPERS oven. They had a higher productivity than the retort furnace batteries that were predominant in the Spanish gas factories.

However, in the mid-1940s, some of the ovens of the chambers were shut down due to repairs or a lack of coal. The increase in the prices of raw materials and the limitation on imports of technological equipment led to deficiencies in the rest of the facilities and services of the factory, as described by the engineers in their reports (Gas Madrid, S.A., n.d. [1947]). The factory also lacked the staff necessary to provide the services correctly. This shortage of workers was acknowledged by the company itself, which complemented the workforce by using subcontracted labourers (Gas Madrid, S.A., n.d. [1947], p. 17). In 1947 the workforce of the Madrid factory was made up of 195 employees.[7]

The fragmentary data available regarding the production of gas in Spanish factories in the 1940s indicate that the Madrid factory of *Gas Madrid* was the second-largest producer in terms of the volume of gas produced and in the tonnes of coal distilled, after the Fábrica de Gas de Barcelona owned by the company Catalana de Gas y Electricidad.

In 1943, the Madrid factory produced 49,210,170 m^3 of gas and 47,538,390 m^3 the following year. There are data available for the years 1945 and 1946 about the type of gas produced. This is important information provided by the engineers of the factory in a *Memoria* (Report), revealing that of the total output a part was coal gas, another blue gas or water gas and a third was mixed gas, also called poor gas, a mixture of water gas and air gas (Alayo and Barca, 2011). The latter two had a lower calorific and light value. In 1946, of the total of 46,381,500 m^3 produced, 77.52 % was coal gas, 17.78 % blue gas and 4.72 % mixed gas (Gas Madrid, S.A., n.d. [1947]). The following year, production was 47,979,450 m^3, far removed from the 87,477,610 obtained in the Fábrica de Barcelona (Sindicato Vertical de Agua, Gas y Electricidad, 1947).

7 This does not include the personnel engaged in cleaning and surveillance tasks (Gas Madrid, S.A., n.d. [1947]).

Due to the difficulties in the supply of coal, during the 1940s, gas production in the factories across the whole of Spain did not cover consumer demand,[8] and the government authorities imposed restrictions on its use, establishing an order of preference for the supply of gas.[9] *Gas Madrid* also applied these restrictions in the Spanish capital. The data referring to the year 1946 show that there were restrictions on 331 of the 365 days of the year. The restrictions were established throughout the day during different time bands and sometimes lasted for up to 14 hours. For example, between the 1 January and 16 March, there were restrictions on the supply of gas from 9 a.m. to 12 p.m., from 5 p.m. to 8 p.m. and from 10.30 p.m. to 7 a.m. (Gas Madrid, S.A., n.d. [1947]).

In addition to the regulations established by Franco's authorities regarding the restrictions on consumption, another factor that influenced it was the number of clients. As previously mentioned, before the outbreak of the Spanish Civil War, *Gas Madríd*'s largest client in the Spanish capital was the City Council through the city's public street lighting service contract which accounted for the majority of the Madrid factory's gas production. The distribution of consumption changed radically after the war, as a result of the progressive electrification of Madrid's street lighting. In 1934, the number of gas street lamps in the city was 19,896 but in the mid-1940s there were only 3,645. Therefore, in 1945, the gas consumed by public street lighting only represented 4 % of the total 38,690,832 m^3 consumed.

Urban street lighting seemed to represent a cumbersome burden for the company, which complained about the difficult relationship with the Municipal Department for Street Lighting which insisted that the public street lighting contract signed by the company in 1922 had not expired. Furthermore, there were about one hundred compressed gas street lamps in different central parts of the city (Puerta del Sol, calle de Alcalá and Plaza de la Cibeles) for prestigious reasons and their conservation represented a "considerable sacrifice" for the company (Gas Madrid, S.A., n.d. [1947], p. 1). Moreover, the conservation of public street lighting caused significant losses for the company, which only in

8 According to the data provided by the Vertical Union of Water, Gas and Electricity, in the mid 1940s, the factories needed an annual quantity of coal of 458,640 Tm., while the official quota that had been granted to them was 350,580 Tm. The figures are very far removed from the real quantities received, which, in 1946 were 258,000 Tm. and 276,602 in 1947. (Sindicato Vertical de Agua, Gas y Electricidad, 1947, p. 10).

9 The energy crisis during the early years of the Franco regime was widespread, not only affecting the supply and consumption of gas but also electricity. In this respect, see Díaz Morlán and San Román (2009) and Bosch (2007).

1946 and 1947 amounted to more than two million pesetas.[10] In this respect, it should be noted again that as a consequence of the autarchic policy that implied the maximum reduction of imports, there was an increase in prices of the materials necessary to maintain these operations and the rest of the company's facilities or new constructions. In 1946, for example, the price of laminated steel increased from 30 % to 40 %, that of wood by 12 %, brass accessories from 40 % to 90 %, sleeves for the street lamps by 75 %, lead pipes by 54 %, the five-light gas metres by almost 59 %, etc. (Gas Madrid, S.A. n.d. [1947]).

The number of clients that the company had in Madrid increased throughout the 1940s, although this growth could be misleading as it was based on a war situation, when many clients had been lost due to the destruction of buildings, evacuations, etc. Furthermore, we should remember the afore-mentioned restrictions that affected all of the company's clients. Therefore, although the number of Gas Madrid's clients increased during the post-war period, we should take into account the above-mentioned factors which prevent us from considering the significant increase in a totally positive way. The clients increased from 28,397 in 1940 to 45,482 in 1947 (Gas Madrid, S.A., n.d. [1947], Sindicato Vertical de Agua, Gas y Electricidad, 1947). The client portfolio grew at a faster pace than that of the population of Madrid in this period, given that the number of inhabitants in the capital grew by 20.6 % while the growth in the number of clients was 60.2 %. We must also consider this increase within the context of the afore-mentioned electricity restrictions that were imposed throughout Spain in this period. As indicated in the company's *Memoria de los servicios técnicos* (Technical services report) of 1946, the new clients "are obtained from either a social group with a high economic position or from aspiring users who have an irremediable need for fuel" (Gas Madrid, S.A., n.d. [1947], p. 16).

With respect to the type of client/consumption, there is data available about their classification for the year 1946. It should be noted here that at that time Madrid had a population of 1,190,831 inhabitants. Of the 44,397 clients recorded by the company in this year, 39,475 (88.91 %) were private homes, 1,175 were classified as "Arts and Trades" (2.64 %), 2,805 corresponded to industries (6.31 %), 457 retail outlets (1.07 %) 128 teaching centres (0.28 %) and 338 Charity and Health establishments (0.76 %). With respect to industries, the majority of them are included in the categories "Culinary" and "Food", followed by laboratories, mechanical industries, graphic arts, railways, the press, military and

10 1 €=166 pesetas.

those engaged in lamp and glass manufacture (Gas Madrid, S.A., n.d. [1947], pp. 12–13).

With respect to the price of gas per m^3, the clients paid 0.60 pesetas until 1946, when the company, after managing its increase, obtained the approval to increase the rate to 0.90 pesetas per m^3. Consumption was measured with metres, the majority of which were owned by the company (close to 67 % in 1945). They rented them out the users at a rate which the company considered unprofitable, even though the difference between the income derived from the hire of the metres and the costs derived from their maintenance was positive, at least in the years for which there are data available (1944–1946). In the 1940s, the complaints and claims made by the clients about the costly and frequent repairs of the new metres due to their poor quality were frequent. This also ratifies the hardship, scarcity and shortage of all types of articles and materials suffered by Spanish society in the 1940s.

In addition to the sale of gas and the hire and sale of metres for measuring consumption, *Gas Madrid* hired and sold other electrical appliances that ran on gas, such as hobs, ovens, grills and heaters, which generated profits for the company although not very high: For example, the profit from sales in the company's showroom in 1946 was 34,107 pesetas,[11] but if we subtract the costs generated by the establishment (rent, staff, etc.) which amounted to 26,500 pesetas, the profit was only 7,607 pesetas. However, we should also add the income obtained from the deposit and hire of these types of appliances, which amounted to 358,963.63 pesetas at the end of that year. On the same date, this type of use included 11,319 gas-run appliances, of which 9,398 were hobs, 1,214 ovens, 327 grills and 594 gas heaters.

4 Conclusions

The Spanish post-war years constituted one of the darkest periods of Spanish history. Popularly known as the "years of hunger", the 1940s were a decade of enormous hardship and difficulties for the Spanish population. In addition to the violent political repression which began after the end of the Civil War on 1 April 1939, severe problems were suffered in every sphere generated by the erroneous autarchic economic policy implemented by the authorities of the Franco dictatorship. The self-sufficiency ideal in a country that lacked essential

11 Corresponds to the sale of 555 appliances: 442 gas hobs, 2 ovens, 111 grills (Gas Madrid, S.A., n.d. [1947]).

resources such as oil, led to a prolongation of the hardship caused by the Civil War, the development of the Second World War and the subsequent international isolation of Spain due to Franco's support of the Axis powers.

The energy sector was one of the most affected by the autarchy, voluntarily imposed by the Franco authorities, particularly the gas industry. The impediments to obtain the coal necessary with which to produce gas and its shortage caused serious problems for operating the factories and the companies that owned them barely survived. One of the most important at that time was *Gas Madrid, S. A.*, founded in 1922. It supplied gas, as a practical monopoly, to the country's capital, a city which then had more than a million inhabitants. Its trajectory and the evolution of the business have been analysed in this study, confirming that in this case, and despite certain advantages with respect to its supply of coal, it also faced enormous complications similar to those suffered by the rest of the gas companies: high coal prices, poor quality coal, the use of raw materials other than coal that produced a lower quality gas, the shortage and scarcity of materials for maintaining the facilities, insufficient labour, restrictions in the supply of gas, clients who were unhappy with the service... In short, a bleak panorama.

References

Alayo, J. C., & Barca, F. X. (2011). *La tecnología del gas a través de su historia*. Barcelona: Fundación Gas Natural Fenosa.

Ayuntamiento de Madrid (1915). *Resumen de los trabajos realizados por las dependencias municipales en el año 1914*. Madrid: Imprenta Municipal.

Ayuntamiento de Madrid (1929). *Información sobre la ciudad. Año 1929. Memoria*. Madrid: Imprenta y Litografía Municipal.

Bosch, F.-X. (2007). Restricciones de energía eléctrica en los primeros años del Franquismo. Las Delegaciones Técnicas Especiales para la regulación y distribución de energía eléctrica, 1944–1958. *Revista de Historia Industrial, 16* (35), 165–186. doi: https://doi.org/10.1344/rhi.v16i35.19833.

Contrato de cesión y suministro de alumbrado con la Sociedad Gas Madrid, S.A., durante veinte años (1922). Madrid: Imprenta Municipal.

Díaz Morlán, P., & San Román, E. (2009). Causas de la restricción eléctrica en el primer franquismo: una aportación desde la historia empresarial. *Investigaciones de Historia Económica, 5* (13), 73–95. doi: https://doi.org/10.1016/S1698-6989(09)70086-4Get.

González Enciso, A., & Matés Barco, J. M. (Coord.) (2006). *Historia económica de España*. Barcelona: Ariel.

Fernández-Paradas, M. (2019a). La crisis del alumbrado de gas en las ciudades españolas durante la I Guerra Mundial. *Historia Contemporánea, I* (59), 127–159.

Fernández-Paradas, M. (2019b). El sector del gas en la Guerra Civil. In M. Fernández-Paradas, & C. Larrinaga (Coords.). *El impacto de la Guerra Civil española en el sector terciario.* (pp. 25–50). Granada: Comares.

Fernández-Paradas, M., & Martykánová, D. (2017). La industria del gas en España en los años 1940 en el contexto de Europa. In I. Bartolomé Rodríguez, M. Fernández-Paradas, & J. Mirás Araujo (Eds.). *Globalización, nacionalización y liberalización de la industria del gas en la Europa latina (siglos XIX–XX)* (pp. 257–278). Madrid: Marcial Pons.

Fernández-Paradas, M., & Rodríguez-Martín, N. (2019). «Una aventura con fatales consecuencias». La incautación de la fábrica del gas de Madrid y la municipalización del servicio público de alumbrado (1917–1922). *Hispania. Revista Española de Historia, 79* (261), 157–187. doi: https://doi.org/10.3989/hispania.2019.006.

Gas Madrid, S. A. (n.d. [1947]). *Memoria de los servicios técnicos. Producción. Redes de distribución. Suministro y consumo. Talleres y obras. Año 1946.* Madrid.

Magaldi, N., & Rodríguez Martín, N. (2020). La incautación municipal de la fábrica del gas de Madrid: los pleitos y su resolución, 1917–1922. In I. Bartolomé Rodríguez, M. Fernández-Paradas, & J. Mirás Araujo (Eds.). *Cercanas pero distintas. La desigual trayectoria de la industria del gas en las regiones del sur de Europa (siglos XIX–XX)* (pp. 329–348). Madrid: Marcial Pons.

Sindicato Vertical de Agua, Gas y Electricidad (Delegación Nacional de Sindicatos). (1944). *Estudio Técnico-Estadístico sobre la Industria Española de Gas*. Madrid.

Sindicato Vertical de Agua, Gas y Electricidad (Delegación Nacional de Sindicatos). (1947). *Datos estadísticos técnicos de las fábricas de gas españolas 1930–1947.* Madrid.

Mercedes Fernández-Paradas

6 *Gas Andalucía S.A.*, the company leading the introduction of natural gas to Andalusia (1987–2001)[1]

Abstract The "Memorandum of understanding for the development of gas in Spain" was signed in 1985 with the aim of promoting the implementation of natural gas. As a result, *Gas Andalucía S.A.* was founded in 1987, with a capital of 1 billion pesetas. The company was in charge of bringing natural gas to the Southern region of Spain (Regional Government of Andalusia). It aims at managing the production and supply of combustible gases, gas appliances and customer technical assistance. This study analyses the main variables of *Gas Andalucía* (shareholders, profits, customers, gas sales, distribution network, etc.). It also examines how manufactured gas was replaced with natural gas and how this energy was introduced between 1987 and 2001, a period in which the company carried out its activities in a regulated market.

1 Introduction

The "Memorandum of understanding for the development of gas in Spain" was signed in 1985 with the objective of promoting the implanting of natural gas which had arrived in Spain, specifically to Barcelona, in 1969, transported by sea. This document gave rise to the founding of *Gas Andalucía S.A.* in 1987, with a capital of one billion pesetas, with the purpose of implementing the gas supply in the Autonomous Region of Andalusia, located in southern Spain. Andalusia covered an area of 87,236 km^2, 17.2 % of the country's territory and its population of 6.9 people accounted for 17.2 % of Spain's total population. It constituted the largest and most populated region of the country.

This chapter analyses the founding of *Gas Andalucía* and the changes in its capital and shareholding. It studies how it replaced manufactured gas with natural gas which began to be introduced in 1987 and how it ceased to supply the manufactured gas that it produced with naphta from 1993. From this year,

1 This text forms part of the results of the of the research project, The Gas Industry in Spain: development and regional trajectories (1842–2008), HAR2017-82112-P, financed by The Ministry of Science, Innovation and Universities of the Spanish Government and ERDF funds.

those municipalities newly incorporated into the network were supplied with natural gas. In the cities of Cádiz and Málaga, the company sold methane and natural gas. The chapter also examines some of the principal variables of the company (profits, clientele, gas sales, length of the distribution network, workforce. . .), particularly those related to the implementation of the gas supply in Andalusia. The process was terminated in 2001. In 2000 the liberalisation of the gas market began which marked the beginning of the end of the regulated market prevailing during the period studied in this chapter. The research is based on the existing literature and on the annual reports of *Gas Natural.*

2 The founding of Gas Andalucía, capital and shareholding

As we have mentioned, natural gas first arrived to Barcelona in 1969. Between 1970 and 1981 it was supplied to 27 municipalities in Catalonia. It began to be supplied to the rest of Spain from 1980. This indicates that it had yet to be introduced in a large part of the territory. In 1988, the Spanish Worker's Socialist Party came to power. In its electoral programme it established the energy policy guidelines, based on savings, increasing energy efficiency and a reduction in the contribution of nuclear energy while favouring a greater contribution of coal and natural gas in relative terms. In order to manage the fulfilment of these guidelines, on 23 July 1985, the public sector, through the Ministry of Industry and Energy, the National Hydrocarbons Institute, the *National Gas Company* (*Enagás*), *Butano* y *Gas y Electricidad*, together with private companies (*Catalana de Gas y Electricidad, Compañía Española de Electricidad y Gas Lebon, Gas Madrid, Gas de Euskadi, Gas de Zaragoza and Hidroeléctrica del Cantábrico*) signed the "Memorandum of understanding for the development of gas in Spain", in which the following objectives were contemplated: (1) The development of the gas industry in Spain; (2) The introduction of natural gas as an alternative energy source; (3) The increase in the share of natural gas in the energy balance to levels similar to those of other European countries; (4) It was anticipated that by 1992 all of the autonomous regions would have natural gas except for Extremadura, Galicia, the Canary Islands and the Balearic Islands. This document represented a milestone in the history of Spanish gas as, used as a base, it enabled an unprecedented increase in the investments made in the gas industry. These investments gave rise to the growth of the distribution network and, in turn, an increase in the number of municipalities supplied with natural gas and its clientele (Fábregas, 1986, 2014, 2018; Ballestero, 2017).

Gas Andalucía S.A. was the company that led this process in the autonomous region of Andalusia. It was founded on 8 October 1987 with a capital of one billion pesetas, with a value of 1,000 pesetas per share, in Seville, where it established its head office. It was created with the objective of implementing the supply of gas for this territory, whereby it "would be engaged in the production, supply and marketing of combustible gases and of the devices that used them and the provision of technical assistance to clients" (Fernández-Paradas, 2009). The founding partners participated as follows. *Repsol Butano S.A.*, affiliate of *Repsol*, owned 33.5 % of the capital, the latter belonged to the National Hydrocarbons Institute. The *Sociedad para la Promoción y Reconversión Económica de Andalucía S.A.*, (*The Company for the Promotion and Economic Reconversion of Andalusía S.A.*) of the Regional Government of Andalusia owned 33 %. *Catalana de Gas S. A.*, owner of the Seville gas factory held 32.57 %. Finally, the *Compañía Española de Gas*, owner of the gas factories of Cádiz and Málaga which formed part of *Catalana de Gas*, had a share of 0.94 %

At the beginning of 1988, based on the stipulations of the "Memorandum", the gas concessions and the *Catalana de Gas* factory and the factories of the *Compañía Española de Gas* in the region were transferred to *Gas Andalucía*. The operation cost 2,784,406,708 pesetas and was partly financed through a capital increase of 969,000,000 pesetas. For this reason, its capital was fixed at 1,969 million pesetas.

Due to its relevance in the introduction of gas in the territory of Andalusia, it is also worth mentioning the signing in that same year of a Collaboration Agreement between the Regional Government of Andalusia and the *Empresa Nacional del Gas*, responsible for the supply and transport of natural gas in the country.[2] Its purpose was to promote the infrastructure of the gas industry. *Enagás* was responsible for constructing the transport infrastructure that distributed piped gas to the municipalities. It supplied *Gas Andalucía*, the company that distributed to the consumers (Gas Andalucía, 1989).

Other important milestone took place at the end of 1991, when *Catalana de Gas* absorbed *Gas Madrid S.A.* and part of the assets of the spin-off *Repsol Butano*. As a result of this operation, *Gas Andalucía* increased its social

2 It should be noted that for a while *Catalana de Gas* had the control of *Enagás*. In 1994 it bought it under the name of *Gas Natural*. But, the beginning of the liberalisation of the gas sector in 1988, which culminated with the Royal Decree of 23 June 2000, implied the obligation to separate the natural gas transport and distribution networks again, and the Technical Management of the System corresponded to the *Empresa Nacional de Gas*. The result was that *Gas Natural* had to gradually shed its capital in *Enagás*, a process that concluded in 2009 (Sánchez Gutiérrez, 2006; Ballestero, 2017; Fàbregas, 2018).

capital to 2.969 billion pesetas and modified its shareholding: *Catalana de Gas* owned 66.9 % of the shares, the *Sociedad para la Promoción y Reconversión Económica* maintained a share of 33 % and the *Compañía Española de Gas* 0.94 %. Therefore, *Catalana de Gas* gained control of the company. In 1992, this company changed its name to *Gas Natural S. D. G. S. A.* and in the year 2000, *Gas Andalucía* became known as *Gas Natural Andalucía* (Fernández-Paradas, 2009; Fábregas, 2014). In 1995, *Gas Natural* had a share of 99.99 % of the capital of *Gas Andalucía* while 0.01 % was owned by *La Propagadora del Gas* (Gas Andalucía, 1996; Gas Natural Andalucía, 2002).

In short, *Gas Andalucía* was controlled by *Gas Natural*, the largest gas company in Spain, which, in just a few years became the world's leading multinational company in the sector. With respect to the distribution of the capital of this latter firm, we will look at the most important changes that took place in the period considered. In mid-1989, the principal shareholders of *Gas Natural* were: *Caja de Ahorro y Pensiones* (*Caixa*), 23.64 %; *Grupo Repsol*, 8.54 %; *Grupo Asland* (6.97 %); *ACC Grup* (4.94 %); *Caja de Barcelona* (4.47 %); and *SGAB* (1.52 %). Together they accounted for 50.1 % of the capital. In June 1990, Repsol was able to buy shares from the principal shareholders of *Gas Madrid*, that is, *Banco Pastor* (33 %) and *Hidroeléctrica Española* (20 %), which gave it the control of 88 % of the capital. Around the same dates, the largest shareholders of *Catalana de Gas* were *Caja de Ahorro y Pensiones* (23.64 %), *Grupo Repsol* (14.27 %), *British Gas* (9.98 %), *Caja de Barcelona* (7 %) and *SGAB* (6.48 %). This means that they controlled 61 % of the capital. A little later, *Repsol* and *Caixa* agreed the merger. As a result, at the end of 1990 the principal shareholders of *Catalana de Gas* were: *Caixa*, 30.45 %; *Grupo Repsol*, 13.74 %; *British Gas*, 9.98 %; and *SGAB*, 6.48 %; the four accounting for 61 % of the capital. At the end of 1991, *Catalana de Gas* absorbed *Gas Madrid* and small distributing companies that had been separated from *Repsol Butano* and the *Instituto Nacional de Industria*. In this way, the leading gas distributor in Spain (*Catalana de Gas*) merged with the second most important distributor (*Gas Madrid*). The capital was distributed as follows: *Repsol*, 30 %; *Instituto Nacional de Industria*, 14 %; *Caixa*, 25 %; and 28,000 small shareholders, 31 % (Fàbregas, 2018).

The grouping of this capital made it possible for *Catalana de Gas* to begin operating in the gas industry outside of Spain. The first change consisted in modifying its name to *Gas Natural*. It seized the first opportunity in 1992, when the Argentine government privatised *Gas del Estado*. *Gas Natural* acquired half of the Buenos Aires division of this company which had almost one million clients. In Spain it had 1.5 million. In the following years, until 2002, it began operating in other South American countries and continued progressing in Spain (Fàbregas, 2018).

The first Board of Directors of Gas Andalucía was made up of Rafael Saqueiros de San Román, as chairman, José Luis Calvo Borrego, vice-chairman, the board members Felipe Cañellas Vilalta, Manuel Domínguez Abascal, Martín Gallego Málaga, Félix Ibáñez de Carlos, José Manuel Manzanedo Díaz, José Moret Quintana, Miguel Ribas Pujol, Ricardo Sánchez de la Moreno, Antonio Téllez de Peralta and Eduardo Torres Vega, Antonio González García as secretary and David Sánchez Díaz as CEO (Gas Andalucía, 1989).

The afore-mentioned operation whereby *Catalana de Gas* acquired *Gas Madrid*, giving the former the control of almost 70 % of the capital of *Gas Andalucía*, altered the composition of Gas Andalucía's Board of Directors. Francisco Badía Vidal and Francisco Mencía Morales became chairman and vice-chairman respectively. Some of the board members also changed. Six of the original members of the board remained: Felipe Cañellas, Manuel Domínguez, Martín Gallego, Félix Ibáñez, Miguel Ribas and Eduardo Torres; and Antonio Blanco Peñalva, Carlos Torralba Gallego, Francisco Javier Soto Chazarri, Eduardo Torres Vega and Diego Vera Hidalgo were incorporated. The position of CEO was held by Pedro de Jorge Manchado (Gas Andalucía, 1992). It can be assumed that the new members were designated by *Catalana de Gas*. There were hardly any changes until 1995. It should be remembered that in this year, its successor, *Gas Natural*, became the shareholder of 99.9 % of the capital of *Gas Andalucía*, which gave rise to the resignation of three board members. Apart from this there were no other changes made to the company's board (Gas Andalucía, 1996). From 1998 the company's chairman was Félix Ibáñez.

3 The end of the manufactured gas cycle in favour of natural gas

A little after the creation of *Gas Andalucía* (1987), the company began to replace manufactured gas (in Andalusia it was made with naphta) with propane, methane and natural gas.[3] The new concessions were supplied with only natural gas from the outset. In order to undertake the so-called gas-changing operations, that is, the conditioning of the clients' installations to receive natural

3 In the territories where manufactured gas had disappeared decades before, as in the case of Galicia, there was no transition from naphta gas to natural gas, the latter was installed directly (Martínez (Coord.), Mirás & Lindoso, 2009).

gas, on 17 May 1989, *Gas Andalucía*, together with *Servicies Energéticos S.A.* founded the *Agrupación Temporal de Empresas Cambio de Gas*, to which it contributed 20 % of the capital. In turn, *Gas Andalucía* participated in the constitution of *Servicios Energéticos* with 15 % of the capital, together with *ESESA* and *EQYSE*, companies of the *Catalana de Gas group* (Gas Andalucía, 1990, 1991).

In 1988, *Gas Andalucía* undertook the following actions. In Cádiz it replaced the manufactured gas produced with naphta with propane air. This is a mixture of air and propane, which has similar characteristics to natural gas. In Seville, it adapted the distribution networks as an essential preliminary step to changing from manufactured naphta gas to natural gas. Furthermore, from the end of this year, although it continued to produce gas with naphta, it used natural gas in the calorific value adjustment phase, also called decarbonisation. In Huelva it began the construction work of the natural gas installations (Gas Andalucía, 1989).

In 1989, in Seville, it used natural gas as a raw material in the decarbonisation phase of naphta gas and in the complementary methane air plant (this product was the result of mixing air and methane gas and has similar characteristics to natural gas), and its contribution accounted for 67 % of the raw materials used to produce gas. In 1990, it began to supply natural gas to the city of Huelva. In this year, the so-called *Gas-Changing Operation* was undertaken in Seville and Dos Hermanas (a municipality close to the city of Seville) together with the *Agrupación Temporal*. It consisted in listing the devices of all of the customers and reviewing the installations. The changing of the devices that began in January 1991 remained pending. In this same year it began to supply natural gas to Seville and to construct the distribution network of Córdoba. Its propane plant in Málaga also started operating. Furthermore, it terminated the changing of devices in Seville, we do not know if it also did so in Dos Hermanas. This meant that all of its clients in the city of Seville only received natural gas (Gas Andalucía, 1990, 1992). In 1992 it initiated the tasks that would enable the sale of natural gas in Málaga and Cádiz, through the construction and implementation of the storage and regasification plants of liquefied natural gas. Similarly, it also implemented the first phase of the construction of the distribution network of natural gas in Córdoba. This enabled it to initiate supply in July of the same year. At the end of 1992, *Gas Andalucía* distributed manufactured gas in Málaga and Seville and natural gas in Córdoba, Huelva and Seville (Gas Andalucía, 1993).

1993 was a relevant year as the company supplied natural gas to all the municipalities in which it operated. This was possible thanks to the start of operations of the liquefied natural gas reception and regasification plants in Cádiz and Málaga. This gave rise to the end of the naphta manufactured gas. In both of these cities, as well as natural gas, it continued to supply methane.

In the subsequent years, the following milestones can be highlighted. In 1997, after *Gas Andalucía* had obtained the concession to distribute natural gas in Jerez de la Frontera, it supplied 13 municipalities that accounted for 36 % of the population of Andalusia. In 1998, the cities of Jaén and Granada were added (Gas Andalucía, 1994, 1999). Then, in 2001, it also started supplying the towns of San Juan de Aznalfarache in the province of Seville and Fuengirola in the province of Málaga. In this year, which marked the closure of a chapter, there were still methane clients in Cádiz and Málaga (Gas Natural Andalucía, 2003). By then, 20 municipalities, including all of the provincial capitals except for Almería and the most populated towns, had a natural gas supply and 47 % of the population of the region had access to it (Gas Natural Andalucía, 2002).

4 A booming business

Next, we will analyse some of the more significant variables that show the development of natural gas in the region of Andalusia which corresponds practically entirely to *Gas Andalucía*. At the end of the 1990s, this company had no competitors. We know that the electrical company *Endesa* began to supply natural gas to towns in the province of Cádiz in the year 2000 (Fernández-Paradas, 2015). Therefore, we will examine the principal variables of the company (profits, clientele, gas sales, length of the distribution chain, workforce. . .) that reflect the growth of its activity (Tab. 1).

The earliest information that we have regarding the number of kilometres of pipes through which *Gas Andalucía* supplied gas to its clients dates to 1993. This year there were 735 kilometres of pipes. The distribution of these pipes shows the predominance of the province of Seville and large territorial inequalities. 53.7 % were in the province of Seville and 28.7 % in Málaga, together accounting for 82.4 % of the total. The rest were distributed between Cádiz (9.1 %), Córdoba (4.8 %) and Huelva (3.7 %). The absence of a network in the provinces of Granada, Jaén and Almería is striking. This is partly due to the fact that they had not received piped gas for a long time (Fernández-Paradas, 2017). In the subsequent years, the length of the network hardly grew. In 1996 it measured 786 km, only 50 km longer, that is 6.9 % more than in 1993. In 1996, there was a greater distribution of the network, although Seville accounted for 50.3 % and Málaga 23.4 %, together representing 73.7 %. Their share had decreased compared with that of 1993. This is because it increased slightly in the other provinces with piped gas and the consumption of natural gas was introduced

Tab. 1: Sales of piped gas, number of clients, kilometres of distribution network, workforce and profits of Gas Andalucía (1988–2001). 1988=100*1

Years	Gas sales (millions of therms)	Number of Clients	Gas sales per client (therms)	Kilometres network*1	Nº. employees	Profits
1988	254.6 100	74,417 100	3,421.3 100	n.d.	185 100	161.3*2
1989	311.7 122.4	75,506 101.5	4,128.1 120.7	n.d.	191 103.2	109.5*2
1990	306.4 120.3	77,296 103.9	3,964 115.9	n.d.	187 101.1	n.d.
1991	345.4 135.7	79,720 107.1	4,332.7 126.6	n.d.	184 99.4	n.d.
1992	438.4 172.2	82,930 111.4	5,286.4 154.4	n.d.	181 97.8	10.7*2
1993	433.7 170.3	88,013 118.3	4,927.7 144	735.4 100	179 96.8	15.2*2
1994	464.3 182.4	94,521 127	4,912.1 143.6	751.4 102.2	121 65.4	99.6*2
1995	465.1 182.7	98,829 132.8	4,706.1 137.6	752.4 102.3	126 68.1	666*2
1996	530 208.2	n.d.	n.d.	786 106.9	125 67.6	355*2
1997	515 202.3	105,138 141.3	4,898.3 143.2	860 116.9	125 67.6	251*2 211*3
1998	584 229.4	112,680 151.4	5,182.8 151.5	991 134.8	138 74.6	234*3
1999	n.d.	n.d.	n.d.	n.d.	n.d.	n.d.
2000	878.9 345.2	n.d.	n.d.	1,314 178.7	n.d.	n.d.
2001	1,094.8 430	182,533 245.3	5997.8 175.3	1,449 197	148 80	n.d.

Source: Gas Andalucía (1989, 1990, 1991, 1992, 1993, 1994, 1995, 1996, 1997, 1998, 1999); Gas Natural Andalucía (2000, 2001). Own elaboration.

n.d.: no data.

*1 Except for the distribution network: 1993=100.

*2. Profits before tax.

*3. Profits after tax.

to Granada and Jaén. From this year the network grew at a faster pace. En 1997 it reached 860 km, in 1998, 991 km, that is, 34.8 % more than in 1988. We do not have the data for 1999. Between 1999 and 2000, an unprecedented increase took place, as in 2000 it had a length of 1,314 km, 32.6 % longer than two years earlier. In 2001, the total length of the network was 1,449 km, that is, 97 % longer than in 1993. It is worth pointing out that, with respect to this year, the distribution network in 2001 was less unequal: 38.4 % in the province of Seville, 18.5 % in the province of Málaga, 14 % in that of Granada, 11.9 % in that of Córdoba, 7.3 % in that of Cádiz and 4.5 % in that of Jaén. Almería still had no piped gas supply.

With respect to the number of clients (Tab. 1), we have a longer series that begins in 1988, when there were 74,417 clients. Until 1991, the growth was slower, at around 1,000–2,000 on average each year, and the number of clients increased by 7.1 % in this three-year period. From then, they grew at a faster pace. For example, in 1992, there were 82,930 clients, that is 3,210 more than in 1991, in 1993 there were 88,013 or 5.083 more than in 1992, in 1994 there were 94,521, that is 6,508 more than in 1993. This trend continued in the following years. In 1998 there were 112,680 clients, 51.4 % more than in 1988, in 2001 there were 182,533, 145.3 % more than in 1988. This means that the years between 1998 and 2001 were those with the highest growth, with a large difference with respect to previous years. From the latter two figures we can draw two conclusions. The first is the greater growth of the distribution network between 1998 and 2001 took place during the increase in clientele, which grew at an even faster pace than that of the network. It is also worth highlighting that the campaigns implemented by the company for the sale of domestic gas appliances, also used by the showrooms, must have been taking effect (Gas Andalucía, 1992, 1997).

With respect to the type of users, in 1989, one hundred percent were "domestic" and "commercial", the latter included those that were neither domestic nor industrial. It is highly relevant that there were no industries that consumed piped gas, including workshops of any size. This indicates that industry used electricity and liquefied petroleum gases as energy sources. Furthermore, piped gas had not reached the market in which it would theoretically be able to most expand its sales, given that the large industries, particularly those in certain sectors such as the chemical or electromechanical sectors, are large energy consumers.

In 1989, households accounted for 97.7 % of the consumption of piped gas and commercial uses 2.3 %. On a provincial level, which then was the equivalent of the respective provincial capitals, we should remember that only the capitals of Seville, Málaga and Cádiz had gas. Seville accounted for 74.3 % of the domestic market, Málaga 17.6 % and Cádiz 8.1 %. The gas supplied for commercial use was distributed as follows: 58.8 % for Seville, 24.2 % for Málaga and 17 % for Cádiz. In Andalusia as a whole, 97.3 % of the supply was for households and 2.3 % was for commercial uses. This means that almost all of the piped gas was supplied to households which considerably limited its development. The province where the highest proportion of piped gas was provided to households was Seville, accounting for 98.2 % of the total, followed by Málaga with 96.9 % and Cádiz with 95.3 %. In a relatively short time, this panorama changed favourably towards a greater diversity in the destination of the gas. We know that in 1994 Gas Andalucía had five industrial clients. This number rose to seven in 1995. In 1996, households were supplied with 54 % of the gas, commercial uses received

37 % and 9 % was supplied to industry. Unfortunately, we do not have data regarding its distribution by province. These percentages remained at similar levels in 1998. For 2000 and 2001 the company reports only provide data for domestic-commercial gas consumption (not broken down) and industrial gas consumption. In the year 2000, domestic-commercial uses accounted for 88 % of the supply and industry 12 %. In 2001, the percentage supplied to industry grew to 20 % (Gas Andalucía, 1990, 1997, 1999, 2001, 2002). In short, we can confirm a considerable increase in consumption in industry; a larger consumer of gas per client than households and commercial uses, which, at least partly, explains the increase in consumption of piped gas at the beginning of the twenty-first century. Also contributing to the growth in sales was the fact that the company won important clients, including the supply to firms installing air conditioning with a heat pump system, the supply of natural gas to hospitals, the supply to the Isla de La Cartuja (Seville) as from the Universal Expo 1992 or compressed natural gas for Seville's bus fleet (Gas Andalucía, 1991, 1992, 1998).

As we can see in Tab. 1, the sales of piped gas increased more than the number of clients and the distribution network. In 1988, sales amounted to 245.6 million therms. With respect to this year, they rose by 20 % in 1989, by 70.3 % in 1993, by 129.4 % in 1998, by 245.2 % in 2000 and by 330 % in 2001. It should be remembered that the number of clients grew at a slower pace. Between 1998 and 2001 they grew by 145.3 %. For this reason, although piped gas sales increased per inhabitant, they did so at a lower intensity than gas sales. In 1988, the average consumption per capita was 3,421.3 therms, in 2001 it was 5,997.8 therms, the highest figure of the period studied and 75.3 % higher than in 1988.

Previously, we analysed the distribution of piped gas sales by use. Now we will examine its distribution across the territory. In 1988 it was distributed as follows: 73.4 % in the province of Seville, 22.2 % in the province of Málaga and 8.4 % in the province of Cádiz. In short, the bulk of *Gas Andalucía*'s business was concentrated in Seville. In 1990, the province of Seville continued to maintain its hegemony with its share lowering slightly to 72.7 % of total sales, followed by Málaga with 17.4 %, Cádiz with 9.8 % and Huelva with 0.1 % (Gas Andalucía, 1989, 1991). The following information corresponds to 1997, the year in which all of the provinces were included in the supply except for Almería. In this year, the province of Seville continued to account for the greatest share, although lower than previous years, with 62.6 % of consumption. A long way behind were the provinces of Málaga (14.3 %), Cádiz (8.5 %), Córdoba (8.1 %), Huelva (6 %), Granada (0.4 %) and Jaén (0.1 %). The last available data correspond to the following year and show only slight modifications in the percentages. Therefore, we can conclude that the distribution of consumption across the territory was highly unequal throughout the whole period studied (Gas Andalucía, 1989, 1991, 1998, 1999).

Another relevant factor is the workforce (Tab. 1). In 1988 the company had 185 employees,[4] in 1989 there were six more. After that the workforce decreased constantly until only 65.4 % of the workers employed in the first year remained. This reduction is due to the closure of the manufactured gas factories of Cádiz and Málaga in 1993, the facilities that replaced them required few workers as they were automated and more labour was not required. From this year, the gas company began to increase its workforce but it did not recover its original size. In 2001 it had 20 % less workers than in 1988.

We only have data for a few years regarding the employees of *Gas Andalucía*. In 1996 it had 125 employees, distributed as follows: directors and technicians, 39, representing 31.2 % of the total; sales representatives and administrative personnel, 40, that is 32 % and professionals of the trade and auxiliary staff, 46, that is 36.8 %. The latter were responsible for servicing and changing the pipes and the customers' installations. In short, taking into account the company's high social capital and its activity in a wide territory, the number of employees was very tight. In 2001, the 148 workers were distributed as follows: directors and technicians, 27 %; sales representatives and administrative staff, 45.9 %; and professionals of the trade and auxiliary personnel 27 %. These figures seem to indicate that the company dedicated more efforts to the sale of its products and required more workers to administratively manage the growth of its clients.

The progress of the distribution network, the gas-changing operations the and construction of plants for propane, methane and the reception and regasification of natural gas, required large investments. Unfortunately we only know the amounts that the company invested for some years. It invested 592.3 million pesetas in 1988, 623 million in 1989, 736 million in 1990, 1,926 million in 1997 and 3,741 million in 1998 (Gas Andalucía, 1989, 1990, 1991, 1999).

Despite these large investments, the company earned a profit, at least in the years for which we have data (Tab. 1). It earned a profit before tax of 151.3 million pesetas in 1988, 109.4 million in 1989. At least from 1992 profits declined

4 Between 1963 and 1969, the workforce of the two gas companies operating in Andalusia, *Catalana de Gas* and the *Compañía Española de Gas* (the latter was controlled by the former after 1965), decreased from 433 to 374 employees, that is, by almost 45 %. This was possible thanks to the replacement of coal gas with the gas produced with naphta in Málaga and Seville and the coal gas and naphta in Cádiz. The new plants required less labour. Fernández-Paradas, 2017.

significantly. In this year they amounted to 10.7 million and in 1993 they were 15.2 million. These reductions coincided with the final years of manufactured gas and the closure of the gas factories of Cádiz and Málaga. After that, profits grew again with fluctuations: it earned 99.6 million pesetas in profit in 1994, 666 million in 1995 (the highest figure in the period studied), 355 million in 1996, 251 million before tax and 211 after tax in 1997 and 234 million after tax in 1998.

However, it seems that when the profits of Gas Andalucía were calculated, the long-term debts that it had with the *Gas Natural Group* were not taken into account. It should be noted that in 1995 *Gas Andalucía* owed 1.6 billion pesetas to this group for loans that it had granted to it. This figure rose to 1.825 billion in 1997 (Gas Andalucía, 1996, 1998). As we have seen, the bulk of the company's expenditure was dedicated to constructing the distribution network and plants for propane and methane and for the storage and regasification of natural gas. With the available data it is not possible to break down how these costs were distributed. With respect to income, 81 % was earned from gas sales in 1991 while 9 % came from the sale of installations and devices. These percentages remained stable with slight modifications until 2001 (Gas Andalucía, 1992, 1999; Gas Natural Andalucía, 2002).

5 Conclusions

The "Memorandum of understanding for the development of gas in Spain" (1985) was signed to promote the provision of natural gas to Spain which was then in its initial phase. It sought to promote natural gas in order to bring its contribution to the same level as other western European countries. In Andalusia, the company responsible for leading this process was *Gas Andalucía*, part of *Catalana de Gas*, the country's principal gas provider, which, a few years later became the largest multinational in the world. Gas Andalucía was founded in 1987 with a capital of one billion pesetas. The amount of public capital is noteworthy, with the Junta de Andalucía having a minority share of 33 %, the rest being held by private gas companies. *Catalana de Gas* had a 33 % share, its affiliate the *Compañía Española de Gas* 0.94 % and *Repsol Butano* 33.5 %. In the following years *Catalana de Gas* increased its share. In 1991 it held 66.9 % and in 1999 then under the name of *Gas Natural* it had a share of 99.9 %.

The period analysed spans from the creation of *Gas Andalucía* until the end of the regulated market in 2001. These years were characterised by large transformations and an increase in activity which was materialised in a significant increase in its distribution network, clients and gas sales. The latter grew with greater intensity than the client network. The year 1993 was a milestone as in this year the company closed the manufactured gas companies of Cádiz and Málaga, From then it distributed methane and natural gas in these municipalities and only natural gas to those town newly incorporated into the supply.

The extension of the distribution network and the increase in the number of provinces being supplied with natural gas (Huelva in 1990, Cordoba in 1991, Granada and Jaen in 1998), increased the number of clients and also potential consumers. However, throughout the period studied there were large differences in the gasification processes on a territorial level with an overwhelming weight of the province of Seville, followed at a great distance by Málaga and the other provinces. This must have constituted an obstacle in the advance of gasification, together with the fact that the immense majority of piped gas consumption was for domestic-commercial use, made up of clients with a lower capacity to demand gas. It is also noteworthy that natural gas did not reach the province of Almería.

Although Gas Andalucía reported profits in all of the years considered, we should also remember the large debt that it had with the *Grupo Catalana de Gas*.

References

Ballestero, A. (2017). *El gas natural en España*. Madrid: Lid Editorial.

Fábregas, P.-A. (1986). *La industria del gas en España. Un ensayo de interpretación histórica*. Barcelona.

Fábregas, P.-A. (2014). *Pere Duran Farell. Biografía*. Barcelona: RBA.

Fábregas, P.-A. (2018). *175 años de compromiso con la energía y la sociedad*. Barcelona: Naturgy Energy Group, S. A.

Fernández-Paradas, M. (2009). *La industria del gas en Córdoba (1870–2007)*. Barcelona: Lid, Fundación Gas Natural.

Fernández-Paradas, M. (2015). *La industria del gas en Cádiz (1845–2012)*. Sabadell: Lid, Fundación Gas Natural.

Fernández-Paradas, M. (2017). El dilema de la industria del gas ciudad en la Andalucía de los años 1960 : renovarso o morir. *Ayer, 107*, 257–584.

Gas Andalucía (1989). *Memoria Ejercicio 1988. Gas Andalucía*. Sevilla.

Gas Andalucía (1990). *Memoria Ejercicio 1989. Gas Andalucía*. Sevilla.

Gas Andalucía (1991). *Informe Anual 1990. Gas Andalucía*. Sevilla.

Gas Andalucía (1992). *Informe Anual 1991. Gas Andalucía*. Sevilla.

Gas Andalucía (1993). *Informe Anual 1992. Gas Andalucía*. Sevilla.

Gas Andalucía (1994). *Informe Anual 1993*. Sevilla.

Gas Andalucía (1995). *Informe Anual 1994*. Sevilla.

Gas Andalucía (1996). *Informe Anual 95*. Sevilla.

Gas Andalucía (1997). *Informe Anual 96*. Sevilla.

Gas Andalucía (1998). *Informe Anual 1997*. Sevilla.

Gas Andalucía (1999). *Informe Anual 1998*. Sevilla.

Gas Natural Andalucía (2000). *Informe Anual 2001*. Sevilla.

Gas Natural Andalucía (2001). *Informe Anual 2002*. Sevilla.

Gas Natural Andalucía (2002). *Informe Anual 2003*. Sevilla.

Gas Natural Andalucía (2003). *Informe Anual 2004*. Sevilla.

Martínez, A. (Coord.), Mirás Araujo, J. & Lindoso Tato, E. (2009). *La industria del gas en Galicia: del alumbrado por gas al siglo XXI, 1850–2005*. Barcelona: Lid, Fundación Gas Natural.

Sánchez Gutiérrez, M. M. (2006). *La regulación del sector del gas natural*. Valencia: Tirant lo Blanch.

Alberte Martínez-López and Jesús Mirás Araujo

7 British investments in the gas industry in Spain: the role of the free-standing companies[1]

Abstract Foreign investment played a relevant role in launching the gas industry in many countries, including Spain. The British, along with the French, were the main investors. In the British case, one of their favorite instruments for foreign investment were the free-standing companies (FSC), whose corporate flexibility provided them with several advantages. The aim of the chapter is the analysis of the profile, behavior, and results of these companies in the context of the Spanish gas industry during the second half of the nineteenth century and the first decades of the twentieth. Primary sources from British and Spanish archives have been used, in order to better contrast the global approach of the FSC to these specific cases.

1 Introduction

The nineteenth century witnessed the introduction of various networked infrastructures that were decisive for the growth of cities (water systems, waste disposal, transportation, communication, energy, etc.). In peripheral countries, the lack of capital and know-how skills made the adoption of those new technologies difficult, so that their implementation was achieved due to technology and capital transfers, which played a key role in their development (Martínez-López, 2020a). Transmission was benefited by the internationalization of the large companies that took part in the construction and modernization of public utilities. Thus, supported by the waves of globalization that began in the nineteenth century, the capitals of the most developed countries sought attractive destinations for their investments (Jones, 2005). As a result, foreign investment played a relevant role in launching those utilities alongside Europe.

One of the most relevant cases was the gas industry, which in many countries was implemented due to the capital exportation flows. Spain was a

1 This text forms part of the results of the research project, The Gas Industry in Spain: development and regional trajectories (1842–2008), HAR2017-82112-P, financed by The Ministry of Science, Innovation and Universities of the Spanish Government and ERDF funds.

peripheral country, with an important growth potential, which attracted the interest of international capital, contributing decisively to boost its economy (Martínez-López, 2020b, p. 211). The British, along with the French, were the main investors. Despite that, this topic has been omitted by the Spanish historiography of foreign investments, except for mining. In the British case, one of their favorite instruments for foreign investment were the *free-standing companies*, whose corporate flexibility provided them with several advantages. The aim of the chapter is the analysis of the profile, behavior, and results of these companies in the context of the Spanish gas industry during the second half of the nineteenth century and the first decades of the twentieth.

2 Gas industry and foreign capital in Spain

The gas industry dates back to the late eighteenth and early nineteenth centuries, when several technological innovations emerged in France and the United Kingdom. This country witnessed the first commercial applications of gas (Thomas, 2018), in addition to being responsible for the first technology transfers to Europe (Tomory, 2011, p. 396). After a shaky beginning, by the 1830s gas began to spread progressively through the European and North American cities (Rose, 1995, p. 21), enjoying in 1840–1910 the monopoly in the urban lighting market (Goodall, 2005, p. 449).

Spain formed part of the second wave of implementation of the gas industry, which began by the 1840s, and which includes Scandinavia, and Central, Southern and Eastern Europe (Martínez-López & Mirás, 2012, p. 128). This stage coincides with a period of globalization of the world economy, which accelerated after the second technological revolution. This process was crucial for the installation of gas and other public utilities in Spain (Broder, 1981), as it went hand in hand with the internationalization of capital, companies, and technology. It was led by large multinationals (Tortella, 2008), and was carried out in parallel with the constitution of important gas groups that had a leading role in the international expansion of the sector (Williot, 2006).

However, the Spanish case is characterized by a later, slow, and modest diffusion process (Sudrià, 1983, p. 97), and by an unbalanced territorial distribution. The most developed region, Catalonia, displays a greater diffusion of gas and an almost absolute dominance of local capital, as compared to the high predominance of foreign promoters in the rest of the country (Fàbregas, 2017, p. 32). In many cases, the introduction of gas was delayed until the 1880s-1890s, immediately colliding with the irruption of electricity, and in fact many cities never even introduced it.

The first city to have gas lighting was Barcelona in 1842. But during the next two decades, implementation was slow. Between 1842–1861, 28 factories were built, and in 1861 the number of towns that were supplied was 25. From 1862 to the late nineteenth century, it spread somewhat more rapidly, as in 1901 the number of towns rose to 82 (Alayo & Barca, 2017, pp. 142–143). But from the 1890s onwards and, above all, after the turn of the century, gas companies had to face a new competitor, electricity. This caused a slowdown in the sector, to which the negative impact of WWI and the postwar period was added, leading to a persistent stagnation until the Spanish Civil War (1936–1939) (Fernández-Paradas, Martínez & Mirás, 2019). In 1934 the number of cities with gas was only 50.

The gas implementation process in Spain was dominated by foreign capital, which played a crucial role in the first steps of this industry (Fernández-Paradas, 2009b, p. 110). The accumulation of capital generated in some pioneering industrialized countries, mainly Britain and France, fostered the growth of their foreign investment in the search for new profit opportunities (Martínez-López & Mirás, 2019, p. 129). Although to a lesser extent, Belgian, German, and Swiss companies also built gas plants in other countries, mainly Switzerland, the Austro-Hungarian Empire and Italy (Williot & Paquier, 2005, pp. 37–44). This international investment facilitated the diffusion of new technologies, specifically new public utilities (water, electricity, trams) and, in particular, gas production and distribution. In Spain, French capital stands out overwhelmingly (Costa, 1983), having a direct impact on the country's economic modernization process (Broder, 1976). British capital was in second place. The leadership of French capital increased constantly during this period. The initiatives of *Lebon et Cie* stand out (Fernández-Paradas, 2015, p. 69), which are framed in the flow of French gas investment, that was mainly oriented towards the Mediterranean area and Eastern Europe (Williot, 2006, pp. 207–208).

British foreign investment in the gas sector was concentrated in the Nordic countries, Portugal, and Latin America, and to a lesser extent in France, Belgium, Germany, the Austro-Hungarian Empire, and the Netherlands. The total volume amounted to £16.5 million in 1865–1914, reaching some relevance between 1865–1899, with two peaks in 1885–1889 and, above all, in 1895–1899, declining later. In relative terms, its importance was small if we consider the period as a whole, since it represented only 8.1 % of British foreign investment in public utilities in 1865–1914, a category that included water, gas, electricity, trams and telecommunications, but also canals and ports. But it fluctuated between 12 %-22 % in 1865–1899, then falls sharply due to the rapid rise of its electric competitor.

Britain was the second investor in Spain, although it was long-distant from France. Quantitatively, in absolute and relative terms, its importance was low. According to Stone, only £25,000 would be counted for the period 1865–1914, which would represent only 0.50 % of British foreign investment in public utilities in Spain in 1865–1914, and 0.11 % of British investment in gas in the same period (Stone, 1999, pp. 242–251 and own calculations). Actually, according to our calculations, which were extracted from the firms' balance sheets, the real (effectively disbursed) British investment in the Spanish gas industry, materialized in the only two long-term companies (*Huelva Gas and Electricity*, and *Anglo-Spanish Gas*), was £43,300 in shares (common and convertible preferred stocks) and £31,000 in bonds, for a total of £74,300. Unlike France, whose presence was focused on larger cities (mainly provincial capitals), where the potential market was more promising (Martínez-López, 2017a, pp. 78–80), the British were located in medium or small-sized cities, due to their lower need for capital and the absence of competitors.

There was a wide variety of factors for the 'landing' of foreign capital in Spain. But, in our opinion, two factors were critical. On the one hand, the lack of experience in financing this type of industry in Spain, due to the absence of a consolidated national financial system. On the other, the aforementioned search for profitable investments by the French and British (Fernández-Paradas, Martínez-López & Mirás, 2019), who would replace the reduced endogenous capital formation.

During the inter-war period foreign investment declined, affected by financial turmoil and incipient economic nationalism in many countries. In Spain, since WWI a substitution process by Spanish capital took place, which intensified during the 1920s. The pressure had been growing significantly since the beginning of the twentieth century, through different legislative actions that progressively cornered foreign capital (Fàbregas, 2003, pp. 116–124). But the distortions caused by the war provoked the temporary closure or the shutting down of many factories, forcing foreign gas companies to sell their assets (Fernández-Paradas, 2009b, p. 120).

Since the dictatorship of Primo de Rivera (1923–30), the constraints were even stronger (Fernández-Paradas, 2009b, p. 119), as the government aimed to 'nationalize' several economic activities, particularly public utilities, putting those services under the control of city councils (Martínez-López & Mirás, 2012, p. 140). In addition, the sector was immersed in a process of business concentration, which was commanded by Spanish capital, and led to the gas industry being 'nationalized' in the third decade of the twentieth century and absorbed by powerful energy groups led by electricity companies. By the Civil

War, practically the last vestiges of foreign presence had disappeared, at least formally (Castro & Matés, 2020, p. 236).

3 The role of British capital in the Spanish gas sector

Given that the set of cities that had gas in Spain was meager, the presence of British capital, entrepreneurs and technicians was necessarily limited. One of the most significant features of British entrepreneurs was that they often proceeded simply by applying for administrative concessions in a city, but in many cases without succeeding in installing the factory or the supply network. Therefore, they acted as simple 'achievers', who gained the contract with the city council, but did not develop the service, and only transmitted the concession to others. Consequently, the rate of failure was high, either due to the inability to implement the facilities or due to the inability to carry out the business.

The first appearances of British citizens in Spain date back to the mid-1840s, coinciding with the first projects in the sector. Specifically, when in 1844–45 the engineer John Burnett Stears presented his proposals to several Spanish and Portuguese city councils (A Coruña, Bilbao, Cádiz, Lisbon, Porto), although in some of them he was unable to get hold of the public auctions (Fernandez, 2000; Cardoso de Matos, 2005, pp. 371–372; Martínez-López (coord.), 2009, p. 24; Fernández-Paradas, 2015, p. 35). He acted on behalf of a British gas group headed by the *Compagnie Générale Provinciale du Gaz*, which was owner of several gas factories in France and Italy (Fàbregas, 2003, pp. 104–105).

Another key figure was William Partington Hurts, who in collaboration with his compatriot, the engineer Edward Oliver Manby, carried out an intense gas promotion activity in the middle of the nineteenth century (Fernández-Paradas & Pinto, 2020). Both focused on trying to obtain concessions for gas lighting in various cities, although many of their attempts were frustrated. Examples of this were A Coruña, where they failed to acquire the concession in 1844, Madrid, where they purchased the public contract in 1846, Seville, where Partington got the concession that same year, as in Malaga, Cádiz, in 1847, and as well as in Valencia, where they successfully acquired the *Sociedad Valenciana para el Alumbrado de Valencia*. Finally, in Santander, Edward Manby's brother, Joseph Lane Manby, tried to obtain the concession, which finally went to his company *Manby, Wilson et Cie* during 1852–1862 (Fàbregas, 2003, p. 17; Fernandez, 2009, pp. 211, 216).

The most notable initiative was the constitution in 1846 - from the company *Manby y Partington* - of the *Sociedad Madrileña del Alumbrado por Gas*, in partnership with English and French capitalists, and well-known members of the Spanish political elite (Tortella, 2000, pp. 54–55). By means of this firm they first of all attempted to gain control of the gas supply to the Royal Palace of Madrid (Simón, 2011, pp. 66–68). Likewise, they founded in Madrid in that year the firm *Empresa General Peninsular para el Alumbrado de Gas*. Through this company, they presented successive proposals in the aforementioned cities.

Nevertheless, some of their projects had to be aborted. In Seville, although they began the construction of the factory, the contract was transferred in 1850 to *Jaime Federico Gregory y Compañía*, from London. The first gas facility would be built by the English firm *York y Compañía*, which was in operation in 1853–1860, the year in which the latter sold the rights to the *Banco General Suizo* (González García, 1981, pp. 9–13, 55). In Malaga they did not even build the factory. In Cádiz, they took over the concession in 1847, through an acquisition from the British firm *Waterton & Cie*, which had bought it the year before from the original concessionaire, the French entrepreneur Charles Lebon (1845). Actually, the concessionaire of the Cadiz auction had been the British citizen Diego Federico Gregory (who was also present in the Seville gas business), who immediately transmitted it to *Lebon, Grafton y Goldsmitdt* (Fernández-Paradas, 2009a, pp. 37–39, 49–51). Yet, the *Empresa Peninsular* went into liquidation in 1852, being forced to sell the gas business in Cádiz to *Manby et Cie*, which transferred it to *Zacheroni et Cie* in 1858. Likewise, they could not fulfill the contract in Valencia, who passed the factory to creditors (García de la Fuente, 1984, p. 87). Finally, the business in Madrid was acquired in 1848 by the Spanish banker and entrepreneur Gregorio López Mollinedo, who in 1857 then sold it to *Crédito Mobiliario Español*, a French capital company (Simón, 1987, pp. 449–453; Tortella, 2000, pp. 54–55).

There was also British presence in other cities, although at times somewhat symbolic, as well as attempts to install gas in towns such as Ferrol or Albacete, which did not crystallize. In Murcia, where in 1864 the definitive concession went to the British firm *William Knicht & Co*, which later gave it to *Colonial and General Gas Co*, and then later to Charles Lebon in 1868 (Montes, 1999). In Córdoba, where in 1852–1870 there were several unsuccessful British proposals, among them those of *York y Compañía* (1858), Duncan Saw (1861), and *William Knicht & Co.* (1863) (Fernández-Paradas, 2009a, pp. 30–35). In Logroño the concession was granted in 1875 to Thomas Rosser, an engineer who was director of the Vitoria gas factory, who transferred the rights to the French firm *Pabst y Compañía* in 1877 (Negueruela, 2011, pp. 113, 123, 138). In Ciudad Real the first concessionaire was the gas factory engineer and contractor Georges Bower, who put it into operation in 1882, although at some point at the end of the century he transferred it to J. O'Farrell (Fàbregas, 1989). Finally, in Santa Cruz de Tenerife the gas factory was established in 1888, run by a British firm that maintained ownership until 1897 (Matos, 2005).

Finally, it is worth mentioning the figure of the engineer William Richards, a 'prototype emigrant British engineer', who was director between 1848 and 1861 of the most important gas company in the country, the *Sociedad Catalana del Alumbrado por Gas*, of Barcelona, and who was also responsible for the construction of several gas factories in Catalonia between 1851 and 1859 (Sabadell, Vilanova, Reus, Tarragona and Manresa), in addition to developing an important business activity of its own in the firm *Richards & Co* (Moyano & Thomas, 2016).

4 The free-standing companies

The *free-standing companies* (FSC) were widely used by Great Britain, although not exclusively, during the golden age of international investment, 1870–1914 (Wilkins, 1998). They differed mainly from multinationals in that from the outset they intended to operate abroad, not to expand from headquarters located in their native country and which generally operated in a single country. On the other hand, especially in the British case, they were often small companies that were financed in the dynamic British capital market, unlike their counterparts on the continent (France and, above all, Germany and Belgium), with larger weight of the Bank financing.

These firms spread from the mid-nineteenth century with the passage of the *Joint Stock Companies Act* in 1856, which instituted the limited liability, and the development of the telegraph, which reduced the moral hazard of asymmetric information. Their compulsory registration in the country where they were constituted, and their capital and bonds issuance in the currency of that country provided broader legal coverage and security to investors, which was particularly necessary for investment abroad. They focused on sectors with a low technological level or on extractive industries, and geographically in countries with little experience in business management, such as Spain.

In Spain's gas sector only two of these types of companies were in operation: *Huelva Gas and Electricity*, and *Anglo-Spanish Gas*.[2] The latter worked in two small towns on the Mediterranean coast: Dénia and Xàtiva. Therefore, these were two different kinds of context and business models: a mining district

2 *Huelva Gas and Electricity*, Reports 1895–1919; *Anglo-Spanish Gas*, Reports 1888–1909; García de la Fuente, 2007; Martínez-López 2017a and 2017b.

of a medium-sized city (Huelva) with a long-run historical establishment of British capital (Cobos, 2005), and the agrarian hinterland of two small and nearby commercial towns, but with no other foreign companies then operating.

The province of Huelva underwent a boost in copper mining in the last third of the nineteenth century, which attracted several foreign companies, mainly British, among which the *Río Tinto Company Ltd* was the most relevant. The exporting nature of the mining activity forced to substantially improve transport infrastructures, such as railways, and the port of Huelva, whose costs were born by British firms. In this context of economic upturn, demographic growth and urban expansion the need to provide Huelva with the modern infrastructures that characterize cities arose: water (1891, German firm), gas (1879, British firm), and electricity (1890, local firm) (Díaz, 1999).

The company that started up the gas production in Huelva was created in 1878, under the name *The Huelva Gas Company Limited*, with registered office in Glasgow and a nominal capital of £25,000. In reality, only £3,000 were disbursed at that time, a rather low figure in comparative terms, although as early as 1895 the total disbursement seems to be recorded. One must bear in mind that the average capital disbursed by Scottish companies in Spain in 1862–1890 was £60,000, although the majority were mining companies, which were more capital intensive (Tennent, 2009, p. 83). It was also clearly lower than the average initial capital invested by all 853 Scottish companies operating abroad in 1862–1914, which was £35,569 (Schmitz, 1997, p. 47). In any case, this mismatch between nominal and paid-up capital was quite common at the time and probably served the desire to impress potential investors giving the appearance of financial strength of the new company that came on the market. Thus, in Scottish companies as a whole operating abroad in 1862–1914, the initial capital invested represented 33 % of the nominal capital (Schmitz, 1997, p. 47).

It is interesting to note that the company shared headquarters and secretary (William Simpson) with *The Huelva Brick and Tile Company*. This firm was founded in 1882 with the aim of manufacturing construction materials -perhaps reclaiming mining wastes from other British companies in the province-, such as bricks, tiles, and pipes. Therefore, *Huelva Gas* would be deploying a vertical integration strategy, with which it would be seeking to promote a subsidiary company that would provide it with pipes and other construction materials. However, it had little success, as it was liquidated in 1886 (Tennent, 2009, pp. 76–77).

Its foundation was part of the aforementioned arrival of British capital in the province of Huelva during the 1870s. The Scottish origin of the company must be highlighted. This was a very fertile territory in business initiatives, especially free-standing companies (FSC), such as *Huelva Gas*. In this sense, it is worth noting the important role played by Scottish entrepreneurs and financial institutions in the creation of the powerful *Río Tinto Company*, or the constitution in Glasgow of the *Tharsis Sulfur and Cooper*, the *Huelva Brick and Tile* or the *Huelva Steam*. The founding of *Anglo Gas* coincided with the late impact of the Joint Stock Companies Act of 1856 on the formation of FSC in Scotland, which took place from the 1870s on.[3] A real comparative advantage of Scottish entrepreneurs as compared with the English ones would be the maintenance in Scotland of the validity of Roman law, over and against the Anglo-Saxon 'common law', which would in part explain the relative importance of Scottish investment in Latin European countries, mainly Spain (Tennent, 2009, p. 299). The common legal tradition would facilitate the Scottish business insertion in the Mediterranean institutional framework.

The professional profile of the managing directors of *Huelva Gas* was nourished in trade, industry, and experts who were linked to gas business, such as accountants and engineers, residing in Glasgow. It was a small, very stable Board of Directors, which was accessed partly by family co-optation but also by professional promotion. This was a group that kept close control of the Huelva factory's activity and was able to assemble an efficient model of organizational structure, which probably largely explains its longevity, well above the FSC average. This was precisely the main cause, in the opinion of Wilkins (1998), of the failure of many of these companies. The technical performance was entrusted to Scottish technicians, whereas a Spanish manager was initially responsible for the economic management, in order to make relations with the local environment easier. The control of the headquarters was reinforced by regular trips of its Directors (secretary or president) to Huelva to inspect *in situ* the progress of the business. Moreover, there was a direct accountability in Glasgow from the local manager. The latter was obliged to refer relevant decisions to the Council.

The first years were the best in financial terms for the company, despite the usual accumulation of municipal debts, probably due to the absence of competitors. During the last decade of the nineteenth century, the Spanish economic crisis, together with the beginnings of electricity competition, the tariff

3 Of 116 FSC that were registered in Scotland in 1862–1885 only 3 were dedicated to gas (in Spain, Italy and Bohemia). Most were mining or agricultural. 8 were located in Spain, being the European country with the highest number, representing 6 % of the paid-up capital (Tennent, 2009, pp. 73, 77, 80, 83).

reduction, and the negative evolution of the exchange rate caused a deterioration in the income statement. Faced with the challenges that were approaching, the company acted resolutely, designing a well-defined strategy on several fronts: improvement and diversification of its gas supply,[4] entry into the electricity market,[5] and financial strengthening to face the high investments required.

During the first decade of the twentieth century, the efforts made by the company to adapt to changing times were positively perceived. The new and more favorable economic context also helped once the end-of-the-century crisis and the deterioration of the foreign position of the peseta had been overcome. During those years the business progressed steadily. Gas sales and, above all, electricity increased, especially in volume served, year after year. This indicates a positive evolution, but also shows the price war that the competitors were developing. In any case, the upward trend until the WWI contrasts with what happened in many Spanish cities (Fernández-Paradas, 2009a, pp. 64–65; Martínez-López (coord.), 2009, pp. 141, 214; Fernández-Paradas, 2015, pp. 132–133). This seems to prove a better comparative result of its adaptive strategy before electrical competition.

Since 1912, the scenario began to be more complicated for the company. Coal became substantially more expensive due to the mining strike in the previous year. A severe blow for the company was the creation in 1913 of a new electricity company, with local capital. WWI had a strong impact on the fragile balance that the company was maintaining. The supply of coal was at risk, and was even more expensive due to higher freight rates. Negotiations were carried out at the highest political level with the Spanish authorities, mediated by British diplomacy, but without results. This forced the closure of the gas and electricity factories in 1917, and their sale two years later to the local electricity competitor.

The second British gas FSC experience in Spain took place, as we have indicated above, in the province of Alicante. The creation of *Anglo-Spanish Gas* in 1886 would be part of one of the outstanding cycles of British investment in the gas sector in the world. The economy of both towns (Dénia and Xàtiva) would be inserted into the production model of the region of

---

4 In 1898 the company decided to provide free gas accessories to some high-consumption homes. That year they set up an exhibition and sales shop for cooking ovens and heating elements, with a reduced rate for the latter, in order to stimulate its dissemination.

5 As an indication of the company's new orientation, its name was changed to *The Huelva Gas and Electricity Company Limited*, in 1896.

Valencia, which was based on export agriculture (wine until the late nineteenth century, and citrus fruits later), and on small hand-crafted industry. But it also was reinforced by the improvement of the roads and ports, and the construction of railways during the second half of the nineteenth century XIX (Palafox, 2001).

In both towns, the concession was obtained by *Gibbons Brothers, Gas Engineers and Contractors*. They immediately transferred it to *Anglo-Spanish*, which was a standard procedure at the time. This agreement probably was linked to the construction of the Dénia factory by *Gibbons Brothers*, since they were the ones who erected it, in an ideal location, that was placed in the lower part of the town (to facilitate gas distribution), between the port and the railway station (for a better supply of coal).

Nominal capital was £200,000, although only £12,490 were disbursed. This paid-up capital was the same until the end of the company. The mentors were a small group of London industrialists, along with the aforementioned *Gibbons Brothers*. Conservative MP James Ernest Spencer also appears. The presence of parliamentarians - normally from the country of destination of the investment - on the Board of Directors was a fairly common practice in foreign companies, especially in public utilities, with the purpose of guaranteeing contacts with political power. The company shows great stability in the Board of Directors.

This stability of the Board contrasts with the bustle, especially in the early years, of legal representatives and local directors. This seems to point at the problems that the English firm tackled in order to recruit trustworthy and professionally solvent native delegates, which was a key issue and always difficult to articulate for foreign companies.

This same business group also owned the *Tuscan Gas Company*, founded in 1876, which had the concessions of six cities in that Italian region. In 1887 it constituted the *Anglo-Portuguese Gas and Water Company*, which obtained the concession for the Portuguese port of Figueira da Foz. This strategy seems to be oriented towards the investment in public utilities in small towns in Mediterranean countries, seeking a market niche with less competition, which would also probably be related to its late implementation. The noteworthy difference between their nominal capital and that actually paid-up, especially in Spanish and Portuguese companies, seems to reveal a significant inability to convince investors that this was an effective strategy. Ultimately, this would force the issuance of bonds, whose stronger security and guaranteed profitability will attract depositors to finance the construction and expansion of the networks. In choosing Dénia, the existence of an active raisin export trade to England - with a peak in the late 1880s - might have influenced, as it was hoped to reduce freight costs of British coal sent to that town, as well as the presence of British merchants, and the creation of a consulate of that country.

According to the small size of the company, the capital was quite scattered among a relatively large number of shareholders (34), with a low degree of concentration.[6] The largest group of shareholders came from connected business and activities, such as industrialists, managers, accountants, engineers, and lawyers. They also used to be the ones with the highest number of shares per capita. At the territorial level, the vast majority of investors (30) resided in London.

As happened in many other Spanish cities, the chronic lack of economic resources of the town councils of Dénia and Xàtiva caused, from the first years, an increasing problem of late payments and delinquency that threatened the financial stability of the company. The end-of-the-century crisis and electricity competition deteriorated business results. These poor results were caused both by a drop in income (lower tariffs) and an increase in municipal delinquencies but, above all, by an increase in costs (that is, coal, due to the deterioration of the exchange rate). The impact of financial expenses to meet the bond interests, as well as the increase in the tax burden must be added. The determining factor in the final crisis of the firm, which was liquidated in 1910, was the increasing electrical competition and the reduction of income that it meant.

5 Conclusions

British investment in the Spanish gas sector was secondary, both in relation to French capital and in relation to British investment in the gas sector at the international level or in urban public utilities as a whole in Spain. Yet, the presence was greater in the technological field, which is more evident in the important role played by British engineers and in technology transfers.

In an early stage, approximately until 1878, British participation was embodied in a series of specific actions that simply aimed at obtaining the concession of the service in various cities. However, and based on the little information available, there was not a consistent and minimally lasting presence of British companies in this period.

The most stable and lasting presence began coinciding with one of the expansive cycles of British international gas investment, in the last quarter of the nineteenth century. The only two confirmed cases of lengthy management

6 Public Record Office (PRO) Anglo-Spanish Gas 1886 BT 31-1554-5011.

materialized under the corporate formula of the *free-standing companies*. This category, which was quite common in foreign British investment, provided flexibility and stronger confidence to investors.

British capital sought its niche in secondary markets: e.g. a medium-sized city and two small Mediterranean towns. In both cases they were located on the coast in order to guarantee a better supply of coal. The large cities markets were left in the hands of French companies, which had more solid bank support.

The installation in Huelva is related to the mining boost and the historical importance of the British presence. It is an interesting example of FSC, as the owners tried a vertical integration and, above all, for having developed organizational capabilities that allowed to tightly control the activities of the company from headquarters.

The investment in Dénia and Xàtiva presents two important peculiarities that, in the end, drove to business failure. Firstly, the fact that these were small towns, which limited expansion and taking advantage of economies of scale. The second handicap was the late start-up of the business, at a time when electrical competition was already beginning to be suffered.

The history of these companies is representative of the evolution of the gas industry in Spain, and also of the difficulties that companies had to face: insufficient demand, municipal delinquencies, and electricity competition. And in the foreign companies, difficulties to hire trustworthy skilled employees, and exchange rate instability. In the end, the critical situation of WWI made the continuity of the activity unviable.

6 References

Alayo Manubens, J. C., & Barca Salom, F. X. (2017). Las técnicas de fabricación de gas utilizadas en las fábricas de gas españolas (1842–1972). In I. Bartolomé, M. Fernández-Paradas & J. Mirás (Eds.), *Globalización, nacionalización y liberalización de la industria del gas en la Europa latina (siglos XIX-XXI)* (pp. 141–172). Madrid: Marcial Pons.

Broder, A. (1976). Les investissements étrangers en Espagne au XIXe siècle: méthodologie et quantification. *Revue d'Histoire Economique et Sociale, 54*(1), 29–63.

Broder, A. (1981). *Le rôle des interets économiques étrangers dans la croissance de l'Espagne au XIXe siècle, 1767–1924* (These d'Etat). Paris: Universitè de Paris I.

Cardoso de Matos, A. (2005). La difusión des réseaux gaziers au Portugal (XIXe siècle). In S. Paquier & J.-P. Williot (Dirs.), *L'industrie du gaz en Europe aux XIXe et XXe siècles. L'innovation entre marchés privés et collectivités publiques* (pp. 359–372). Bruxelles: Peter Lang.

Castro-Valdivia, M., & Matés-Barco, J. M. (2020). Los servicios públicos y la inversión extranjera en España (1850–1936): las empresas de agua y gas. *História Unisinos, 24*(2), 221–239. doi: 10.413/hist.2020.242.05.

Cobos, J. (2005). *La Huelva Británica*. Sevilla: Fundación José Manuel Lara.

Costa Campí, M. T. (1983). *Financiación exterior del capitalismo español en el siglo XIX*. Barcelona: Universidad de Barcelona.

Díaz, M. A. (1999). *Huelva: la construcción de una ciudad*. Huelva: Ayuntamiento de Huelva.

Fàbregas, P.-A. (1989). Gas Ciudad Real c.1882–c.1920. Castilla - La Mancha. Papeles de trabajo, Programa de Investigación Histórica del Grupo Catalana de Gas.

Fàbregas, P.-A. (2003). *La Globalización en el siglo XIX: Málaga y el gas*. Sevilla: Ateneo de Sevilla.

Fàbregas, P.-A. (2017). La estrategia de la implantación de la industria del gas en España (1826–2010). In I. Bartolomé, M. Fernández-Paradas & J. Mirás (Eds.), *Globalización, nacionalización y liberalización de la industria del gas en la Europa latina (siglos XIX-XXI)* (pp. 21–44). Madrid: Marcial Pons.

Fernandez, A. (2000). Urbanización e implantación de nuevas tecnologías urbanas: algunas reflexiones sobre los casos de Burdeos y Bilbao al final del siglo XIX y principios del XX. *Scripta Nova. Revista Electrónica de Geografía y Ciencias Sociales, 69*(10).

Fernandez, A. (2009). La primera economía política del gas en Santander (desde 1852 hasta la competencia de la electricidad). *TST. Transportes, Servicios y Telecomunicaciones*, 16, 206–225.

Fernández-Paradas, M. (2009a). *La industria del gas en Córdoba (1870–2007)*. Barcelona: Lid Editorial y Fundación Gas Natural.

Fernández-Paradas, M. (2009b). Empresas y servicio de alumbrado público por gas en España (1842–1935). *TST. Transportes, Servicios y Telecomunicaciones*, 16, 108–131.

Fernández-Paradas, M. (2015). *La industria del gas en Cádiz (1845–2012)*. Barcelona: Lid Editorial y Fundación Gas Natural Fenosa.

Fernández-Paradas, M., Martínez-López, A., & Mirás-Araujo, J. (2019). The gas companies in Spain, a long-term approach (1842–2018). *Business History*. doi: https://doi.org/10.1080/00076791.2019.1683162. Accessed 2020 July 24.

Fernández-Paradas, M., & Pinto Tortosa, A. J. (2020). ¿Emprendedor o «conseguidor»? William Partington Hurts y el despegue de la industria española del gas. In I. Bartolomé, M. Fernández-Paradas & J. Mirás (Eds.), *Cercanas pero distintas. La desigual trayectoria de la industria del gas en las regiones del sur de Europa (siglos XIX-XX)* (pp. 349–365). Madrid: Marcial Pons.

García de la Fuente, D. (1984). *La Compañía Española del Gas, S. A.: Más de cien años de empresa*. Paterna: CEGAS.

García de la Fuente, D. (2007). *La luz de gas también brilló en Dénia*. Dénia: Regidoria de Cultura.

González García, A. (1981). *El Gas en Sevilla (cien años de historia)*. Sevilla: Artes Gráficas Salesianas, S.A.

Goodall, F. (2005). Entrepreneurs, Engineers and the Growth of the British Gas Market. In S. Paquier & J.-P. Williot (Dirs.), *L'industrie du gaz en Europe aux XIXe et XXe siècles. L'innovation entre marchés privés et collectivités publiques* (pp. 449–459). Bruxelles: Peter Lang.

Jones, G. (2005). *Multinationals and Global Capitalism from the Nineteenth to the Twenty-first Century*. Oxford: Oxford University Press.

Martínez-López, A. (2017a). La Anglo-Spanish Gas y su actuación en España, 1886–1910. *TST. Transportes, Servicios y* Telecomunicaciones, 32, 78–100.

Martínez-López, A. (2017b). Transición energética y capital extranjero: Huelva, 1878–1919. In I. Bartolomé, M. Fernández-Paradas & J. Mirás (Eds.), *Globalización, nacionalización y liberalización de la industria del gas en la Europa latina (siglos XIX-XXI)* (pp. 215–236). Madrid: Marcial Pons.

Martínez-López, A. (2020a). Capital extranjero y energía: Madrileña de Gas, 1846–1935. *Investigaciones de Historia Económica - Economic History Research, 16*(1), 1–11. doi: https://doi.org/10.1016/j.ihe.2018.04.002. Accessed 2020 July 23.

Martínez-López, A. (2020b). Inversión extranjera y abastecimiento de agua: Algeciras, 1895–1952. *História Unisinos, 24*(2), 209–220. doi: 10.413/hist.2020.242.04.

Martínez-López, A. (coord.), Mirás, J., & Lindoso, E. (2009). *La industria del gas en Galicia: del alumbrado por gas al siglo XXI, 1850–2005*. Barcelona: Lid Editorial y Fundación Gas Natural.

Martínez-López, A., & Mirás Araujo, J. (2012). The City as a Business: Gas and Business in the Spanish region of Galicia, 1850–1936. *Continuity and Change, 27*(1), 125–150. doi: https://doi.org/10.1017/S0268416012000082. Accessed 2020 June 30.

Martínez-López, A., & Mirás Araujo, J. (2019). Organizaciones profesionales y difusión tecnológica: la *Société Technique de l'Industrie du Gaz en France*, 1874–1900. In J.M. Matés-Barco & A. Torres-Rodríguez (Eds.), *Los servicios públicos en España y México (siglos XIX-XX)* (121–145). Madrid: Sílex.

Matos, R. (2005). L'industrie gazière à Tenerife (Canaries). Le rôle des capitaux allemands et helvétiques (1906–1933). In S. Paquier & J.-P. Williot (Dirs.), *L'industrie du gaz en Europe aux XIXe et XXe siècles. L'innovation entre marchés privés et collectivités publiques* (pp. 373–379). Bruxelles: Peter Lang.

Montes Bernárdez, R. (1999). *La Energía que ilumina. Historia de la iluminación en la Región de Murcia (1797–1935)*. Murcia: CajaMurcia.

Moyano, F., & Thomas, R. (2016). William Richards and the Unrecorded Success Abroad: A British Engineer in the Spanish Gas Industry in the Nineteenth Century. *The International Journal for the History of Engineering & Technology, 86*(2), 124–146. doi: https://doi.org/10.1080/17581206.2016.1223934. Accessed 2020 July 1.

Negueruela, E. (2011). *Historia del alumbrado público en Logroño*. Logroño: Ayuntamiento de Logroño - Instituto de Estudios Riojanos.

Palafox, J. (2001). La tardía industrialización de la economía valenciana. In L. Germán et al. (Eds.), *Historia Económica Regional de España: Siglos XIX y XX* (pp. 390–412). Barcelona: Crítica.

Rose, M. H. (1995). *Cities of Light and Heat. Domesticating Gas and Electricity in Urban America*. University Park, PA.: Pennsylvania State University Press.

Schmitz, Ch. (1997). The Nature and Dimensions of Scottish Foreign Investment. *Business History, 39*(2), 42–68.

Simón Palmer, M. C. (1987). La instalación del gas en Madrid (1832–1856). *Anales del Instituto de Estudios Madrileños*, 24, 445–463.

Simón Palmer, M. C. (2011). *La Real Fábrica de Gas de Madrid*. Barcelona: Fundación Gas Natural.

Stone, I. (1999). *The Global Export of Capital from Great Britain 1865–1914. A Statistical Survey*. Basingstoke: Macmillan Press.

Sudrià, C. (1983). Notas sobre la implantación y el desarrollo de la industria de gas en España, 1840–1901. *Revista de Historia Económica - Journal of Iberian and Latin American Economic History, 1*(2), 97–118.

Tennent, K. (2009). *Owned, monitored, but not always controlled: understanding the success and failure of Scottish Free-Standing Companies, 1862–1910* (Thesis). London School of Economics and Political Science, London.

Thomas, R. (2018). The development of the manufactured gas industry in Europe. In J. Craig, F. Gerali, F. Macaulay, F. & R. Sorkhabi (Eds.), *History of the European Oil and Gas Industry* (pp. 137–164). London: The Geological Society.

Tomory, L. (2011). Gaslight, distillation, and the Industrial Revolution. *History of Science, 49*(4), 395–424. doi: https://doi.org/10.1177/007327531104900402. Accessed 2020 May 17.

Tortella, G. (2008). El capital extranjero en la formación del capitalismo español. In J. Tascón (Ed.), *La inversión extranjera en España* (pp. 31–47). Madrid: Editorial Minerva.

Tortella, T. (2000). *A Guide to Sources of Information on Foreign Investment in Spain 1780–1914*. Amsterdam: International Institute of Social History.

Williot, J.-P., & Paquier, S. (2005). Origine et diffusion d'une technologie nouvelle au XIXe siècle. In S. Paquier & J.-P. Williot (Dirs.), *L'industrie du gaz en Europe aux XIXe et XXe siècles. L'innovation entre marchés privés et collectivités publiques* (pp. 21–51). Bruxelles: Peter Lang.

Williot, J.-P. (2006). La diffusion de la technologie gazière française dans le bassin méditerranéen: de la construction des usines à gaz à la mise en place des réseaux de gaz naturel (années 1840–1980). In M. Merger (Ed.), *Transferts de technologies en Méditerranée* (pp. 207–219), Paris: Presses Universite Paris-Sorbonne.

Wilkins, M. (1998). The Free-Standing Company Revisited. In M. Wilkins & H. G. Schröter (Eds.), *The Free-Standing Company in the World Economy, 1830–1996* (pp. 3–64), Oxford: University Press.

María José Vargas-Machuca

8 Rural credit banks: Credit cooperatives for the land. The case of Andalusia (1902–2000)

Abstract Rural credit banks emerge as a formula to cover the collective requirements of financial resources in the rural world, at a time when access to credit under efficient conditions was difficult for farmers. Despite their geographic and functional expansion, these entities have maintained a close territorial link.

The aim of this chapter is to analyse the history of Andalusian rural credit banks during the 20th century. The first entities of this type in Andalusia emerged at the beginning of this century with some delay compared to other European countries and with less momentum than in other areas of Spain. Since then, numerous small-scale entities have been created, mostly linked to Agrarian Trade Unions or as credit sections of agricultural cooperatives. Since the middle of the century, the Andalusian sector of rural savings banks began to take shape with institutions that, for the most part, remained operational until the end of the century.

1 Introduction

The cooperative societies of any nature appear as a manner to meet the common needs of a group of people. In the case of the credit cooperatives, its origin is determined by the group requirement of financial resources when the access to credits in efficient conditions is very difficult for their partners.

Currently, Spanish credit cooperatives are a group of institutions, mostly of small dimension, that, under the legal form of cooperative societies, have the aim of meeting the financial needs of its partners, but also third parties. Originally, they appeared linked to different scopes of activity, that is why there are three types: rural, popular and professional credit banks. Nevertheless, in these three cases, the business has developed into a lower operative specialisation and the difference among them has blurred (Vargas Vasserot, 2015).

The first Spanish credit cooperatives appear at the end of the 19th century, with a little delay regarding other European countries. Since then, a sector that, in spite of its geographic and functional expansion, has kept a close territorial link, was being formed.

Although, over time, this group of institutions became established in the Spanish banking system, it has always kept a relatively minor market share than banks and savings banks. However, their intense territorial similarity has allowed them to reach a relative important importance in some localities or geographic areas, even getting to exceed banking institutions (Palomo Zurdo, Sanchis Palacio and Gutierrez Fernandez, 2011).

The aim of this chapter is to analyse the development of credit cooperatives in Andalusia in the 20th century. From their origin at the beginning of the century until their consolidation in the last quarter of the century. This work approaches basically rural credit banks given that, in spite of the fact that there were some experiences as credit cooperatives of another nature, their life and success was very brief.

The study of the history of these entities is not easy because of, principally, a lack of documentation (Titos Martinez, 2003). To go in depth in their first stages, it would be necessary to turn to the memories that each of them publish annually. Nevertheless, this is not always easy, as many of these rural credit banks do not keep these copies of such documents. Therefore, we will use information gathered in the bibliography published on that subject, together with, for the final part of the 20th century, the data gathered by the National Union of Credit Cooperatives in their statistical annual directory,[1] as well as the Banco de España (Bank of Spain) in its Statistical Bulletin and its Official Registry of Institutions.

This chapter is divided into five parts based on the chronological development of these institutions. First of all, the grounds of the credit cooperatives and the rural credit banks in Spain and Andalusia are analysed. Next, we will study the development of the credit cooperatives in Andalusia in three different stages: the first third of the century, from the Spanish post-war period to the great changes of the Spanish financial system in the sixties decade, and the last quarter of the century. Last, the main conclusions drawn from this work and the consulted bibliographic references.

2 History: The origin of credit cooperatives and rural credit banks

The cooperative societies, in general, appear due to the desire of a group of people to meet a common requirement. Regarding the credit cooperatives, its

---

1 This Annual directory has changed its name since the beginning of its publishing. We will refer to it in this work with the name "Statistical Annual Directory of the Credit Cooperatives".

origin is determined, equally, by the group need of financial resources, when the access to credits in efficient conditions in the market is very difficult for their partners (Belmonte Ureña, 2007).

The first credit cooperatives appear in Europe in the second half of the 19th century, in a time period of important political and economic tension, together with the crisis in European agriculture (Soler Tormo, 2002). Reorganising and modernising the agricultural production involved strong capital investment what, for many farmers, meant the need to resort to credits. However, the rare development of the financial system and the concentration of the banking business in very little hands made it difficult to access financing for these agents that had to face excessive interest rates. In that context, credit cooperatives had an appropriate response as they could offer lower interest to the ones required by banks and private moneylenders (Martinez Soto, 1994).

A fight against the usury and Christian-inspired mutualism would be the base to develop the first credit cooperatives in Germany (Soler Tormo, 2002). These institutions were based on the Friedrich W. Raiffeisen's ideas, who stood up for the credit cooperative movement as the best solution to dispose of the usury and the need to get financing through bankers (Nieto Gonzalez, Belmonte Ureña & Nieto Gonzalez, 1998). This cooperating system and other similar ones (Durand in France, Cerruti in Italy, etc.), as well as other methods of lay nature (official mutualism in France, Luzatti and Wollemborg in Italy and Schulze-Delitzsch & Hass in Germany, etc.) quickly spread over the whole European continent (Martinez Soto, 2000).

Regarding Spain, the first institutions of that kind appeared in the last years of the 19th century, with a little delay regarding the other countries in Western Europe.

Nevertheless, there are authors (Belmonte Ureña, 2007; Titos Martinez, 2003) that consider that credit cooperatives in Spain had their precedent in the so-called public granaries, non-profit institutions that, since the 15th century, were founded in most Spanish towns. The excess of grain was kept there to lend it to farmers that needed it or to consume it in times of shortage (Carasa Soto, 1983).

In Andalusia, during the second half of the 19th century, public granaries were not very important nationally regarding the number, but they were regarding the volume of operations, carrying out an activity highly over the rest of the organisations of this kind (Bernal, 1991). In the first years of the 20th century, public granaries continued having certain importance, even that their funds were not enough to cover the enormous resources required by the modernisation of the sector (Sanchez Picon & Navarro Perez, 2001).

Afterwards, corruption and abuses meant, in not few cases, the decline of these institutions that, in their last years, did not have many benefits due to their rare resources and the limitation of credit that they could provide (Rodero Franganillo, 1974).

Although there were some prior efforts to establish credit cooperatives as such in Spain, we can say that the first practical implementation of Raiffeisen's ideas was in 1881, when the Rural Credit Bank of Savings, Loans and Assistance of Jabali Viejo in Murcia was established (Martinez Soto, 2003a). Since then, the credit cooperative movement has suffered a relative motivation promoted, in many cases, by the Catholic clergy; and continuing with the German model whose approaches had brought to our country some scholars of this matter such as Diaz de Rabago, the Padre Nogues (Father Nogues) and the Vizconde de Eza (Viscount of Eza) (Rodero Franganillo, 1974).

At the beginning of the 20th century, the Administration, the Church and certain groups of owners drove with eagerness the cooperative organisation in rural areas (Garrido Herrero, 1995). In fact, the first credit cooperatives that appeared in Spain at the beginning of the new century were linked almost exclusively to the agricultural activity (Conde Rodriguez, 1995).

In Andalusia, the first references about credit cooperatives are from 1902. That year Francisco Rivas Moreno was designated Delegate of the Spanish Tax Office in Granada, who, driven by his concern about the poorer classes, had previously founded several socially inspired institutions such as savings banks and rural credit banks in other parts of Spain. In his new destination, he started the processes to implement agricultural organisations of that kind in several localities. Although in the capital that plan had a higher first acceptance, the transfer of Rivas Moreno to Valencia only six months after his arrival, caused the weakening of the eagerness and the failure of the project (Titos Martinez, 2005).

All these first experiences were ground-breaking for a system that would be driven by the approval, in 1906, of the Agricultural Trade Unions Law (Spanish law), that promoted the creation of numerous cooperatives in the form of "agricultural trade unions" and rural credit banks, autonomous or linked to the previous ones (Martinez Rodriguez & Martinez Soto, 2008).

Since then, the Catholic Agricultural Trade Unions have started to quickly spread, many of them with rural credit bank, which were included in the National Catholic Confederation of Spain.

3 The first decades of the 20th century

In 1904, the first census of agricultural trade unions and rural credit banks included a total of 129 agricultural trade unions with a rural credit bank in Spain, of which eight were located in Andalusia. Since that year, the development of these institutions in this territory had been a little irregular. The number of rural credit banks in Andalusia is reduce in the twenties decade, concurrently to what happens at a national level, and it is recovered in the prior years to the Spanish Civil War, in order that, according to the Anuario Estadistico de España (Spanish Statistical Annual Directory) and the Agriculture General Directorate, in 1933 there was a total of 29 rural credit banks in Andalusia (Titos Martinez, 2003; Martinez Soto, 2003b).

Globally, these institutions and, especially, rural credit banks, suffered an expansion stage in the first third of the century. Nevertheless, the growing process was stopped by the Spanish Civil War and got slowed down in the subsequent years (Garrido Herrero, 1995; Gamez Amian, 1998). However, during this period, the development of these institutions in Andalusia was smaller than in other areas of the country where the cooperative movement was more important, such is the case of Valencia, Catalonia and Castile Leon (Rodero Franganillo, 1980).

From the legal point of view, the first regulation that regulates, scarcely, the credit cooperatives is the Royal Decree (in Spain) of 12 July 1917 of agricultural credit, which intended to organise the sector, joining the bodies that, at that moment, were directing the agricultural loans: public granaries, agricultural associations, agricultural trade unions and rural credit banks. It regulated the credit cooperatives, such as those of which the business purpose shall be the credit for partners and other agricultural cooperative associations (Terron Muñoz, 1987).

In 1925, the Military Governing Body of the Spanish Dictatorship creates the National Service of Agricultural Credit (Gamez Amian, 1998), the official body that would be responsible for that financing method and that, in 1962, would come to be named as the Banco de Credito Agricola (Rural Credit Bank).

4 The sector's organisation: From the post-war period to the sixties decade

After the digression of the Spanish Civil War, in 1942, the Cooperation Law (Spanish law) is approved, with which cooperatives get to be linked to the Trade Union Organisation and the National Union of Territorial Unions of

Land Cooperatives (Palomo Zurdo, 2004). Likewise, this Law established a classification in the group of rural credit banks: the credit sections of the land cooperatives (depending on those), the rural credit banks of first level (local and regional) and those of second level or provincial whose partners were the land cooperatives of the province where the headquarters were located (Server Izquierdo & Melian Navarro, 2001; Terron Muñoz, 1987).

Once the main consequences of the battle were overcome, the number of credit cooperatives increased again due to, not only the urgency to cover the new financial needs of the economic development, but also because many of them were used by other institutions to avoid the prohibitions that imposed the statu quo in which the Spanish banking system was absorbed during the first 20 years of the Franco regime. These restrictions did not concern the group of credit cooperatives that, at that moment, were not fully considered as part of that sector.

Since then, new rural credit banks have started to occupy the Andalusian territory, mainly those of a local nature, being mainly congregated in the province of Cordoba, Granada, Jaen and Seville (Rodero Franganillo, 1974). Nevertheless, many of these institutions would not remain over time nor would they get to become true financial institutions. In fact, in the Cooperative Societies Registry of the Regional Government of Andalusia there are more than 30 credit cooperatives created between 1947 and 1965, of which there would not be any later records in the Registry of Institutions of the Banco de España (Bank of Spain). In most of the cases, it would be local rural credit banks or credit divisions of agricultural cooperatives that, back then, would also be named rural credit banks, and that then did not meet the needed requirements to be able to get the condition of credit institution under the supervision of the Banco de España (Bank of Spain).

In spite of all these experiences that did not get to become established, it can be said that, since the end of the fifties begins the final configuration of the rural credit banks systems of the region. These are institutions that, once they are registered in the Banco de España (Bank of Spain), they are maintained, most of them until the end of the 20th century.

In 1957 the Caja Rural Nacional (National Rural Credit Bank) (CRUNA, for its Spanish initials) is established as a credit cooperative society of second level, with the aim to solve the difficulties that started to appear regarding the lack of union among the rural credits banks in Spain (Belmonte Ureña, 2007). This institution contributed to the final start of the sector at the beginning of the sixties and, especially for the establishment of provincial rural credit banks (Palomo Zurdo & Valor Martinez, 2001). As a result of this boost, that same year, the first "modern" credit cooperatives in Andalusia are born: the Caja Rural Provincial de Jaen (Rural Credit Bank in Jaen), an institution that is still working as of today.

In the next 13 years, 16 rural credit banks were founded in Andalusia (Tab. 1). It is worth mentioning the supremacy of the Cordoba province as destination of these new societies as seven of them were set up in this territory.

Tab. 1: Rural credit banks created in Andalusia since 1957 (Entities that were registered with the Bank of Spain)

Foundation year	Rural credit bank	Dimension	Province
1957	C.R. Provincial de Jaén	P	Jaen
1958	C.R. San José (Torredonjimeno)	L	Jaen
1958	C.R. Nª Sª del Rosario (Nueva Carteya)	L	Cordoba
1959	C. R. Nª Sª Madre del Sol (Adamuz)	L	Cordoba
1961	C. R. Los Pedroches (Pozoblanco)	L	Cordoba
1962	C.R. Nª Sª del Campo (Cañete de las Torres)	L	Cordoba
1962	C. R. Nª Sª de Guadalupe (Baena)	R	Cordoba
1962	C.R. Provincial de Málaga	P	Malaga
1963	C.R. Provincial de Almería	P	Almeria
1964	C.R. Provincial de Córdoba	P	Cordoba
1964	C.R. Provincial de Sevilla	P	Seville
1964	C.R. Utrera	L	Seville
1965	C. R. Caja Rural de La Carlota	L	Cordoba
1967	C.R. Provincial de Huelva	P	Huelva
1968	C.R. de Morón de la Frontera	L	Seville
1969	C.R. Provincial de Cádiz	P	Cadiz
1970	C.R. Provincial de Granada	P	Granada
2000	C.R de Almería y Málaga (Cajamar)	-	Almeria
2001	C.R. del Sur (Huelva y Sevilla)	-	Seville

C.R.= Caja Rural (Rural Credit Bank)
Nª Sª= Nuestra Señora (Our Lady)
Dimension = P (Provincial), R (Regional) & L (Local)
Source: Author, based on Statistical Annual Directory of the Credit Cooperatives (1973 & 1974), Titos Martínez (2003, pp. 269–270) & Official Registry of Entities of the Bank of Spain

The development of these institutions is very diverse. In the group of the provincial rural credit banks, all of them keep their activity until the end of the century (since the nineties without the "provincial" description), except the one in Cadiz that was acquired by the Caja de Ahorros de San Fernando (Saving Bank in San Fernando) in 1986. Several years later, in the transition of the century, the ones in Malaga, Almeria, Huelva and Seville would be each involved in concentration processes from which Cajamar and the Caja Rural del Sur (Rural Credit Bank of the South) would appear, located in Almeria and Seville respectively.

Among those of local or regional dimension, more changes occur. The Caja Rural Provincial de Cordoba (Provincial Rural Credit Bank of Cordoba) absorbs the one in Los Pedroches in 1979 and the one in La Carlota in 1991. On the other hand, the Caja Rural San Jose (San Jose Rural Credit Bank) in Torredonjimeno is dissolved in 1989, turning into the credit division of an oil cooperative under the same name, once the Banco de España (Bank of Spain) did not authorise the Caja Rural Provincial de Jaen (Provincial Rural Credit Bank in Jaen) to absorb it. Regarding the Caja Rural de Moron de La Frontera (Rural Credit Bank in Moron de La Frontera) (Seville), in the Registry of Institutions of the Banco de España (Bank of Spain) there is evidence that it stopped working in February of 1980 by agreement of the Executive Council, but there is no more specific information about the causes that motivated it nor the specific destiny of the institution.

Besides the rural credit banks, during the sixties decade, another four non-agricultural credit cooperatives were founded in Andalusia, and their activity was more limited than that of the prior ones: the Caja Central del Ahorro Popular (Central Popular Saving Bank) in Seville (1963–1974); the Caja Latina de Credito (Latin Credit Bank) in Cordoba (1966–1975); the Cooperativa de Credito y Fomento Industrial (Credit and Industrial Development Cooperative) in Cordoba (1967–1976) and the Caja de Credito (Credit Bank) in the South of Malaga (1969–1979). The fact that this modality of credit cooperatives did not have that much success in this region makes us think that, in many cases, the rural credit banks in Andalusia served to meet the financial needs of non-agricultural cooperatives that, in other areas, have been covered by popular or professional credit cooperatives (Carbonel de Masy, 1973).

Thus, during the sixties and seventies decade, the sector faced a double process, that does also take place nationally. On the one hand, new institutions appear, at a provincial level as well as lower levels because of the conversion of many credit divisions of agricultural cooperatives into rural credit banks. On the other hand, an important restructuring takes place, which affects significantly these last ones, so that they disappear, they become integrated into bigger ones as new branch offices or they are absorbed by the provincial ones

(Martin Mesa, 1988). As a consequence, the global number of these institutions is reduced.

From the legislative point of view, in the middle of the decade of 1960, a process of legal changes is nationally started, which means the end of the banking statu quo, which had been kept during the prior years with the relaxation of the borders to get into the sector and open new branch offices. Besides, these measures implicated the beginning of the process to include the credit cooperatives in the Spanish financial system.

In 1964, the Decree of the 26th of March, entailed the reorganisation of the functions of the Caja Rural Nacional (National Rural Credit Bank) and the subjugation of rural credit banks to the coefficients covering and the management of the Spanish Tax Office Ministry. Likewise, it recognised numerous benefits for the banks that obtained from the Banco de España (Bank of Spain) the category of "qualified". Among others, they were allowed to participate in the distribution of the official credit of the Banco de Credito Agricola (Bank of Agricultural Credit) with similar conditions as the ones of the rest of the collaborating institutions (Terron Muñoz, 1987). That encouraged the creation of provincial rural credit banks, in many cases promoted by the existing local banks, with the intention to access the official agricultural credit and to reorganise the association and consolidation ways. In fact, Andalusia gets to have eight of these institutions, one in each province, all of them "qualified", except for the one in Cadiz. At the same time, the creation of Territorial Unions of Cooperatives (UTECOs, Spanish initials) was also extended, which were closely linked to rural credit banks or to other credit cooperatives (Palomo Zurdo & Mateu Gordon, 2013).

Finally, in 1971, the autonomy of these institutions is approved and they come to be subdued, exclusively, to the Banco de España (Bank of Spain). However, the most important regulation of this change process would be the Royal Decree (Spanish decree) 2860/78 of the 3rd of November about credit cooperatives. This regulation and its development through several ministerial orders in the two next years would entail a total and final integration of credit cooperatives in the Spanish financial system.

5 The end of the century: Crisis, remediation and recovery

The positive development of these institutions is interrupted by a significant crisis that, between 1971 and 1983, in an environment of general banking difficulties, reached a high number of rural credit banks. This situation, that affected 20 rural credit banks in the whole country, had important consequences in four banks in Andalusia, mainly in the Caja Rural Provincial de Jaen (Provincial Rural Credit Bank in Jaen). This bank was taken over in 1982 by the Banco de España (Bank of Spain) and needed a very considerable volume of public financial aid (27,160 million of pesetas (old Spanish currency)) to face the situation resulting for its excessive risk concentration with UTECO and the Agricultural Provincial Cooperative in Jaen (Martin Mesa, 1986). Likewise, the Caja Rural Provincial de Sevilla (Provincial Agricultural Bank in Seville) was taken over by the Banco de España (Bank of Spain) in 1983, even that it got to solve the situation. The Caja de Malaga (Bank of Malaga) did also need an important remediation plan in 1984 with which it was able to recover, while the one in Cadiz ended being acquired by the Caja de Ahorros de San Fernando (Saving Bank in San Fernando) in 1986 (Titos Martinez, 2003).

This recession implied the establishment of a Remediation Plan (between 1983 and 1992) and the signing of an association agreement with the Rural Credit Banks and the Banco de Credito Agricola (Rural Credit Bank) with the aim of strengthening the sector and providing support to guarantee its future.

In May of 1984, the Associated Group BCA-CRA (Rural Credit Bank-Associated Rural Credit Banks) was constituted between the Rural Credit Bank and 57 rural credit banks, to which some more would later be added. All the rural credit banks in Andalusia, except for the one in Torredonjimeno and the Caja Rural Provincial de Cadiz (Provincial Rural Credit Bank in Cadiz), are included in this project from the beginning (Martin Mesa, 1987). This agreement benefited the remediation of the banks involved in the crisis, its reorganisation and the channelling, through them, of the official agricultural credit, what entailed a new impetus for the sector. Likewise, this agreement implicated the dissolution of the Caja Rural Nacional (National Rural Credit Bank) whose functions were absorbed by the Group.

At the same time, in 1983, the Deposit Guarantee Fund of the credit cooperatives was created, which would also execute an important role in the remediation process of the sector.

The agreement with the Rural Credit Bank started to weaken when, in 1989, some rural credit banks decided to leave it and create the Spanish Association of Credit Cooperatives, as an institution to unite the sector, and the Banco Cooperativo Español (Spanish Cooperative Bank), as its banking operative branch. In the creation of this new institution participated the 24 banks promoting the project together with the German cooperative bank Deutsche Genossenschaftsbank (DG Bank) (Palomo Zurdo, 1995). To this project, of the Andalusian institutions, have been initially involved the seven provincial banks that participated in the Associated Group BCA-CRA (Rural Credit Bank-Associated Rural Credit Banks) (all of them except the one in Cadiz). The five local and regional banks active at that time were kept in that last Group, and these would be included in the Banco Cooperativo (Cooperative Bank) some years later.

Together with the brand-new bank and as common management instruments, two companies were created: the Rural Company of Computer Services and the Insurance Agricultural Group (RGA, Spanish initials). These four bodies came to work cooperatively under the name of "Gupo Caja Rural" (Rural Credit Bank Group), especially from 1995. The concentration of credit cooperatives through the creation of groups responds to an integrated strategy that allows them to keep operating in the financial market under common and solidarity principles, but without losing the individual competitive advantage of each of them (Melian Navarro, 2004).

The dissolution of the agreement would also be favoured by the Spanish public banking restructuring process at the beginning of the nineties decade which, in 1991, would lead to the integration of the Banco de Credito Agricola (Rural Credit Bank) in the Spanish Banking Corporation Argentaria which, in turn, would be privatised in the following years.

The Credit Cooperatives Law (Spanish law) in 1989 and its Regulations of 1993 are a new manner to understand these financial intermediaries with their two different purposes as cooperative societies and credit institutions. However, this regulation has an additional character regarding the one approved by the Autonomous Communities with legal competences on this matter. In that way, in Andalusia, the Decree 158 (Spanish decree) of the 10th of August of 1983 regulated the competencies of the autonomous government in respect of the credit cooperatives. In 1985, the Andalusian Cooperative Societies Law (Spanish law) was promulgated, being replaced by a new legal text when the Law 2/1999 of the 31st of March was approved. This new law establishes, among other matters, a new control and inspection system that is considered as a competence for the autonomous government.

The deep crisis suffered by the group of rural credit banks during the first years of the eighties decade entailed, among other things, an important decrease in the number of rural credit banks in Spain. In 1977 there were 200 registered, in 1985, 146, and five years later, that number came only to 107, according to the data of the Anuario de Cooperativas de Credito (Annual Directory of the Credit Cooperatives) of the UNACC (National Union of Credit Cooperatives). This decrease, in many cases, is due to absorptions by other rural credit banks or by banks or savings banks, although some liquidations did also occur (Palomo

Zurdo and Valor Martinez, 2001). Regarding Andalusia, this decrease does also occur, but less intensely, going from 18 banks to 13 between 1977 and 1990.

Once these difficulties were overcome, the banks continue with their activity until the last years of the century, when a new impetus takes place in the sector concentration process. Regarding that, the first experience takes place in Andalusia where, in 2000, Cajamar Caja Rural (Cajamar Rural Credit Bank) appears as a result of the merger of the Caja Rural de Almeria (Rural Credit Bank in Almeria) and the Caja Rural de Malaga (Rural Credit Bank in Malaga), two banks that, in return, had previously integrated the agricultural cooperative and the rural credit bank in Murcia in Campo de Cartagena (1989) and the credit cooperative Grumeco in Madrid (2000). It is the first creation case of a SIP (Spanish initials) Institutional Protection System in Spain. A SIP is a new manner to integrate companies that had been created with the Directive 2006/48/CE Directive, transposed to the Spanish legal system in 2009 through various dispositions. Regarding the credit cooperatives, it entailed to group under one institution that worked as the group head a group of smaller cooperatives that mutualised their results and balanced their internal risks from 0 to 100, while it allowed them to keep their identity and trade name as well as certain legal and operative independence (Palomo Zurdo and Gutierrez Fernandez, 2012). In this way, at the end of the 20th century, after this new integration phase, the number of credit cooperatives located in Andalusia was a total of 11, all of them with agricultural nature.

This is a process of concentration of the sector at a national level, as a consequence of the generalised adjustment of the Spanish banking system. This tendency shall be intensified in the first decade of the 21st century driven, not that much by the authority's decisions, but by the wishes of the sector itself (Fajardo Garcia, 2011).

On the other hand, during the last years of the 20th century, the sector starts nationally a territorial expansion project that takes the credit cooperatives to an important growth regarding the number of their offices. A business retail banking model based on the closeness with the client together with other factors such as the intensification of the competition in the financial system, the need to find new business opportunities and the changes in the traditional operative, took these banks to get out of their regular acting field. This expansion started generally in adjacent provinces or regions where there were no institutions of that type. But, over time, it was expanding to areas in the scope of the credit cooperatives that became their competitors (Palomo Zurdo & Sanchis Palacio, 2008). On occasion, the territorial growth was derived from the processes of merger and acquisition of institutions with different acting geographic areas.

This process entailed an oversizing of the network of branch offices of these banks (the same that occurred with the savings banks) what would later entail a true encumbrance when the financial crisis fully affects the Spanish banking system in the first years of the 21st century (Gutierrez Fernandez, Palomo Zurdo & Romero Cuadrado, 2012).

In this expandable context, during the last years of the 20th century, the Caja Rural de Almeria (Rural Credit Bank in Almeria) kept a growing level of its distribution network that is very higher over the rest of the Andalusian and Spanish rural credit banks. In fact, when in 2000 Cajamar appears because of its merger with the Caja Rural de Malaga (Rural Credit Bank in Malaga), the 567 offices of this new bank are the 49 per 100 of the total branch offices of the Andalusian rural credit banks and a 15 per 100 of the total credit cooperatives nationally. The other banks located in Andalusia suffer a development keeping with the country average, excepting the local banks that, at the end of the 20th century, only keep one office located in the original locality (Vargas-Machuca, 2017).

As it has been explained, this geographical expansion was not limited to the region. Once the legal rules for that were made flexible, the interest in these banks grows as they grew outside their traditional scope, both geographical and operational (Soler Tormo, 2002). This trendy took the Caja Rural de Almeria (Rural Credit Bank in Almeria) to start operating in the Murcia province (1989) when it included the Caja del Campo (Land Bank) in Cartagena, which was absorbed by the bank that year, and to acquire the network of branch offices that the Banco Urquijo (Urquijo Bank) had in the metropolitan area of Barcelona (1990). The Caja Rural de Malaga (Rural Credit Bank in Malaga) has also expanded its scope with offices in Cadiz (1990), Madrid (1992), Melilla (1996) and Ceuta (1998). Likewise, the Caja Rural de Granada (Rural Credit Bank in Granada) buys the Banco Zaragozano (Bank of Zaragoza) six of its offices in Galicia (2000) even that it will finally sell all of them to the Caja Rural Gallega (Rural Credit Bank in Galicia) one year later (Titos Martinez, 2005). In this way, at the end of the year 2000, Andalusian rural credit banks kept a total of 270 branch offices outside the autonomous community.

Nevertheless, despite this geographical expansion, rural credit banks maintained an important territorial link. In the same way, the operative homogenisation with other banks and the loss of specialisation, did not prevent these institutions from keeping some differentiating characteristics of their activity with respect to the rest of the components of the banking system. However, in these last years, rural credit banks and, in general, all the credit cooperatives have given the impression of wanting to moderate their component strictly agricultural, to emphasise a new style of regional banking destined for families and small and medium businesses (Vargas Vasserot, 2015).

From the point of view of the business volume, the main characteristic to be highlighted among the rural credit banks in Andalusia is the size heterogeneity. Among all of them, stands, by far, the Caja Rural Provincial de Almeria (Provincial Rural Credit Bank in Almeria) that, before its merger with the one in Malaga, represented a little more than the 30 per 100 of the total of the resources obtained and the 40 per 100 of the credit investment of these banks in Andalusia. Once the two banks were integrated, the resulting company, Cajamar, would become the more important credit cooperative regarding the size, not only in Andalusia, but also nationally (Vargas-Machuca, 2017).

6 Conclusions

The first credit cooperatives appear in Spain at the end of the 19th century, with a little delay regarding other central European countries. The first experiences of these institutions were linked, almost exclusively, to the agricultural scope. These approaches arrived late to Andalusia, where the first references to this type of banks are from the first years of the 20th century. They were rural credit banks linked to agricultural trade unions, very frequent at that time.

After a development phase, stopped by the Spanish Civil War, the sector suffered a double process until the middle sixties decade. On the one hand, an important expansion regarding the number of banks and, on the other hand, the trend to integrate banks, because of the mergers of the local ones by the provincial ones, as well as the liquidations and dissolutions. From all the credit cooperatives that appear in these years, only 21 get to get registered as such in Official Registry of Institutions of the Banco de España (Bank of Spain). It is likely that, the other ones were only credit divisions from other agricultural cooperatives (that at that time were also called rural credit banks) that, did not get the authorisation from the Banco de España (Bank of Spain) to operate autonomously, or got integrated with the rural credit banks of their correspondent provincial scope.

Regarding Andalusia, it can be said that the configuration of the regional sector of credit cooperatives is carried out between 1957, when the Caja Rural Provincial de Jaen (Provincial Rural Credit Bank in Jaen) was created, and 1970, the year when the Caja Rural Provincial de Granada (Provincial Rural Credit Bank in Granada) was founded. Although the sector suffers an important crisis at the beginning of the eighties decade, once its main consequences are overcome, an expansion stage starts, which will entail the consolidation of this group of banks in the Andalusian banking outlook.

Between these two dates, a total of 16 rural credit banks of varied scopes (local, regional and provincial) are founded, and four non-agricultural credit cooperatives. These last ones with little trajectory, when disappearing by dissolution or absorption on the part of others before 1980. Due to these same prior causes, some rural credit banks also disappear from the Andalusian financial outlook before the end of the 20th century. Finally, in 2000, this territory embraced the headquarters of 12 rural credit banks, two of which (Rural Credit Banks of Almeria and Malaga) were in that year integrated into a new bank, Cajamar.

Individually, the main characteristic to be highlighted among the rural credit banks in Andalusia is the size heterogeneity. Among all of them, stands, by far, the Caja Rural Provincial de Almeria (Provincial Rural Credit Bank in Almeria) regarding the business volume as well as the number of offices. Once the two banks were integrated, the resulting company, Cajamar, would become the more important credit cooperative regarding the size, not only in Andalusia, but also nationally.

At the beginning of the 21st century, the configuration of rural credit banks sector would be disrupted as a consequence of the concentration processes in the group of credit cooperatives, intensified as a result of the crisis of the Spanish banking system and driven, not only by the authorities decisions, but also by the wishes of the sector itself.

References

Banco de España (1975–2000). *Boletín Estadístico, Instituciones financieras, Información obtenida de los Estados de Supervisión.* http://www.bde.es/bde/es/secciones/informes/boletines/Boletin_Estadist/.

Banco de España. *Registro Oficial de Entidades, Consulta de datos históricos de las entidades.* http://app.bde.es/ren/html/inicio.htm. Access date July 20, 2020.

Belmonte Ureña, L. J. (2007). *El sector de cooperativas de crédito en España: un estudio por comunidades autónomas.* Sevilla: Consejo Económico y Social de Andalucía. Recovered from: https://www.juntadeandalucia.es/export/drupaljda/1_1505_cooperativas_credito.pdf. Access date July 22, 2020.

Bernal, A. M. (1991). Pósitos, cillas, tercias y economía agraria en Andalucía. In M. D. Gil Pérez; M. Torres Hidalgo & N. Ramírez Moreno (Eds.), *Pósitos, cillas y tercias en Andalucía. Catálogo de antiguas edificaciones para almacenamiento de grano* (pp. 51–73). Sevilla: Consejería de Obras Públicas y Transportes. Dirección General de Arquitectura. Junta de Andalucía.

Carasa Soto, P. (1983). Los pósitos en España en el siglo XIX. *Investigaciones Históricas: Época Moderna y Contemporánea*, 4, 247–304.

Carbonell de Masy, R. (1973). Cooperativas de crédito-no rural en Andalucía: ¿son instituciones necesarias para su desarrollo? *Estudios Cooperativos*, 30, 71–77.

Conde Rodríguez, C. (1995). Las cooperativas de crédito en España. *REVESCO. Revista de Estudios Cooperativos*, 61, 127–140.

Fajardo García, G. (2011). How viable are Spanish credit cooperatives after recent bank capitalization and restructuring regulations? *CIRIEC-España, Revista de Economía Pública, Social y Cooperativa*, 73, 151–170.

Gámez Amián, A. (1998). *El crédito institucional a la agricultura en Andalucía (1768–1936)*. Málaga: Universidad de Málaga.

Garrido Herrero, S. (1995). El cooperativismo agrario español del primer tercio del siglo XX. *Revista de Historia Económica*, 13(1), 115–144.

Gutiérrez Fernández, M., Palomo Zurdo, R. & Romero Cuadrado, M. (2012). La expansión territorial como factor motivador de la reestructuración del sistema financiero español: el caso de las cajas de ahorro y las cooperativas de crédito. *REVESCO. Revista de Estudios Cooperativos*, 107, 7–34. doi: https://doi.org/10.5209/rev_REVE.2012.v107.38746.

Junta de Andalucía. *Registro de Sociedades Cooperativas de la Junta de Andalucía, Consulta Pública*. http://www.juntadeandalucia.es/economiainnovacionyciencia/ConsultaSociedades/rscl/inicioConsultaSociedades.do. Access date July 20, 2020.

Martín Mesa, A. (1986). Crisis y saneamiento de la Caja Rural Provincial de Jaén. *Boletín de la Cámara Oficial de Comercio e Industria de Jaén*, 42, 16–27.

Martin Mesa, A. (1987). Un nuevo modelo orgánico de las Cajas Rurales españolas: especial referencia a las andaluzas. *Revista de Estudios Regionales*, 17, 71–102.

Martín Mesa, A. (1988). *La crisis de las cajas rurales españolas y el nuevo modelo del cooperativismo del crédito agrario*. Granada: Banco de Crédito Agrícola – Instituto de Desarrollo Regional de la Universidad de Granada.

Martínez Rodríguez, S. & Martínez Soto, A. P. (2008). Los pioneros del cooperativismo agrario de crédito español (1880–1920). *CIRIEC-España, Revista de Economía Pública, Social y Cooperativa*, 63, 89–112.

Martínez Soto, A. P. (1994). El papel del crédito y la financiación en la agricultura capitalista (1850–1970): Una primera aproximación a un campo multifactorial. *Noticiario de Historia Agraria*, 4(7), 39–66.

Martínez Soto, A. P. (2000). Cooperativismo y crédito agrario en la Región de Murcia, 1890–1936. *Historia Agraria*, 20, 123–167.

Martínez Soto, A. P. (2003a). Los orígenes del cooperativismo de crédito agrario en España, 1890–1934. *CIRIEC-España, Revista de Economía Pública, Social y Cooperativa*, 44, 57–104.

Martínez Soto, A. P. (2003b). El cooperativismo de crédito en España, 1890–1934. Modelos, sistemas de gestión y balance de su actuación. *Historia Agraria*, 30, 119–150.

Melián Navarro, A. (2004). El fenómeno concentratorio como estrategia de crecimiento en las cajas rurales españolas. El Grupo Caja Rural. *REVESCO. Revista de Estudios Cooperativos*, 82, 89–112.

Nieto González, F. J., Belmonte Ureña, L. J. & Nieto González, J. L. (1998). Las Cajas Rurales en Andalucía en el período 1990–1996: Evolución y situación. *Revista de Humanidades y Ciencias Sociales*, 16, 81–108.

Palomo Zurdo, R. J. (1995). *La banca cooperativa en Europa*. Madrid: Unión Nacional de Cooperativas de Crédito y Asociación Española de Cooperativas de Crédito.

Palomo Zurdo, R. J. (2004). El crédito cooperativo español en el marco de la UEM: crecimiento y expansión territorial. *Mediterráneo Económico*, 6, 110–132.

Palomo Zurdo, R. J. & Gutiérrez Fernández, M. (2012). El desajuste del crédito en el sistema bancario y la acción de la economía social: el camino de la reestructuración. *REVESCO: Revista de Estudios Cooperativos*, 109, 138–169. doi: http://dx.doi.org/10.5209/rev_REVE.2012.v109.40653.

Palomo Zurdo, R. J. & Mateu Gordon, J. L. (2013). Las sociedades cooperativas de crédito en España: antecedentes históricos, evolución y adaptación estratégica ante la crisis financiera. In G. Lejarriaga Pérez de las Vacas, S. Martín López, & A. Muñoz García (Eds.), *40 años de historia de las empresas de participación* (pp. 502–526). Madrid: Escuela de Estudios Cooperativos de la Universidad Complutense de Madrid, Editorial Verbum.

Palomo Zurdo, R. J. & Sanchis Palacio, J. R. (2008). Un análisis del crédito cooperativo en España: situación actual, expansión territorial y proyección estratégica. *Estudios de Economía Aplicada*, 26(1), 27–41.

Palomo Zurdo, R. J. & Valor Martínez, C. (2001). *Banca cooperativa: entorno financiero y proyección social*. Madrid: Unión Nacional de Cooperativas de Crédito.

Palomo Zurdo, R. J., Sanchis Palacio, J. R. & Gutiérrez Fernández, M. (2011). Efectos de la crisis financiera sobre la innovación en la reorganización de los sistemas bancarios: los sistemas institucionales de protección en las entidades financieras de ámbito territorial. *Innovar: Revista de Ciencias Administrativas y Sociales*, 21(39), 179–190.

Rodero Franganillo, A. (1974). *Las cajas rurales españolas*. Madrid: Ediciones ICE.

Rodero Franganillo, A. (1980). Las cajas rurales andaluzas. Un instrumento financiero para el desarrollo. *Revista de Estudios Regionales*, II(Extra), 481–501.

Sánchez Picón, A. & Navarro Pérez, L. C. (2001). Algunas cuestiones en torno al crédito agrario en Andalucía (1800–1936). *Áreas: Revista Internacional de Ciencias Sociales*, 21, 165–184.

Server Izquierdo, R. J. & Melián Navarro, A. (2001). Evaluación de la eficiencia de las entidades financieras en las secciones de crédito de las cooperativas. *Investigación Agraria. Producción y Protección Vegetales*, 16(1), 87–104.

Soler Tormo, F. V. (2002). La identidad cooperativa como garantía de futuro: Las cooperativas de crédito ante la trivialización de sus principios. *CIRIEC-España, Revista de Economía Pública, Social y Cooperativa*, 40, 215–242.

Terrón Muñoz, F. (1987). Las Cajas rurales españolas: nacimiento, auge y perspectivas del cooperativismo agrario crediticio en España. Granada: Universidad de Granada.

Titos Martínez, M. (2003). El sistema financiero en Andalucía: tres siglos de historia (1740–2000). Sevilla: Instituto de Estadística de Andalucía. Recovered from: https://www.juntadeandalucia.es/institutodeestadisticaycartografia/historicas/sistemafinanciero/SistemaFinanciero.pdf. Access date July 10, 2020.

Titos Martínez, M. (2005). *Historia de la Caja Rural de Granada (1970–2005)*. Granada: Fundación Caja Rural de Granada.

UNACC (several years). *Anuario Estadístico de las Cooperativas de Crédito*. Madrid.

Vargas Vasserot, C. V. (2015). Las cooperativas de crédito y su posición dentro del modelo cooperativo. Integración frente a diferenciación en el marco de la reforma del sistema financiero. *REVESCO, Revista de Estudios Cooperativos*, 117, 50–76. doi: http://dx.doi.org/10.5209/rev_REVE.2015.v117.48145.

Vargas-Machuca, M. J. (2017). Las cooperativas de crédito andaluzas en el siglo XX: origen y consolidación del sector. *REVESCO, Revista de Estudios Cooperativos*, 124, 175–214. doi: https://doi.org/10.5209/REVE.54925.

Leonardo Caruana de las Cagigas

9 The jump in quality of Spanish insurance companies between 1966 and 2000

Abstract The Spanish insurance sector in the period 1966–2000 is characterised by two well differentiated periods. The first one was marked by slow growth until 1986, with a difficult beginning when the insurance companies lost the branch of occupational accidents that represented 29.1 % of all their activity, and by the global crisis of 1973, which hit Spain especially hard. The second period was one of rapid expansion starting with the country's entry into the EEC, explained by the economic growth of the country and a significant increase in cultural standards, which led to a demand for more life insurance, pension plans, health insurance and multi-risk insurance. These changes also brought about serious problems in the most characteristic branch, that of automobiles, and was one of the causes of the crisis in La Unión y el Fénix and La Estrella, as well as the success of MAPFRE and Mutua Madrileña, among others.

1 Introduction

In terms of growth, the evolution of the Spanish insurance sector in the period 1966–2000 is marked by two very different stages. The first was one of slow growth until 1986, with a difficult beginning when the insurance companies lost the occupational accidents branch, which represented 29.1 % of all their activity, and the 1973 global crisis, which affected Spain severely. The second phase, from 1986 onwards, saw rapid expansion linked to a variety of factors, including the rise in the country's economic level and cultural standard, which led to a sharp increase in demand for more life insurance, pension plans, health insurance and multi-risk insurance; the entry into the EEC (today the European Union or EU), which attracted European foreign investment that contributed to a "soft" restructuring of the sector (Herrando, 1991); the acceleration in the formation of the Single Insurance Market in Europe; the incorporation of managers more aware of the importance of internationalisation; and the presence of new intermediaries and competitors, mainly emerging among commercial banks and savings banks. These changes also led to serious problems in the most significant insurance branch, that of automobile insurance, and was one of the causes of the crisis at entities such as La Unión y el Fénix and La Estrella, as well as the success of MAPFRE and Mutua Madrileña, among others.

2 The economic growth of Spanish insurance companies

In 1966 there were 842 registered insurance entities in Spain, a figure that dropped to 557 in 1985 and to 354 by 2000 (Tortella, 2014, p. 300). In this way, the less efficient insurance companies disappeared and the average size of the companies increased. If we look at the "degree of penetration" (ratio of premiums to GDP), the progress of Spanish insurance was as follows: 2.3 % in 1964, 3.2 % in 1990 and 6.7 % in 2000. The definitive take-off of insurance in Spain was clearly brought about by the regulatory changes of the 1980s, and above all with the entry into the EEC, which allowed the ratio of 5 % of GDP, the characteristic threshold of developed countries, to be comfortably exceeded by the end of the 1990s. Two factors contributed decisively to this growth. The first was the sector's capacity for innovation, incorporating new coverage and services, and boosting the sale of those that were rarely bought in isolation by including them in multi-risk policies. The second was a more dynamic commercial action, largely supported by the development of new marketing channels, among which that of bancassurance, especially for life insurance, took on special importance.

3 Life insurance

Despite the fact that during the 1970s and the beginning of the 1980s in Spain, financially very solvent products were developed to facilitate savings for the elderly, their acceptance was very limited. From a financial point of view, life insurance played a significant role in the generation of savings in developed countries. For example, in the United Kingdom it accounted for more than 40 % of the increase in savings between 1980 and 1981, and in the United States, Germany, Sweden and the Netherlands it was also a significant percentage. In France the percentage was clearly lower than in those countries, but even so it was more than six times higher than in Spain. If the citizens of these countries invested so much in life insurance, it was because they had developed a pension culture. Only Italy was similar to Spain.

In 1984 the biggest competitor to life insurance was the public pension system, which according to several analysts was threatened with bankruptcy. In an international congress held between April 25 and 27 of that year, both the Secretary of State for the Economy, Miguel Ángel Fernández Ordóñez, and the Minister of Economy and Finance, José Borrell, made known their concerns about the future of the system. This concern was based on two fundamental factors: the country's economic weakness during those years, and the rising life expectancy. The two politicians warned about how difficult retirement could be for everyone, and that perhaps the pension offered by the state would not be enough to cover the necessary minimums. This opinion was not shared by the representative of the General Union of Workers in the insurance sector who asserted: "We must put an end to the existing catastrophic idea about the future of Social Security since, although at this time there is room for complementary systems (private pension plans), these are no panacea," (*La Vanguardia*, 27 April 1984, p. 67). In the newspaper *ABC* on 18 September 1984, it stated: "It has been scientifically proven that life is extended by an average of twenty years" (ABC de Sevilla, 18 September 1984, p. 50). This reality was confirmed by the National Institute of Statistics. Over a longer period of time, life expectancy actually increased from 50.1 years in 1940 to 78.71 in 1998. Therefore, the number of retirees with pressing financial needs receiving a social benefit was growing. For this same reason, the government recommended that private pension plans be taken out. In fact, there was no other solution than to freeze average pensions, and especially high pensions. For these reasons, private insurance strengthened its offer with retirement life insurance, which was given different trade names: Systematic Retirement Plan, Systematic Pension Plan, Systematic Insurance Plan, Retirement Savings, Adjustable Retirement Plan, Personal Retirement Savings Insurance, etc.

Another determining factor in the growth of life insurance was the behaviour of interest rates. Since the end of the 1970s, the yields on Spain's long-term public debt had risen substantially, reaching yields of around 15 % a year, to which tax allowances and deductions were added. This rise, a consequence of the high inflation rates of the so-called Transition years, was later maintained under the socialist government, especially at the end of the 1980s and beginning of the 1990s, with the economic policy of the Minister of the Economy Carlos Solchaga (high rates, strong peseta). This situation allowed life insurance providers to invest their reserves in assets with high profitability and little or no risk, and to offer policyholders an attractive return (6 % technical interest already computed in the calculation of the premium, and an annual share in profits of another five or six percentage points) with a good profit margin for the insurance company. Thus, long-term life insurance competed very well with the term deposits of banks and investment funds, which were the possible alternatives in those years. However, the fall of interest rates in the 1990s to unanticipated levels had another effect, that of shortening the differential between short- and long-term interest rates, sometimes even with the interest rate curve inverted, which eliminated the attractiveness of medium- and long-term investments, producing a greater concentration of savings in short-term instruments, where life insurance competed poorly with bank deposits and investment funds.

In those years there was also a very striking episode with the single premium that was spectacularly successful and competed with bank deposits, supported by its tax advantages. The sudden cancellation of these advantages shortly thereafter led to the collapse of that market, which also generated a major crisis in life insurance companies in 1989–1990. The fleeting success of single premiums was brought about by the Law of the Tax Regime of Certain Financial Assets of 29 May 1985, which offered single-premium policies a fiscal advantage over treasury notes, with the treatment of returns as capital gains and not as returns on movable capital, so that they were not subject to withholding taxes (Pérez, 1992). When, at the end of 1988, the Ministry of Finance modified its criteria and considered that these products were purely financial operations and that they should therefore be subject to the tax burden inherent in investment income, their attractiveness disappeared.

4 Non-life insurance, 1966–2000

The dominant insurance activities in 1966 were automobile insurance and occupational accident insurance, which together accounted for more than 60 % of all premiums. In that year, the provision of the latter type of insurance by corporations was prohibited, while the mutual insurance societies of employers became subject to the control of Social Security and had to split off their remaining insurance activities into an independent entity. The idea behind such a rule was that workers' compensation insurance could not be considered a "business". If in 1900, due to the incipient development and small size of the public sector, the only real option was the coverage of this insurance by the private sector, by 1966, due to the economic progress of the country, it was understood that it was now possible to use public institutions to administer it, since a country that was on the verge of modernisation could bear a greater tax burden, which would allow it to have a wider public coverage. For the insurance sector, the nationalisation of occupational accident insurance brought about considerable damage, which affected 292 entities and lead to the loss of 834,264 policies and 8.921 billion pesetas of annual premiums, that is, 29.1 % of the insurance business. This loss was alleviated by the growing demand for automobile insurance, which became the dominant branch with 30 % of private insurance in 1971, and 33.9 % in 1990, falling to 19.5 % in 2000.

5 Automobile insurance between 1966 and 2000

The finest example of this progress was the Mutua Madrileña Automovilista, which, despite the lack of a commercial network, increased its volume of premiums due to the legal requirement to take out auto insurance and the good terms the company offered. Such was the success of this company that by 1980 the Mutua was the second largest Spanish insurance company in terms of premium volume despite its specialisation in one insurance branch and one city.

The rapid growth of the vehicle fleet prompted the enactment of the Law on the Use and Circulation of Motor Vehicles, dated 24 December 1963, whose regulations were approved by a decree dated 19 November 1964, and a decree law dated 22 March 1965, which established compulsory automobile insurance. In fact, the 1963 law had already established the prohibition of the circulation of vehicles that did not have their corresponding compulsory civil liability insurance, although this obligation did not become effective until 1 June 1965. The penalties for non-compliance were very severe, between 1,000 and 5,000 pesetas and even the impounding of the vehicle.

At that time, the car was one of the most highly prized consumer goods, and the growth of the automobile industry was spectacular. This led to a sharp increase in the number of insured persons. For example, in 1966, 2,384,000 compulsory auto insurance policies and 2,519,000 voluntary auto insurance policies were taken out. But only five years later these two figures had almost doubled; in 1970 there were 4,009,000 compulsory and 4,027,000 voluntary auto insurance policies. But for the insurance companies these years were actually problematic owing to the lack of adequate knowledge of the management methods of this insurance, but also to the low profitability that the companies obtained from it. In fact, in some cases we found negative profitability in the technical results due to the high accident rate. Part of this problem was due to the relative age of the vehicle fleet, which was one of the causes of the large number of accidents. According to research carried out by the Banco Urquijo Research Department in 1970, vehicles were replaced every 11.2 years in cars, trucks and vans (Banco Urquijo, 1970, p. 33). This situation seemed fairly stable despite the growth in the number of vehicles and drivers. In any case, the ageing of the fleet only explains part of the accident rate. The sharp increase in the number of accidents was also basically due to three additional factors: on the one hand, drivers were poorly prepared, on the other, the roads of the 1960s were not in a suitable condition to withstand such intense traffic, and most vehicles lacked protective features for drivers. The terrible consequence of the combination of these three factors, plus the age of the fleet, was the high number of people killed and injured and the large amount of property damage. In round figures, accidents basically doubled between 1966 and 1970, which means that accidents grew at almost the same rate as the number of vehicles. The Spanish accident rate had no comparison with the surrounding countries. In 1964 the number of people killed on Spanish roads per 10,000 vehicles was 12.5, while in France it was 7 and in Italy 9.6 (*Boletín de la Revista Seguros*, 70 (1967), pp. 230–231). The situation improved over time and in 2000 there were 1.82 deaths per 10,000 vehicles; this was due to safer vehicles, better roads and more cautious drivers.

In 1966, and in reference to compulsory insurance, the management of claims had an estimated cost for companies of 1.362 billion pesetas, while the volume of premiums received for this product amounted to 2.985 billion. Thus, the cost of the claims represented 45.6 % of the total value of premiums collected for compulsory insurance. But the situation deteriorated in 1970, when the cost of claims reached 3.237 billion pesetas while the premiums amounted to 4.815 billion pesetas, so the cost had jumped to 67.2 %. The situation with respect to voluntary insurance followed a different trajectory. In 1966 there were 1,241,000 claims with an estimated cost of 4.494 billion pesetas, and the premiums amounted to 6.442 billion pesetas; therefore, the ratio of claims to premiums was 69.8 %. In 1970, there were 1,925,000 claims with a cost of 7.426 billion pesetas, and the premium income was 11.265 billion pesetas, so the ratio was 65.9 %. Jaime Argüelles Armada, President of La Unión y el Fénix, which was at that time the largest company in the sector and in the auto insurance branch, expressed satisfaction in June 1967, before the general meeting of shareholders, stating that "the claims actually paid represent 21 % [of the premiums]" and thus the profit was very high. This encouraging situation soon changed. The claims payment procedures were extremely slow and generated a backlog of unpaid claims. For this reason, but also because of the increase in the number of claims, the management of auto insurance was becoming less lucrative. By 1970, the situation had worsened dramatically; for example, La Unión y el Fénix no longer had a positive technical result in the auto branch. The sector was urgently calling for an updating of premium rates, while redoubling its efforts in the selection of policyholders in order to reduce the number of bad drivers (Board of Directors, La Unión and el Fénix 1971, May 18). To make matters worse, management costs rose due to the growth in salary costs, which in reality were starting from very low levels, and logically required a strong correction.

In 1973, at the general meeting of La Estrella, its president, Gabriel de Usera González, described the situation of compulsory car insurance as "stagnant in a static price position" that "produces an endemic deficit." In his opinion, "only with a true spirit of sacrifice can one continue to practice" the provision of automobile insurance. Usera advocated an "automatic corrective index" of rates. The situation in the automobile industry was so worrisome that companies were not looking to increase the volume of policyholders, but to reduce the volume of claims, that is, to eliminate bad drivers from their portfolios. In Usera's company, La Estrella, instructions were even given to all offices and agents to reduce the sale of auto policies, because the ultimate goal should be to balance the portfolio. Specifically, the goal for 1975 was to reduce by 50 % the weight of car insurance, down from the goal of 55 % the previous year (Board of Directors' 1974, May 16).

As Gabriel de Usera argued in the board meeting, between 1967 and 1971 the industrialisation of the country had caused a "worsening of the risk, as has happened throughout the world. This effect has manifested itself in a very accentuated way in the automobile sector due to the striking increase of the National Automobile Fleet" (Minutes of the General Meeting of La Estrella from 26 June 1974). Teodoro Flores Gómez, Professor of Economic Structure in the Faculty of Economic and Business Sciences of the University of Bilbao, explained the increase in accidents by drawing attention to other factors: on the one hand, the deficiencies in the road infrastructure in terms of safety, and on the other, the mountainous Spanish terrain, which made driving even riskier (Flores, 1972, pp. 287–313). Another difficulty for the sector stemmed from the problems inherent in excessive fragmentation. In 1971 there were 162 companies offering car insurance; 68.1 % of these were Spanish public limited companies, 18.4 % were mutual societies and 13.6 % were foreign companies (*Seguros*, special statistics issue, 1972, p. 39). It was clear that there was excess supply, that is, too many companies, which were often uncompetitive. In 1971 the top ten insurance companies received 38.2 % of all premium income, and half of the companies accounted for 92.5 %. The combined market share of the other 80 companies was therefore only 7.6 % and they seemed destined to disappear.

But this lack of profitability was also largely the result of administrative rigidity, not only in the insurance rates. In the automobile industry, for example, a high level of reserves was required, and companies were subject to the rigid authorisation scheme provided for in the 1954 law. Professor Flores Gómez considered that the "technical deficits" were not as alarming as they seemed, because they were due to the fact that the companies had allocated excessive amounts to reserves. For his part, Gabriel Usera gave a different explanation in the prestigious *Revista de Hacienda Pública Española*: "the general trend of the market is a gradual worsening of the technical results, in which general expenses and then external management expenses have considerable weight, these being the two dimensions on which one must operate in order to obtain more favourable results," (Usera, 1970). In his opinion, the other two aspects that needed to be improved were the fight against fraud and the profitability of the reserves. The winners in this whole process were the policyholders. The companies offset the technical losses with financial gains derived from the investment of their reserves. Therefore, policyholders were sharing in the financial returns of the insurance companies.

Only one company, Mutua Madrileña, was successfully escaping from this auto insurance predicament. With the only exception being 1963, its technical results were always positive. Mutua Madrileña focussed its activity in this branch through direct sales, and in only one city: Madrid. In 1966 it was the fifth largest company in the branch of voluntary auto insurance, and by 1975 it was number two in the entire insurance sector, such was the importance of auto insurance at that time (*Seguros*, extraordinary statistics issues 1967 and 1976). The key to its impressive results was that its costs were very low. It did not have a network of branch offices with sales representatives. Moreover, like the other mutual societies, it did not have to pay back its shareholders, and could return part of each year's profits to its members through discounts on the premiums for the following year, so that its prices were very competitive compared to its rivals. In addition, its directors received no salary, no per diem and no shares. Another advance in the 1960s was the introduction of computerised policy management, a process made easier by the uniformity in the type of risk (Mutua Madrileña Automovilista, 1980). While Gabriel Usera saw in general costs a ceiling that prevented the obtainment of better technical results, this did not greatly affect Mutua Madrileña.

At that time, it was predicted that the great capacity of this branch to generate supplementary business would end up making the company that dominated it the leader in the Spanish insurance sector. This is what happened with MAPFRE, which went from being the leader in the sector to the leader in the industry. In 1970 it was the ninth largest insurance company in the country, and by 1983 it was number one. Of course, this success should not be attributed exclusively to auto insurance, but there is no doubt that it was key to achieving it.

The company that was the leader in the insurance sector for decades, and that continued to be the reference for many, La Unión y el Fénix, had a dismal track record in the auto insurance branch, with negative technical results in the three-year period 1988–1990 (11.973, 11.027 and 9.583 billion pesetas, respectively; Minutes of Board of Directors Meeting of 27 February 1991). Mario Conde, President of La Unión y el Fénix, stated in that meeting what was obvious: "It is absolutely untenable to maintain an income statement with such a high technical loss." Felipe Puyol Plans, the CEO, pointed out the advisability of creating a specific company for the complicated management of automobile insurance, a solution that probably came too late for the company.

In spite of all the difficulties, during these years there were positive aspects in the evolution of the sector, particularly the reduction in the number of accidents, which can be attributed to several factors: firstly, the greater prudence of drivers, perhaps due to the lack of fuel; secondly, the improvements introduced in the safety of the vehicles and the roads; and, finally, that the public administration became more involved in the inspections of automobiles through the technical inspection of vehicles.

In the 20th century, traffic accidents in Spain caused the death of some 250,000 people and injured a further 14 million; in other words, figures similar to those brought about by the Civil War. The corresponding figures on a global scale are chilling. In the last century, traffic accidents are thought to have caused 35 million deaths worldwide, a figure halfway between the number of victims of the First and Second World Wars, and left 500 million people seriously injured. At the end of the 20th century, the total annual cost of traffic accidents in Spain could be estimated at two trillion pesetas, that is, half of the income from tourism (these figures are from Luis Montoro, professor of Road Safety at the University of Valencia and director of the University Institute of Traffic and Road Safety, compiled in *El País*, 13 January 2000).

The available studies indicated that in 75 % of cases, accidents were caused by human error as a result of negligence, by speeding, by sleep-deprived driving or by the consumption of alcohol or drugs; only 5 % of accidents were caused by mechanical failure, with deficiencies in infrastructure causing another 20 %. In addition, there was an obvious problem of the ageing of the car fleet; 30 % of vehicles were over ten years old, a problem compounded by the bad habit of not regularly inspecting the car.

The ranking of automobile insurance companies changed substantially during this period. Only three of the ten companies that occupied the top ten positions in 1965 were still in the top ten in 2000: Plus Ultra (CGNU), Winterthur and Catalana Occidente; the newcomers to this esteemed list were four large European insurance companies (Allianz, AXA, Generali and Zurich) and three Spanish mutual companies specialising in automobile insurance: MAPFRE, Mutua Madrileña and Pelayo.

6 Industrial insurance

In Spain, the traditional market of the large industrial insurance companies operated with a practically unique rate set by the sector's employer, UNESPA (*Unión Española de Entidades Aseguradoras y Reaseguradora*, inherited from the *Sindicato Nacional del Seguro*) and even with a standard policy (the combined fire policy). There was a "simplified rate" for the most straightforward risks. The insurance of large companies was centred on a small number of insurers (mainly the subsidiaries of banks and MUSINI), which exchanged shares in co-insurance and even developed "non-aggression" practices. It was, therefore, an uncompetitive and poorly professionalised market, offering unsophisticated coverage with high premiums, partly as a result of premium rigidity and the absence of a risk management culture, both on the part of the insurers and the companies themselves. Insurance for small and medium-sized companies was mostly taken out by the representatives or local agents themselves, who had little training.

This situation began to change at the end of the 1970s, and gave way in the last two decades of the 20th century to an open, more competitive and efficient market, as a result of the concurrence of several factors: the challenges that the 1973 oil crisis generated in the insured companies, which prompted them to work towards lowering the cost of their insurance; the arrival of the large multinational insurance companies (AXA, Allianz, Zurich, Generali, etc.), which could offer better coverage than Spanish insurance companies at competitive prices; the privatisation of the INI companies; and the sale by the big banks of their industrial and insurance subsidiaries.

Spanish insurance companies had to adapt quickly to this new playing field. They created or strengthened technical departments specialised in the identification, evaluation and control of risks (Sáez, 1994) and had to modify their reinsurance policies to optimise the efficiency of their assignments to reinsurers. The insured companies also equipped themselves with risk managers, and turned to brokers to find the best offers. This led to the establishment of the large international brokerage firms in Spain, where traditionally there had only been one large national firm, Gil y Carvajal, and both the insurers and the insured companies paid increasing attention to prevention.

Another problem that insurance companies had to deal with in the 1990s was the increase in risk, which in many cases was difficult for one company to cover in isolation, requiring the formation of pools of Large Risks and of Environmental Risks, which took over from the *Pool Atómico Español* (created in 1964). The Large Risk Pool was set up in 1991 on the initiative of

Álvaro Muñoz, President of MUSINI. The large insurance companies of that time participated in it: La Unión y el Fénix, MAPFRE, Generali, AXA, Caser, Groupama, etc. According to the Second Community Insurance Directive, large risks were considered to be those of companies that met at least two of the following parameters: more than 900 million pesetas in assets on the balance sheet, a turnover of more than 1.8 billion pesetas, and an average of at least 250 employees throughout each financial year. The Environmental Risk Pool, also promoted by MUSINI, was created in 1994 to cover risks generated by environmental pollution. It was initially made up of 21 insurance companies, with the capacity to cover environmental risks valued at almost one billion pesetas.

The field of business insurance also includes two branches with very specific characteristics: credit insurance, which allows companies to cover themselves against the risk of non-payment of amounts invoiced to their clients, and surety insurance, through which firms can offer a guarantee of compliance with the obligations they assume in their relations with third parties. Until the mid-1970s, these types of insurance were marketed practically exclusively by the *Compañía Española de Seguros de Crédito y Caución*, whose shareholders included the *Consorcio de Compensación de Seguros* (the Insurance Compensation Consortium, which provides compulsory government catastrophic risk insurance) and some insurance companies.

Starting in the mid-1980s, the large investments made by the State in infrastructure led to a sharp increase in the purchase of surety insurance in the construction sector, as well as in the number of entities operating in this field, which resulted in a drop in premiums that caused the technical results to be very low or even negative. Credit and surety insurance in Spain went from a volume of premiums of 3.2 billion pesetas in 1980 to more than 10 billion in 1988. The improvement in the management of the branch allowed the accident rate to fall significantly in subsequent years, to 50 % or 60 % of the premiums, compared to more than 100 % in 1983. The increase in the number of entities operating in these branches resulted in a drop in rates, but also led to faster claims management and better service to the companies that took out this insurance.

The official statistics of the DGSFP (General Directorate of Insurance and Pension Funds) and those of UNESPA and ICEA, as they are structured by branch, do not provide overall data on business insurance. However, by grouping together data from the branches most closely linked to business activity, some approximate data can be compiled. According to the DGSFP, their volume of premiums at the end of 2000 was 2.7689 billion, including multi-risk insurance for industry (515.5 million) and business (331.8 million), civil liability (713.7 million), financial losses (65.2 million), transport (336.3 million), credit and surety (367.6 million) and other damage to property (438.8 million). The largest entity was MAPFRE, with a market share of 12.3 %, followed by Generali (10.4 %) and Zurich (8.6 %).

7 Multi-risk insurance

One of the most important innovations in the insurance industry was the multi-risk policy, whose generalisation in all non-life insurance branches was part of the commercial strategy of the companies, with the goal of providing a comprehensive solution to the needs of the client. Multi-risk insurance emerged at the beginning of the 1950s in the United States, where it saw strong expansion, and from there it moved to Europe. In Spain, some entities did sell these policies in the 1960s, but its generalised expansion took place in the 1970s. The first multi-risk insurance that appeared on the market was home insurance, and almost at the same time commercial insurance. Later, other types were developed, including policies for homeowners associations, hotels, workshops, offices, etc. (Marín, 1983).

It should be noted that the strong growth of these types of insurance occurred in parallel with the development of the Spanish economy itself. It is clear that the insurance companies were able to offer a product that facilitated its purchase by future clients, and that contributed decisively to increasing the level of insurance in the country. Thus, while Spanish homes were hardly insured in the 1960s, by the end of the 20th century it was common for them to have multi-risk insurance, just like businesses or homeowners associations. Although the level of insurance was already high in the large industries at the beginning of the 1960s, this new type of insurance was also successful in the industrial companies; while in 1983 the industrial multi-risk premiums were 479 million pesetas, by 1987 they exceeded 10 billion, and these multi-risk policies represented more than 50 % of the insurance of industrial establishments.

In 1989, multi-risk insurance reached second place in terms of the volume of premiums for non-life insurance branches, although it has since moved down to third place, surpassed by the health branch. The highest volume of multi-risk insurance is that of home insurance, which has been growing in line with the number of Spanish middle class employees. Multi-risk insurance premiums represented 6.5 % of total premiums in the sector in 1985, while by 1990 they reached 8 %. This demand was maintained throughout the 1990s, so that in 2000 the volume of premiums reached 2.452 billion euros. 50 % of that total corresponded to home insurance, another 20 % to industrial multi-risk, almost 15 % to commercial insurance and a little over 10 % to homeowners' associations.

8 Health insurance

This branch enjoyed remarkable growth in the second half of the 1950s and in the 1960s, with more than 150 groups of professionals who provided medical services to the public for a fixed monthly fee. The Insurance Market Regulation Act of 1954 forced these groups to become insurance companies. The services these policies offered covered benefits not included in the public health services until 1967 and reached ever broader layers of society, especially in the 1990s when their demand skyrocketed to become the third largest branch by volume of premiums, surpassed only by life and automobile insurance. Between 1987 and 1997, premium growth averaged more than 16 % per year, evidence of its success and driven by the strengthening of the middle class in Spain.

One of the reasons for the increase in demand for health insurance in the 1980s was the deterioration of Social Security services, a circumstance that was well exploited by insurance companies to boost the supply of "health policies", with a growing range of products adapted to the demand for increasingly complete and sophisticated services by consumers with growing purchasing power. This process also had the support of the unions, which demanded in many labour agreements the contracting of collective medical insurance for their members.

The growth of the health sector was also boosted by the mutual societies of the public administrations – Mutualidad General de Funcionarios Civiles del Estado (MUFACE), Instituto Social de las Fuerzas Armadas (ISFAS) and Mutualidad General Judicial (MUGEJU) – which offer their members an alternative coverage to the Public Health Service through agreements with private insurance companies, affecting two million people. For the insurance companies, these agreements have the advantage of providing them with a large mass of insured persons, but they also come with disadvantages: the companies cannot select risks, since it is the civil servants themselves who freely choose the insurance company; and the premium is capitative, that is, the insurance company receives a fixed amount per capita regardless of the number or nature of the services provided to each patient. In addition, the negotiation of the agreements is from a position of strength on the part of the mutual societies and the revisions to the premiums do not cover the increases in health care expenses derived from the proliferation of medical tests and the ageing of the insured population.

MUFACE came into being with the law of 27 June 1975 for civil servants, which established in article 19: "Health care shall be provided by the *Mutualidad General de Funcionarios Civiles del Estado*, either directly or by agreement with other public or private entities or establishments." This system of agreements represented an effort aimed at simplifying and rationalising the service, in line with the provisions of the Social Security Act of 28 December 1963, which sought uniformity throughout the state by eliminating the "not few inequalities" that existed among civil servants, whose care was covered by a large number of mutual societies offering very different services. The origin of these mutual societies was very old (some dated from the last third of the 18th century and had been maintained from 1975 on a voluntary basis). The new law established the progressive reduction of the subsidies they received, and the non-provision of subsidies for the incorporation of new civil servants. Initially, there were three companies that agreed to cover the MUFACE demand: Adeslas, Sanitas and Asisa. Adeslas, created in 1990, had the Agbar group (Aguas de Barcelona) as its largest shareholder, which made it possible for it to acquire and absorb other insurance companies in subsequent years; Asisa is a large cooperative of doctors; and Sanitas, founded in 1954, was acquired in 1989 by the British group BUPA (British United Provident Association), which boosted its growth. The health insurance sub-sector underwent a strong process of concentration in the final decades of the 20th century. Many small insurance companies specialised in this branch were absorbed by others and 79 were liquidated by the CLEA (*Comisión Liquidadora de Entidades Aseguradoras*).

9 Conclusions

In the period 1966 to 2000, the Spanish insurance sector was significantly modernised and surpassed the 5 % threshold of GDP penetration. There were clearly two stages, one from 1966 to 1985 and the other from the integration of Spain into the Common Market in 1986 to 2000. A traumatic change took place in 1966 when private insurance companies lost their right to deal in occupational accident insurance. This was offset by a spectacular increase in automobile insurance, which became the driving force behind the growth of the insurance industry in Spain. The 1973 crisis and the industrial restructuring of the 1980s boosted the development of industrial insurance with a marked effort to improve prevention, forced in part by a more complex and competitive insurance industry that had become international starting in the 1980s. The management of large risks drove the development of large insurance pools and the participation of the state was materialised with the greater presence of the Insurance Compensation Consortium.

Similarly, along with the country's economic growth, a large number of other insurance products became significantly more relevant, such as multi-risk insurance, which, as its name indicates, includes a range of coverage in one policy, with the most typical example being home insurance. However, this is also the case for life insurance and particularly private pension plans, due to the fact that there was a thriving middle class in Spain that had already taken out private health insurance, with special emphasis on the demand from public sector employees.

References

Anuario Estadístico de Accidentes (2009). Dirección General de Tráfico.

Banco Urquijo (1970). *La industria del automóvil en España*. Madrid.

Boletín de la Revista Seguros, 22 (1963), 70 (1967).

Fernandez, M. (18 September 1984). El futuro de las pensiones. *ABC* de Sevilla. p. 50.

Pinazo, F. (13 January 2000). El tráfico se ha cobrado 250.000 vidas en España en el siglo XX. *El País*.

Flores Gómez, T. (1972). *El seguro privado en la estructura económica nacional*. Madrid: Colegio Nacional de Agentes de Seguros.

Herrando Prat de la Riba, L. (1991). Evolución del sector asegurador y previsión frente al Mercado Único de 1992. *Boletín de Estudios Económicos*, 142, 107–118.

Marín Lario, J. J. (1983). *Efecto de los seguros multiriscos en el mercado*. Madrid: ICEA.

Mutua Madrileña Automovilista (1980). *La Mutua Madrileña Automovilista a través de sus primeros 50 años*. Madrid.

Pérez de Laborda, J. (1992), Memorándum sobre el contencioso de las primas únicos. *Revista Española de Seguros*, 70, 13–27.

Saéz Castillo, J. (1994). 1984–1994. Una década en los seguros industriales. In *Diez años de gestión de riesgos y de seguro en España*. Madrid: AGERS.

Seguros, special statistics issue, 1972.

Seguros, special statistics issues of 1967 and 1976.

Tortella, G., Caruana, L., García Ruiz, J. L., Manzano, A. and Pons Pons, J. (2014). *Historia del seguro en España*. Madrid: MAPFRE Foundation.

Unanimidad en la creación de fondos privados de pensiones, salvo CC.00. (27 April 1984). *La Vanguardia*. p. 67.

Usera, G. de (1970). Panorama del seguro privado español. *Hacienda Pública Española*, 5, 109–121.

Primary sources

Documents from the Board of Directors of La Unión y el Fénix Español.

Documents from the Board of Directors of La Estrella.

Miguel Muñoz Rubio and Pedro Pablo Ortúñez-Goicolea

10 The impact of First World War on neutral countries' railways: The Spanish case

Abstract The railway systems of neutral countries during First World War also felt the effects of the conflict, and the Spanish economy was among those severely impacted by the war, although there were sectors that benefitted from the opportunities which would not have otherwise existed in times of peace. These opportunities included the chance to do business and engage in exports. In contrast, other sectors were negatively affected by the conflict, which had a major impact on passenger and goods transport and affected the cost structure of railway companies. During the years of the Great War, as in other countries, whether neutral or not, inflation was running rife, which put even greater pressure on running costs. In Spain, railway companies were subject to strong regulation, and the lack of any flexibility to adapt prices to the dramatic conditions triggered by the war only served to heighten their production and institutional crisis.

1 Introduction

Probably more than any other previous circumstance, the First World War (WW1) marked a before and after in human history.

This rather generic affirmation is also true when we speak about Spanish railway companies. For these companies, the period corresponding to WW1 was one of inflection. These companies, or at least the largest of them, entered this period with relatively good results, in a relatively good health and with their business in good order. By the time the war ended, however, these companies were completely unbalanced. What is more, and what proved more serious in the long run, was the fact that the delay – by the political powers – in taking measures to reduce the impact of this conflict probably played a key role in – and largely explains – the ending of the system through which concessions were awarded for the introduction of railway services Spain, which had been first introduced in 1855 (Comín, Martín, Muñoz and Vidal, 1998).

Feinstein, Temin and Toniolo said that "in pre-1914 peacetime economies, the role of the state was extremely limited" (Feinstein, Temin & Toniolo, 2008, p. 21). This affirmation would seem justified in the case of the Spanish railways. Before WW1, this such activity predominantly lay in private hands, albeit subject to state regulation. After the war, the state began to finance the railways via subsidies which rendered the previous system of concessions unsustainable. This opened the way for a growing tendency for state intervention and increasing effective control over concessionaires. As previously noted, WW1 was a watershed for the railway companies; it marked the true "turn" of the century, much more than any specific year.

We show that although Spain remained neutral during WW1, it was very much affected by this conflict (Carreras & Tafunell, 2004). In particular, this study centres on the railway and its role as a strategic sector.[1] We also seek to demonstrate that the instability of successive Spanish governments during this period, combined with the complexity of the problems associated with the regulation of this sector, impeded the taking of any rapid action that might have helped to palliate the impact of the war. In fact, the first really important political decision related to this issue was not taken until 26 December 1918; by this time, the conflict was over and the main damage had already been done and irreparable.

Bearing this in mind, we shall proceed according to the line of argument and narrative process explained immediately below. After the first few months of global conflict, whose main effect was to cause a certain degree of paralysis in rail traffic, the Spanish railway sector experienced an increase its volume of transport. This was reflected in a greater density of traffic, a larger volume of merchandise being transported, and a change in its nature with respect to the tendencies of previous years. All of this had a major impact on infrastructure. The logical consequence of this should have been an increase in investment, but this did not occur. Instead, complaints from users about delays, the accumulation of merchandise at stations, damage to material, higher repair costs, the deterioration of infrastructure and difficulties replacing it were the final results of a number of very complicated years.

2 The economic impact of the WW1 on Spanish railway companies

Contrary to what might have been expected in a neutral country, the Spanish railway network and companies operating it were affected by WW1. The effects of the conflict were not only measured in terms of the destruction caused by the bombs or by the priority given to the use of means of transport and transport infrastructure for the mobilisation of troops, the wounded, munitions and

1 Rollo and Pires (2012), study Portugal, which although left neutrality in 1917, its territory was not affected by the war. It is a similar to Spanish case.

military logistics. The railway network also played a strategic role in neutral countries.

This was reflected in the report from the Board of Directors of the rail operator *Norte* to its shareholders when, in 1915, it presented its trading results corresponding to the first year of conflict: "The results for the period, which we explain in detail in the present Report, show – as could not be otherwise – the pernicious impact that the great crisis produced by war in Europe has had on all areas of economic activity associated with the operations of our network".[2]

In this section, we shall examine the nature of this impact on transport, networks and companies.[3] We have sought to use data relating to the two largest Spanish railway companies: *Compañía de los Ferrocarriles del Norte de España,* (hereinafter *Norte*) and *Compañía de los Ferrocarriles de Madrid a Zaragoza y Alicante* (hereinafter *MZA*) (Muñoz & Ortúñez, 2013a, b).

We have opted to present the most relevant data on railway operations corresponding to the years of conflict within a wider chronological context which provides a better view of the main tendencies. The best way to evaluate the density of traffic carried by the network was judged to be by expressing the total number of passengers or tonnes of haulage carried per kilometre. The transport tendencies for both the number of passengers and volume of haulage carried during the war years showed a sharp break with previous years. Although there had been continuous growth in business before WW1, it had not occurred at the rate experienced during and after this conflict. *Norte* and *MZA* went from approximately 500 million passengers per kilometre each to 1,500 in 1923. The turning point in the trend came during the years of the Great War, with the figure having reached 1,000 million by 1918. In the case of goods, the trend was fairly similar. The figure rose from some 900 tonnes per kilometre to 1,800 in 1923, when during the war it had stood at 1,650. This clearly reflects how the Spanish economy had changed during the war years. This increase in the figures was by no means temporary, but was to become consolidated in the years that followed.

Not surprisingly, a similar pattern can be observed for absolute volumes of transport. Figures rose from approximately nine million passengers, both in *Norte* and in *MZA*, to 19 million in 1918 and 28 million in 1923, while in the case of goods, the figure increased from five million in 1900 to 11 million in 1923, reaching 10 million during the years of the conflict.

---

2 Report of the Board of Directors of the *Norte* which was approved by the General Meeting of Shareholders held on 8 May 1915 (relating to the fiscal year 1914).

3 The source used for this, can be found in the database: http://www.docutren.com/EstadisticasHistoricas/ferroestad.asp (consulted on 30 August 2020).

When average distances and densities of traffic increase, so too does the absolute quantity of freight carried. It was only possible to deal with the increase in the total amount of freight carried combined with the increase in tonne/km and passengers/km by either by loading freight into each wagon and people into each carriage, and/or by increasing the number of wagons and/or carriages used on each trip and/or the number of trips made. However, these three options were not always technically possible. It remains to be established, though it will be difficult to do so, whether the Spanish rail network reached its saturation point at any time. This would seem to have been the case based on data for the two biggest operators in the Spanish network. The locking systems of the time, plus the widespread presence of single tracks, would certainly have limited the volume of circulation possible within the network. Acquiring more traction and transport material in the middle of the war would have been almost impossible, so the only options available would have been to accept delays or to increase the use of whatever resources were available. This no doubt resulted in a major outlay on both infrastructure and on the material required to run railway operations. In short, and as we shall see below, there was a spectacular increase in costs in all the accounting categories.

The railway companies had, however, increased their investments at the beginning of the 20th century. Both *Norte* and *MZA* substantially increased the number of locomotives and wagons that they possessed between 1911 and 1914 (with increases ranging from 13 % to 60 %). These increases were in line with those experienced in traffic. They had not, however, been able to foresee the coming of WW1; as a result, their expansion proved totally insufficient to meet the intensification of business that came with the wartime scenario.

The general tendencies in railway traffic during WW1 reflected changing situations. At first –until September 1915, according to the companies– there was a deep recession, to the extent that many wagons were surplus to need. This was followed by a period of growing, yet covered, demand that lasted until August 1916. This was when the period of crisis and abnormal demand began, and when there were not enough wagons to meet day-to-day demand. On top of these difficulties came those occasioned by the ship building companies and their preference to cover the demand for tonnage of the warring factions.

All of the railway operators agreed on the tremendous importance that cabotage had for Spain.[4] They thought that the increase in freight charges during the war years, as a consequence to the lack of available tonnage, contributed

4 Compare with Frax and Matilla (1988); according to their data, between 1860 and 1920, maritime cabotage traffic represented 12 % of the total national traffic traded by

to the disappearance of shipping from Spanish ports as it went in search of higher earnings elsewhere, while that which stayed also imposed extraordinary increases in its prices. This contributed to the overloading of the railway network as the general public found itself faced with the obligation of finding overland transport, with this offering the cheapest and safest way to travel in contrast to the risks inherent to maritime expeditions. The state had tried to dictate certain measures in an attempt to remedy the situation, which gave veracity to the arguments of the railway companies, but the measures applied were ineffective. The Royal Decree of 20 October 1917 made it obligatory for port to port traffic that exceeded 500 kg in weight to be carried by maritime transport. However, the prices that were applied were too high and therefore the public tended to fraction the freight loads sent. This had the end result of making the measure ineffective; what is more, it caused the number of shipments made by train to multiply and thereby increased the workload at the railway stations. If the cabotage system had worked normally, traffic would not have been displaced and the railway network would have become less congested. These problems explain the previously cited increase in the density of rail traffic.

Together with this, there were difficulties obtaining coal supplies, at both the national level – due to transport problems – and internationally – because it was not exported. The poor quality of Spain's own coal resulted in more breakdown incidents affecting locomotives, which also needed to consume more coal. According to Maristany, coal consumption by the trains operated by *MZA* increased from 15 kg/km before WW1 to 22 kg/km during the war.[5]

In the middle of what Spain's rail operators denounced as the excessive demands placed on the system as a result of WW1, other economic sectors took advantage of the situation to increase their profits. This generated an inflationist trend in the face of which the railway companies saw their costs appreciably increase. As a result, despite the increase in rail traffic, their operating results stagnated, mainly due to the impossibility of increasing their fares and

---

rail. Also consult Frax (1981); according to calculations carried out by these sources, it can be deduced that in the years corresponding to WW1, based on the total volume of merchandise transported by both rail and cabotage, 24.75 % was transported by cabotage; in contrast, in the years prior to the war (1908–1913), this same value was 29.46 %. In other words, the descent in the traffic of merchandise in the form of cabotage suffered by the railway companies during the WW1 was real.

5 Interview with Eduardo Maristany (manager of *MZA*) in *El Sol*, Friday, 13 December 1918, year II, nº 376, p. 4.

freight rates.[6] This question of pricing became one of the key issues amongst the complaints made by the railway companies.

The rail operator *Norte* considered that the exceptional situation had arisen as the result of a perfect storm of accumulated factors. Amongst these, it is possible to identify, in first place, the brusque and significant increase in the demand for all types of transport associated with a number of good harvests and the intensification of Spain's industrial production in response to the demands of WW1; the latter resulted in a series of large and urgent orders. Secondly, *Norte* underlined the impact that the frequent strikes by railway workers had on its operations during these years; the associated lack of capacity to deal with the intense traffic produced largely explains why the lines and stations had become so congested.

Those responsible for *MZA* put the emphasis on the fact that – as previously noted – before the war, they had had sufficient material to carry out their work, but had still invested. In fact, between 1910 and 1914, *MZA* received 176 locomotives, 574 carriages and 7,788 wagons and goods vans. Furthermore, between 1901 and 1914, the company had also invested fixed material to the tune of 104 million pesetas. However, all of this effort proved insufficient due to the increase in traffic that followed the first months of WW1. Between 1913 and 1917, the number of tonnes of merchandise transported increased by approximately 25 %.[7] This was a disproportionate increase, but apparently conjunctural and completely unexpected. The lack of available transport resources in this situation could not be exclusively blamed on the railway companies; they had previously carried out investment and were suddenly faced – as if that were little – with the almost impossible task of acquiring more material.

The locomotives were not constructed in Spain and it became increasingly difficult to obtain them from abroad. As far as other types of railway material and rolling stock were concerned, Spanish manufacturers encountered great difficulties in obtaining certain components, while the rate at which the material depreciated became more and more of an issue than its reparation and

---

6 *Archivo Histórico Ferroviario* (hereinafter AHF) C/2/4 (3), July 1920. The economic data will be studied in greater detail later. For the moment, they have been used to better define the question that we are currently examining, which refers exclusively to *MZA*. Between 1900 and 1919 the company's increase in income was 158 %, but its costs rose by 365 %. Over the same period, its coefficient of exploitation increased from 40 % to 72 %.

7 AHF C/2/1 "The current transport crisis: data requested from the *Dirección General de Obras Públicas* (*General Directorate for Public Works*)". 21 December 1917.

substitution, due to its more intensive use. Thus, the increase in demand for transport produced by the war was accompanied by a reduction in the material available. It is also necessary to bear in mind the amount of broken material. This became more and more abundant as the war dragged on. This is also included in the statistics, even though it was never used, because it was not written off either.

All of these issues provide us with a better understanding of the conjuncture that WW1 brought with it and help to explain some of the problems that mortally wounded Spain's railway operators. Artola observed that the crisis associated with the war had dynamited the suppositions on which the Spanish railway system had been based (Artola, 1978, p. 417). And what were these suppositions? They would initially seem rather simple to deduce: first and foremost, that low operating costs would allow favourable coefficients of exploitation and that the demand for railway transport would reflect the lack of dynamism in the rest of the country's productive sectors at the time. This would explain the low levels of income generated by the exploitation of their activity. However, the war marked a complete change from that previous situation and the existing regulation proved an obstacle to increasing income in line with the increase in expenditure resulting from the increase in demand and in the costs of operation. There was certainly an incapacity to satisfy all of the demand for transport that was generated and this became particularly evident from August 1916 onwards, when failings in the wagon stock began to be detected on a day-to-day basis.

As we said before, the conjuncture of the increase and intensification in the traffic was not interrupted with the end of WW1. In reality, the war not supposed a change of cycle for the railway companies, but also for the whole of the Spanish economy, which also found itself immersed in what was the start of a process of structural change (Carreras & Tafunell, 2004) and (Carreras, Prados and Rosés, 2005). It was, in fact, the whole period that caused this imbalance in the railway business. The catalyst was WW1, but there was no subsequent return to "normality"; the regulatory system that had been designed between 1844 and 1855 ceased to serve its purpose.

WW1 favoured the making of quick profits in many sectors. This was a consequence of an unprecedented increase in demand and new opportunities to export that had previously been almost unknown to the majority of Spain's productive sector. This unbridled activity called for much greater transport capacity than had previously been required. The demand for rail transport also increased because it was cheap. However, both of these circumstances ran contrary to the possibilities and interests of the country's railway operators.

While practically all other sectors were making money, these companies saw their maximum fares and freight rates frozen at a time of alarming increases in production costs. The cost structure of the largest Spanish railway companies was profoundly modified by the war, and especially after 1915. With the increase in demand, there was a notable intensification in the use of the infrastructure and material. This was accompanied by increases in the prices of all the sector's inputs, including labour costs. This spectacular increase in costs gave rise to a definitive change in the system of railway concessions, with respect to how it had previously worked. Even so, it was not until 1923 that a new regulatory system was introduced. For *MZA*, the company for which we have some of the most precise details, comparing prices with those of 1913, it is evident that by 1920 the cost of rails had increased by 201 %; in 1919, that of coal had increased by 322 %, creosote by 428 %, smoke tubes by 570 %, wheel rims by 857 % and ingots of tin by 978 %. The cost of staff, which in 1913 was 36 million pesetas, had risen to 106.5 million pesetas in 1922. Similar increases occurred in the cost of other materials which we have omitted.[8] Very similar increases affected the rest of the railway companies. The data which we have for the French company *Nord*, present similar proportions. In 1913, the price to *Nord* of a tonne of coal was 17.50 francs, as opposed to 47.50 francs in 1916 and an average of 198 francs in 1920. Rails received from the USA cost 490 francs instead of 186 in 1913, while sleepers imported from Brazil passed from costing 5 francs before WW1 to 8 francs in 1916. By 1919, the prices of all these materials had suffered even greater increases: bars of low-carbon steel increased in price by 640 % and ingots of iron by 765 % (Caron, 1973).

To finish this description of the desolate panorama that WW1 bequeathed to the concessionaires of the Spanish railway system, it is necessary to look at what happened in terms of their results (which we will do through net income, Tab. 1). Although something has already been mentioned relating to the growth in demand and increase in costs, this was not accompanied by any modification to the fare and freight rate system. The results of this set of special circumstances proved disastrous for the rail operators. Only *MZA* managed to make a profit in each financial year of its operation. This includes taking into consideration the

8 These data were obtained from AHF C/71/160 *Estudio de Rafael Coderch sobre las primas supletorias de gestión de las explotaciones ferroviarias. Datos estadísticos de la explotación de MZA*. (Study by Rafael Coderch of the supplementary premiums associated with the management of railway operations: statistical data on the operations of *MZA*) June 1921.

financing costs. The collapse hit the two largest companies from 1916 onwards; this was the year in which the effects of the increases in traffic and operating costs were most noted. In fact, the *Ministro de Fomento* (Minister for Public Works) qualified 1917 as "inadmissibly disastrous".[9] At the start of the 20th century, *Norte* and *MZA* showed positive net income, albeit only just. There was a general trend of growth and improved results until 1913. In 1912, which was the best year in terms of results, *MZA* recorded a profit of 29 million pesetas, and *Norte* close to 15 million. By the end of WW1, *Norte*'s losses were close to 20 million while *MZA* was returning a profit of just three million. The "inadmissibly disastrous" results recorded during the war were due to the inflexibility to increase income while costs were spiralling. This is the only explanation since, as we have seen, passenger and freight transport numbers were growing.

The companies only managed to escape from this abyss when the government approved an increase of 15 % in the fares and freight rates which were applied to passengers and merchandise at the time. This measure was taken on 26 December 1918 and enabled a return to the results of previous years.

3 Institutional instability

Relevant questions would include: What did the political powers do in the meantime? and, what measures were taken in response to this set of problems and their impact on users? The answers are provided by the facts, and these are very simple: no measures were taken by the Spanish governments of the time to help the railway sector. Furthermore, nothing was done to try to solve the underlying problems associated with the existing system of regulation, such as those related to the rescuing of concessions. Nor was anything of a more specific nature done which, through an adjustment of fares and freight rates, for example, could have reduced the impact of the conjuncture of WW1 on the companies. The intervention of the state during this period was limited to a single measure, which was adopted on 26 December 1918; in other words, when the war had already finished.

There were 18 different governments and 23 different Ministers of Public Works in Spain between 27 September 1913 and 15 September 1923 (Artola, 1993). If we were to reduce this period to dates closes to the beginning and ending of WW1: between the end of 1913 and November 1918, there were 10 governments

9 Meeting held on 5 September 1918 between the minister and representatives from Spain's four main railway companies. AHF C/3/27 (2).

Tab. 1. Net income *MZA* and *Norte*. (Millions of pesetas at current value)

YEARS	MZA	NORTE
1900	4.4	0.0
1901	5.1	0.2
1902	8.9	0.9
1903	5.9	2.1
1904	3.0	-3.5
1905	4.3	-0.8
1906	12.4	-0.4
1907	14.3	9.8
1908	15.2	9.0
1909	17.4	8.9
1910	20.6	12.5
1911	20.8	14.0
1912	28.6	14.9
1913	23.2	13.6
1914	17.1	8.2
1915	21.3	11.1
1916	20.4	10.6
1917	15.5	-1.2
1918	2.7	-19.9
1919	16.7	9.6
1920	17.0	22.1
1921	18.1	30.7
1922	21.5	23.0
1923	22.1	21.4

Source: https://www.docutren.com/EstadisticasHistoricas/Ferroestad/norte05.asp and https://www.docutren.com/EstadisticasHistoricas/Ferroestad/mza05.asp

(approximately 2 per year) and 8 ministers of different profiles (more than one and a half per year). These figures reveal a period of great political instability. In fact, these five years constitute one of the periods of greatest instability in the contemporary history of Spain (Jordana & Ramió, 2005). Negotiating, discussing, studying measures, getting to know the sector and the situation of the companies, became an almost impossible task for such volatile governments.

At the same time, this situation of instability was very difficult to manage for those operating the concessions, as the person with whom they had to deal changed too often and with them the criteria that had to be followed.

Complying with the requirements and characters of one group and the other was not, therefore, an easy task. And that is to say nothing of the ministers themselves: by the time they wanted to deal with a certain problem, there had already been a change of government.

Perhaps the most solid attempt to deal with the sector and change the existing regulation made during these years was that developed by Francisco Cambó, who was Minister for Public Works (The Ministry of Public Works was the one responsible for railways) between March and November 1918, during the period known as the National government, which was presided over by Antonio Maura.

Cambó understood that the problems that affected the concession-holding companies were, on the one hand, different in function of the size of each company and, on the other, of two types: permanent and conjunctural. There was not only the crisis caused by WW1; two important errors had also been made. These were: having considered the railways to be a private business rather than a public service; and having thought that once the initial investments had been made and the lines constructed, the chapter relating to investment could be closed. As we have already mentioned, although this was true, by the end of the war, the Spanish economy had been transformed and the traffic did not fall back to the low pre-war levels.

Immediately after assuming the role of Minister for Public Works, and with these questions clearly in mind, Cambó began to draw up the bases for a project of *Ordenación ferroviaria* (Railway organisation). These plans were drafted many times, and up to ten different pre-projects were prepared during Cambó's eight months in front of the Ministry. It is possible to know this project quite well because it is well-documented in the archives of the company *MZA*. The minister informed the companies, frequently met their representatives, and tried to introduce solutions into the pre-projects which had previously been discussed and agreed with them.

The first thing that Cambó proposed was the need to consider that whatever action he might take should begin with the early rescue of all the concessions that were then in the hands of the railway companies. This was an enormous task, because it first required an agreement as to how to establish the amount of time that still legally corresponded to the concessionaires for the exploitation of the business. The concessions had been granted on different dates and also with different expiry periods and there were even some, for example, without any end date. Once this had been achieved, it would then be necessary to establish the payment procedure and the quantity of money that should be paid for the rescue. The legislation in force at the time had established one: it should be based on the average number of products obtained during the five years preceding the moment of rescue. However, given the fact that the years previous to the rescue had corresponded to such an anomalous period of operation, because of the war, it was agreed that these should not be the years used for such calculations. It can be seen that it was no easy task to reach the final goal and even less so in the situation of recognised political instability corresponding to the period.

In fact, Cambó noted, in a book that he wrote some years later, in reference to his eight months as Minister for Public Works, that when he realised that the government was going to be incapable of resolving the problem, he decided to adopt a series of partial solutions. If the project should not be approved, these were to remain as a present reality which would make it possible to resolve the conjunctural problem and they would improve the situation of the companies when the rescue occurred. However, he did not have time to implement either one thing or the other.

Cambó had manifested on repeated occasions – and even when he did not form part of the government – his preference for the state to directly intervene in the railways by rescuing the concessions. That rescue was to carry with it first a rational geographical grouping of the railway network and then the subsequent leasing of the operations of the rescued lines to various different private companies which would then operate them on behalf of the state, via a participation in the proceeds.

He took the trouble to insist – both at conferences and in writing – on the difference that existed between a rescue and direct administration by the state. A rescue was necessary to solve the difficulties facing the railway at that time. There was a need: to extend the amount of doubletrack; to increase the total number of kilometres in the network, above all in those areas where a private company would never have risked its capital; to resolve the problems that the railway began to cause in the major urban centres; and to construct new stations and loading platforms, etc. . . However, all of this did not imply that, at a later date, it should be the state which would appoint the staff, establish the timetables, or determine the trains, their routes, their commercial agreements, etc. . . . in short, that would carry out daily operations.

As can be appreciated, the idea of the minister with respect to the railway was that the state should carry out a radical intervention to sanitise and reorganise the sector and then return it to private companies with them operating as tenants. The rescue was initially to be limited to the four main companies. Once their concessions had been restructured, based on geographical criteria, four new networks would emerge, one of which would be directly exploited by the state so that it could serve as a point of reference and help to keep the other three tenancies in line. There would therefore always be a point of comparison and a network to look to.

As carrying out this plan would be slow, and in order to try to escape from the most immediate difficulties that the companies were facing, Cambó asked the Boards of Directors of the four largest companies to submit their proposals for remedying the situation. On 2 September 1917, they sent a letter in which they requested an increase of 25 % in all of the fares and freight rates in force at the time.[10] After various negotiations with the companies, the minister prepared a draft bill in which increases of up to 15 % in the maximum fares and freight rates were authorised. Note that the increase proposed by the companies would have affected current fares and freight rates, with some of these being below the maximum values authorised by the conditions of the concession. And it was precisely the legal maximum values that the increase proposed by the minister affected. This project was passed by the Senate, but it was left stranded in the Congress by the fall of the Maura government. It proved very controversial and caused heated discussion in both its passage through parliament and before public opinion.

The next government, which was in office outside the period studied in this work, was presided over by García Prieto. It was in power for barely a month and then, on 5th December, the Count of Romanones presided over a new cabinet in which the Marquis of Cortina took charge of Public Works. Following the suspension of the parliamentary sessions on 15th December, the new minister passed the Royal Decree of 26 December 1918, which approved an increase of 15 % in the fares and freight rates applicable at the time; in other words, there was a reduction in real terms with respect to the proposal previously made by Cambó. The authorisation for this increase should have ended on 11 November 1921, but it was subsequently extended. However, almost immediately, it proved insufficient for the companies due, above all, to the improvements in terms that they had conceded to their workers. In 1919, the increases in salary that were awarded ranged from 20 % to 35 %, plus an extraordinary amount added to one monthly payment[11] and to the continuous increases in the prices of raw materials. As a result, the increases in resources obtained following the increase in fares and freight rates were not used to intensify the transport capacity of the railway service. The railway companies were particularly affected by the Royal

10 AHF C/98/218.

11 Junta Superior de Ferrocarriles (*Higher Board of Railways*) (1940), vol. I, p. 16 and that discussed in the previous pages.

Decree of 3 April 1919, which established an eight-hour working day for all tasks and, as a consequence, forced them to increase the size of their workforces.

Cambó did not achieve his objectives and those who came after him sidestepped the problems of the large companies with an urgent, but insufficient, solution to the problems which, in 1924, were destined to finally bring to an end the regulatory regime of the Spanish railway sector that had been established in the middle of the 19th century (Muñoz Rubio, 1995).

4 Conclusions

Studying a regulated strategic sector at the time of a special conjuncture, such as a period of war, allows us to draw several conclusions and lessons which history can share with the present.

1. WW1 had a profound effect on the Spanish railway sector. This had been regulated in another time and for other circumstances times and could not deal with either the increase in traffic or with the operating costs in an autonomous way.
2. It was necessary to bolster the income for the companies, but this required action by the state. Only the State could authorise any increase in what companies charged. When it became clear that income was insufficient, government weakness prevented it from acting without delay. It has been shown that companies' transport activity actually grew during this period, although their results did not. It was circumstances outside the concessionaires' control that led to these difficulties in terms of viability. Amongst these, we have highlighted the impact of inflation, although other factors were also involved: labour conflicts, difficulties maintaining the pace of investments, and so on.
3. The state, as regulator, responded late and often insufficiently. It is true that managing the conjuncture of a war, even in a neutral country, was not an easy task, but the division of parliament into a series of small groups and the instability of the government made it impossible to take quick decisions. Institutional stability and good public policies form the basis for the normal development of economic activities. If an extraordinarily difficult situation, in this case the Great War, is not able to bring people together to overcome differences and so solve the serious problems affecting both companies and citizens alike, then such problems can eventually lead to even greater difficulties.
4. As well as being a fundamental factor for explaining structural change in the Spanish economy and its growth during the 1920s, WW1 also explains

the change in cycle that Spanish rail transport underwent; this involved an important and sustained increase in the traffic of both passengers and freight. Said increase continued until the early 1930s, when transport figures began to reflect the decline in the Spanish economy and, gradually, that of the railway system itself.

5. The existing regulation failed to offer a good system for establishing fares and freight rates or a good system of incentives to ensure that when the dates for line rescue arrived, the state would receive the infrastructure and transport material in good condition. Fare and freight rate controls, but with a greater degree of flexibility in the way they are established, would seem necessary characteristics for a good system of regulation. For this reason, when the regulator is the state, it is necessary for it to have an autonomous, independent, control body that not only supervises, but also warns of, the difficulties that companies subject to its regulation may face. This body must even have the capacity to adopt extraordinary response procedures for special circumstances, which must later be approved by the legislature. In this way, it would be possible to prevent a paralysed legislature delaying strategic decisions.

References

Artola, M. (1978). La acción del Estado, in M. Artola (dir.), *Los ferrocarriles en España (1844–1943)*, vol. 1 (pp. 341–454). Madrid: Banco de España.

Cambó, F. (dir.) (1918–1921). *Elementos para el estudio del problema ferroviario en España*. Madrid: Artes Gráficas Mateu.

Caron, F. (1973). *Histoire de l'exploitation d'un grand résau. La Compagnie de chemin de fer du Nord*. Paris: École Pratique des Hautes Études.

Carreras, A. & Tafunell, X. (2004). *Historia Económica de la España Contemporánea*. Barcelona: Crítica.

Carreras, A. & Tafunell, X. (coords.) (2005). *Estadísticas Históricas de España: siglos XIX y XX*. Bilbao: Fundación BBVA.

Carreras, A., Prados de la Escosura, L., & Rosés, J. (2005). Renta y Riqueza, in A. Carreras & X. Tafunell (coords.), *Estadísticas Históricas de España: siglos XIX y XX*, vol. 3 (pp. 1297–1376). Bilbao: Fundación BBVA.

Comín, F., Martín, P., Muñoz, M. & Vidal, J. (1998). *150 Años de Historia de los Ferrocarriles Españoles*. Madrid: Fundación de los Ferrocarriles Españoles.

Feinstein, C. H., Temin, P. & Toniolo, G. (2008). *The world economy between the world wars*. Oxford, University Press.

Frax Rosales, E. (1981). *Puertos y comercio de cabotaje, 1857–1934*. Madrid: Banco de España.

Frax Rosales, E. & Matilla Quiza, Mª. J. (1988). Transporte, Comercio y Comunicaciones, in M. Artola (ed.), *Enciclopedia de Historia de España. Economía y Sociedad* (pp. 191–263). Madrid: Alianza Editorial.

Jordana, J. & Ramió, C. (2005). Gobierno y Administración, in A. Carreras & X. Tafunell (coords.), *Estadísticas Históricas de España: siglos XIX y XX*, vol. 3 (pp. 973–1.026). Bilbao: Fundación BBVA.

Junta Superior de Ferrocarriles (1940). *Antecedentes y Datos para el estudio del problema ferroviario*. 6 volumes. Madrid.

Muñoz, M. (1995). *Renfe (1941–1991). Medio siglo de ferrocarril público*. Madrid: Ediciones Luna.

Muñoz, M., Sanz, J., & Vidal, J. (1999). *Siglo y medio del ferrocarril en España, 1848–1998. Economía, Industria y Sociedad,* Madrid: Fundación de los Ferrocarriles Españoles.

Muñoz, M. & Ortúñez, P. P. (2013a). Los transportes y las comunicaciones: la transición de modelos tradicionales a industriales, in A. González Enciso & J. M. Matés (eds.), *Historia Económica de España* (pp. 209–241). Barcelona: Ariel.

Muñoz, M. & Ortúñez, P. P. (2013b). Los transportes y las comunicaciones en la España de la primera modernidad, in A. González Enciso & J. M. Matés (eds.), *Historia Económica de España* (pp. 551–591). Barcelona: Ariel.

Rollo, M. F. & Pires, A. P. (2012). Transports under the First World War: the case of Portuguese railways, in A. McCants, et al. (eds.), *Railroads in historical context: constructions, cost and consequences*, vol. 2 (pp. 139–150). V. N. Gaia: Inovatec.

Pablo Alonso Villa and Pedro Pablo Ortúñez-Goicolea

11 Car manufacturers in Spain and Portugal during the second half of the 20th century. A comparative historical perspective

Abstract This chapter analyses the historical evolution of automobile manufacturers in two neighbouring countries that have close ties; Spain and Portugal. In both cases, although on a different scale, this sector is one of the main driving forces of the national economy. Compared to other European countries, the automobile industry in Spain and Portugal had scarcely got off the ground by the mid-20th century, since when it has followed quite different paths in the two countries. This work tries to determine the characteristics of car manufacturers in each country, and the consequences, in terms of expansion, to emerge from the strategies adopted.

1 Introduction

If it was the railways which revolutionised transport in the 19th century, it was the motorcar which took over this mantle in the 20th, with this sector becoming one of the mainstays of European and North-American industrialisation in the 20th century. It was the United States – through *Ford*, *General Motors* (*GM*) and *Chrysler* – who led production of this new means of transport throughout the 20th century, although the country's position came to be less dominant after the 1950s, when vehicle production began to increase sharply in the main western European nations – France, the United Kingdom, Germany, and Italy – as well as in Japan. It was after this point that these countries entered the era of mass production (García-Ruiz, 2001), through manufacturers such as *Volkswagen*, *Renault*, *Citroen*, *Peugeot*, *Morris*, *Austin*, *FIAT*, *Toyota*, and *Nissan*.

In the expansion and internationalisation strategy of multinational manufacturers it was common practice to make direct investments in other countries and to sell manufacturing licences. By the mid-1960s, the brands of the seven leading manufacturing countries were assembled at 350 plants spread over 53 countries. Twenty years later, these figures had risen to 620 and 90, respectively, with developing countries playing a key role in attracting these investments. According to Biggart and Guillén (1999), the idea of having an automobile industry proved attractive to these countries for a number of reasons. Automobiles were expensive items and importing them meant that large amounts of currency were leaving the country. Moreover, they were essential to creating wide communication and transport networks, added to which their manufacture entails major spin-off effects towards other industries, thus spurring the country's industrial development. Furthermore, they were a symbol of success and economic prosperity.

Countries that were still in the early stages of industrial development such as South Korea, Taiwan, Argentina, Brazil, Spain or Portugal provided the location for major multinational manufacturers. This chapter aims to draw a comparison between the leading manufacturers who have operated in two peripheral countries in western Europe; Portugal and Spain. In the mid-20th century, the two countries were still developing and evidenced certain similarities in terms of their political regime as well as in the protection which the country's industrial policy afforded to their economies. The pages that follow will show how the size of the domestic market, the industrial policy in place, the development of their subsidiary industries and the investment strategies of overseas manufacturers are the main factors which account for the different dynamic followed by car manufacturers in these two Iberian countries.

2 1950–1973: The rise of the sector in Spain and the start of production in Portugal

The 1950s heralded a turning point in the history of the automobile sector in Spain. Thanks to two national manufacturers – *SEAT* and *FASA* – mass production of passenger cars began. However, the same cannot be said of Portugal, since it was not until the 1960s, following the protectionist industrial policy implemented by the government, that vehicle assembly began on a permanent scale, and it was not until the 1980s, with the *Renault Project*, that actual manufacturing commenced.

The shortage of vehicles in Spain in the 1950s and the protectionism towards the domestic market – coupled with the fact that *Ford* and *GM* had quit the market – created the ideal conditions for the appearance of business initiatives (Catalan, 2000). Said decade saw the emergence of the two main car manufacturers Spain has been home to; *SEAT* and *FASA*. The setting up of the former in 1950 was due to private interests as well as to those of the Spanish government who, through the National Institute for Industry (INI), held a major stake in the company's social capital. The agreement involved the Italian company *FIAT*, who bought 6 % of the social capital and awarded the manufacturing licence, thereby providing its *know-how*. The aim was to produce 10,000 units of the 1.400 model each year. The decision was made to set up the factory in Barcelona thanks to the area's good communication by sea and its industrial structure, which meant that local suppliers could be used to provide certain parts (Catalan, 2000). The facilities were opened in 1953 and by 1956 over 10,000 units were being produced.

For authors such as Catalan (2000), *SEAT's* success was in part due to the protectionist market policy and in part was the result of the company's business strategy. *SEAT* could draw on the technology of one of the leading European manufacturers of the period, *FIAT*. In addition, the decision was taken to set up in Barcelona, where the Marshallian type economies that could be benefitted from were present. Initially, the Barcelona factory was mainly charged with assembling the parts from Turin – to which certain nationally manufactured parts were added so as meet the nationalisation quotas imposed by law – although the factory quickly shifted to full-scale vehicle production. To achieve this, it drew on a large group of approximately 650 national firms that were able to meet the great demand for parts and components. In the early 1960s, the value of the parts imported accounted for only 1 % of the vehicle's final sale price. The plant was in a position to easily meet the requirement of 90 % domestic production of the components included and which the ministerial order of July 1964 had imposed on foreign manufacturers operating in Spain.

Equally decisive for the success achieved was the company's business strategy of manufacturing a cheaper vehicle than the 1400, namely the 600, which was far more accessible for a Spanish market that was still subject to low levels of income at the time. Nevertheless, as the tastes – and the disposable income – of Spaniards changed, the range of models available expanded. Better quality and better priced vehicles thus began to appear on the market. The company's production figures speak for themselves; rising from just over 1,300 vehicles in the first year of production to over 31,000 by 1960 and reaching 280,280 by 1970. These figures meant that they led the way in sales in the domestic market until the mid-1970s, with over 50 % of the total.

The early 1950s also saw the creation in Valladolid – an inland city with a rich industrial history – of *FASA*, with 100 % local capital, to manufacture *Renault* vehicles. The company remained in Spanish hands until the mid-1960s when *Renault* acquired a major stake in the capital (49.9 %) and took over control of the company, which is when the company changed its name to *FASA-Renault*. As did *SEAT*, it initially assembled the parts brought in by rail from France, to which it added some parts provided by local suppliers. However, it was soon to start manufacturing the high value components of the vehicle – engines and gearboxes – as well as bodywork and chassis. To achieve this, it undertook a vertical integration strategy, creating two mechanised subsidiary companies in the mid-1960s, – *FAMESA* and *FACSA* – and purchasing a third, *ISA*, for the gearboxes. The production capacity of these subsidiary companies enabled it to supply the assembly lines of *FASA-Renault* as well as export to *Renault* itself (Fernández de Sevilla, 2013). By the mid-1960s, the level of nationalisation of all the models manufactured in Valladolid stood at around the 90 % demanded by the government as of 1964.

The first model to be launched by the company was the 4CV in 1953. By 1958, the year in which production of the model ceased, output had reached 6,800 units. The number of models manufactured increased during the 1960s. During those ten years, five new models of different quality and price came onto the market, and by 1970 the total number of vehicles manufactured in Valladolid had reached 98,720. This figure was still some way off what *SEAT* was producing, but it did enable the company to gain a foothold in the market during the 1960s and first half of the 1970s, with its share ranging between 20 % and 25 % (Fernández de Sevilla, 2013, pp. 39–50).

The range of Spanish vehicles available was completed with the appearance of a further two manufacturers, both of passenger cars as well as commercial vans and trucks. The main passenger car manufacturers were *Citröen Hispania*, who opened a factory in Vigo in 1957 to produce not only cars but also industrial vehicles, and *Munguía Industrial*, who set up in Bilbao in the same year to manufacture the so-called Goggomobil under German licence. Ten years later an agreement between *AUTHI* and *BMC* was reached to manufacture the Morris 1100, which had become very popular in the British market, at Landaben (Navarra).

Prominent in the field of industrial vehicles were the public company *ENASA* (through its Pegaso brand), *Motor Ibérica* (Ebro), and *Barreiros* (own brand). This latter company, founded in 1954, and specialising in the manufacture of trucks with its own engines, reached an agreement in 1963 with *Chrysler* to manufacture its models in Spain. Yet there were more, such as *IMOSA*, set up in 1950, who manufactured *DKW* vans under a German licence, *Auto Union*. 1954 saw the emergence in Jaen of *Metalúrgica de Santa Ana*, who built engines and jeeps under licence from *Rover*. In the latter half of the 1950s, a further two truck and van manufacturers appeared; *FADISA* (in 1956 under licence from *Alfa Romero*) in Avila, and *SAVA*, in Valladolid in 1957, using British technology from BMC (Catalan, 2000; García-Ruiz, 2001).

The protectionist industrial policy which, in addition to demanding a specific quota of national parts, imposed excise duties on imported vehicles, favoured the emergence and development of business initiatives in the sector.

The number of car registrations grew substantially as Spaniards' income rose, increasing from 2,545 passenger cars registered in 1950 to over 50,000 in 1960 and to almost 400,000 by 1970. Unlike what had occurred in the first half of the 20th century, when the number of vehicles had mainly consisted of imports, during this period it was domestically produced cars, which included local parts, that met the growing demand for vehicles. Between 1960 and 1973, imports accounted for an average of only 6.8 % of all car sales, and 7.8 % of industrial vehicles.[1] Moreover, in 1971 exports of vehicles outstripped imports for the first time, evidencing a major shift in the comparative advantage of the Spanish car industry (Catalan, 2000, p. 137).

In Portugal, the car industry did not emerge until the 1960s, and up until the 1980s was characterised by assembly rather than by manufacture. The required boost, which arrived late and was very limited in scale, came through the second incentive programme, the *Plan de Fomento* (1959–1964). Prior to this, in the 1950s, the opening up of the Portuguese economy after the end of the second World War had led to the appearance of local initiatives aimed at cooperating – under technological licences – with European manufacturers. Some were of great interest and promised success, yet met with fierce opposition from the *lobby* of importers and dealers,[2] who pressured the government relentlessly to deny permission to purchase overseas licences. This was the case with firms such as *SOREFAME* and *Produtos Estrela* (*PE*). A further two projects, perhaps those of greatest relevance, were evaluated and finally rejected by the Portuguese authorities in the second half of the 1950s. One of them, headed by the businessman António Champalimaud, sought to establish an agreement with *SIMCA*, similar to the one signed by the Spanish firm *SEAT* with *FIAT*. Yet, once again the pressure from the *lobby* of importers led to the project being abandoned. The other, *Indústria Portuguese de Automóveis*, sought to manufacture a small utility vehicle using the combined technology of *Astra* and *British Anzani*. As happened with the previous ventures, they were denied authorisation to manufacture (Barros & Sousa, 2007), and there is evidence of only one company (*UTIC*) having been able to assemble vehicles in the late 1950s.

On the demand side, the 1950s witnessed a sharp rise in the number of car registrations, almost all of which were imported. The number of vehicles, both

1 Figures calculated using data on vehicle registrations and imports in Spain from García-Ruiz (2001).

2 These made up the Guild of Importers, Agents and Dealers of Automobiles and Accessories, which dates back to the 1930s (Sousa, 2005).

in terms of passenger cars as well as commercial vehicles, registered in 1960 was twice that of 1950. On average, during this period, approximately 16,180 vehicles were registered each year, such that the total number in the country rose from 89,254 to over 216,000.[3]

It was not until the 1960s that Portugal joined the general trend of other developing countries by creating a national automobile industry. To achieve this, the government put through a law regulating the sector. December 1961 saw the approval of the "law on assembly", which formed part of the II *Plan de Fomento* (Simões, 2000). As its very name suggests, this law was designed to favour assembly-related activities, not manufacturing, which proved to be the case.

The new phase that commenced after the approval of this law was characterised by a policy of import substitution which, up to that point, had accounted for the number of cars on the roads in Portugal. The aim was twofold: on the one hand, to create a new industry of vital importance to the country's economic development, and on the other, to improve the balance of payments by producing in the country itself goods which up until that point had been imported. The "law on assembly" restricted vehicle imports after 1963, meaning that only 75 units per year and per brand could be purchased from overseas. Above this limit, only *CKD* could be imported, to which 15 % of national components had to be added to the value of the vehicle. This represented a very low level of nationalisation compared to what was established, for instance, in Spain. The decree also established a percentage of local content (60 %) after which vehicles were deemed to have been manufactured domestically, a figure that was not reached until the 1990s. In late 1967, a new provision increased the required rate of nationalisation slightly to 20 % in 1968, and 25 % after 1969.

Given this regulatory framework, many international manufacturers wanted to remain in the Portuguese market which, despite only being small, was attractive given its low levels of motorisation – 53 inhabitants per passenger vehicle in 1961, a figure way below other countries in western Europe, except Spain and Greece[4] – and which showed good prospects for growth in demand

3 Figures calculated using the information on registrations from Portuguese annual statistics.

4 Data taken from Guerra (1990). During the first third of the 20th century, levels of motorisation in Spain were higher than those of Portugal. However, after the Civil War and the Second World War, Portugal narrowed the gap, and in fact overtook Spain until the late 1960s.

(Guerra, 1990).[5] These manufacturers had two ways of entering the Portuguese market: one was to make direct investments by creating subsidiary production companies, sometimes with a local capital stake, which would assemble the *CKD* produced in their home countries; the other was to grant manufacturing licences to Portuguese companies.

In 1965, the Portuguese automobile industry consisted of 18 assemblers, most of whom had set up after 1963. Six firms – *Ford Lusitana, Lda., General Motors de Portugal, Lda., FIAT Auto Portuguesa, S.A., Indústrias Lusitanas Renault, S.A., Citroën Lusitana, S.A.*, and *IMA* – were subsidiaries of overseas manufacturers or were partly owned by them.[6] The first three were mainly controlled by the parent companies. For its part, *Renault* controlled only 5 % of the capital of *Indústrias Lusitanas Renault, S.A*, with the rest being shared between *FASA*, 75 %, and *SAEAR*, 20 % (Fernández de Sevilla, 2013). *Citroën* owned 20 % of the capital of its Portuguese subsidiary, *Citroën Lusitana, S.A.*, with a further 20 % lying in the hands of the Spanish subsidiary, which had been operating in its neighbouring country since 1957, and the rest being shared amongst local investors. Only *IMA* had a symbolic contribution from the British firm *BMC*. The remaining 12 companies who made up the Portuguese automobile sector at the time, prominent amongst whom were *SOMAVE* and *MOVAUTO*, were owned by national capital, generally underwritten by business agents who purchased manufacturing licences from different international carmakers. The ban on selling imported vehicles forced many of these commercial companies to transform their activity and to direct it towards assembly so as to be able to continue selling the vehicles which until that point they had been importing.[7]

There was a huge range of vehicles available in Portugal – with over 50 carmakers – and models – 474 including passenger cars and freight vehicles. Total production grew rapidly after 1963, when the ban on imports was introduced. In both that year as well as in the next the majority of companies began to assemble the imported *CKD*. Figures rose from 1,098 vehicles – passenger and commercial vehicles – in 1963 to 41,069 in 1965, a number which represented over 90 % of registrations that year.[8] The number of vehicles

5 In that same year, for example, France had a motorisation ratio of nine inhabitants per vehicle, as did the UK, while this stood at 6 in Sweden and 24 in Italy.

6 National Guild of Automobile Assembly and Manufacturing Industries (GNIMFVA), annual reports, several years, and Sousa (2005).

7 GNIMFVA, annual reports, 1965–1970.

8 Data taken from the reports of GNIMFVA and Portuguese annual statistical reports.

continued to grow and by the early 1970s national production exceeded 84,000 units.[9]

Up until the early 1970s, the subsidiaries of *Ford* and *GM* were the main assemblers in the Portuguese market, holding a joint share in excess of 35 % of the total. However, these two were soon joined by others involving local capital whose models started to become popular. By the early 1970s, it was *SOMAVE*, *MOVAUTO* and *IMA* who controlled, in an equal proportion, the market with over 46 % of output. Lagging slightly behind were the subsidiaries of *Ford* and *GM* with a joint share of 27 %. These were the years which first witnessed the arrival of capital from Japan, specifically *Toyota*, with 27 % of the capital of the recently created *Salvador Caetano*.

In order to operate, all of these companies were obliged to meet with the requirement of 15 % nationalisation. This was raised to 20 % in 1968 and to 25 % one year later.[10] According to overall estimations made by the Portuguese Association of Automobile Manufacturers (ACAP), between the mid-1960s and late 1980s assemblers on average used local elements up to 35 % of the vehicle's value.[11] Yet of this figure, only some 16 % corresponded to parts and components – of low value, such as batteries, inner tubes and paintwork – with the rest corresponding to salaries, energy consumption and even insurance (Guerra, 1990). The importance of the ancillary industry was, therefore, minimal and was to remain so for at least a further two decades. In 1975, the first year for which data are available, there were 72 firms in Portugal dedicated to manufacturing parts, components and bodywork for vehicles, employing 5,505 workers. By 1985, the number of firms and workers had risen to 104 and 9,267, respectively. Yet the level of nationalisation still stood at around a mere 16 % during this period. Moreover, the parts included were still low value, such as screws, casings, inner tubes, and paintwork.[12]

Despite the increase in national production, the Portuguese car industry evidenced a number of major weaknesses that prevented it from being on a par with its neighbour Spain in this respect. One of the problems facing assembly firms was the scant development of ancillary industries, which was true of the rest of the metal industry as a whole. According to the figures calculated by Lisbon (2002), using Portugal's *Estatísticas Industriais*, metallurgical firms in

9 GNIMFVA, annual reports, several years.

10 Decree no. 23042, of 29 November 1967.

11 ACAP, annual reports, several years.

12 Data taken from Portuguese annual statistical reports and from Guerra (1990).

1960 represented, out of the whole of industry, twice the number in terms of gross value added (GVA), reflecting the fact that they were still highly labour intensive activities. Up until the 1980s, the sector had to a large extent been formed by small family firms which had little machinery and a very limited production level. A comparison of this industry's figures with those of Spain reveals how far behind Portugal was. By the mid-1970s, there were 72 companies supplying parts and bodywork compared to the 1,500 in Spain (Ortiz-Villajos, 2010). The same was true of jobs, with 5,505 and 50,000 workers being employed, respectively. In terms of parts manufactured and the extent to which they were included, the difference was overwhelming. By the early 1960s, the two principal Spanish manufacturers, *SEAT* and *FASA*, incorporated over 90 % of local parts in their models, which included those of greatest value; engines and gearboxes. In Portugal, the rate of national parts included was less than 16 % between the mid-1960s and the late 1980s, and the contribution from local suppliers was characterised by low-value parts. Moreover, the large number of brands and models on the market triggered demand from assemblers for a wide range of parts, which prevented the specialisation of the already weak ancillary industry.

Another problem, in this case caused by the strategy adopted by the assembly companies themselves, concerned the characteristics of their production system, which prevented production or assembly in any standardised manner. The array of vehicles available spanned a vast number of brands and models. These were assembled in very short runs and needed long preparation times as well as a reorganisation of the production chain between the different batches. Low levels of investment coupled with high production inefficiency – substantial intermediate costs[13] – meant reduced economic profitability (Sousa & Diogo, 2012). Spanish manufacturers, on the other hand, adapted the range of models – both in terms of price and quality – to the demand at each moment.

The third major problem was workers' low skill levels which, on many occasions, meant that certain sophisticated machinery and technology could not be incorporated into the production plants.[14] Sousa and Diogo (2012) point to this shortcoming in the specific case of the firms *MOVAUTO* and *Salvador Caetano*. Spanish manufacturers were not faced with this problem, since the

---

13 Lourenço (1978) estimated that for 13 models sold in the Portuguese market in the early 1970s, the cost of assembling them was between 17 % and 37 % higher than the cost of importing the finished vehicle.

14 This question is recurrent in the annual reports of GNIMFVA for the period.

cities where they had set up already enjoyed a long-standing industrial tradition and could draw on workers who were skilled and specialised in the metal sector. Such is the case of *SEAT* in Barcelona (Catalan, 2017), and *FASA* in Valladolid (Alonso & Ortúñez, 2019).

There is widespread agreement amongst researchers concerning the limited role played by Portuguese industrial policy during this period in the growth of the car industry, particularly when compared to that implemented in Spain, where policy favoured initiatives and encouraged multinationals to share technology. In any case, the Portuguese market was too small for any company to operate at a minimum scale in terms of international efficiency (Guerra, 1990).[15] The only possibility lay in exports, yet Portuguese firms were in no position to compete even with the Spanish market, which was in turn less developed than the leading European countries. Moreover, the pressure exerted by the car importers and dealers' *lobby* in certain cases shaped the focus of the automobile sector's industrial policy.

3 Expanding overseas. The transformation to exporting: 1973–2000

The 1970s and early part of the 1980s witnessed a period of turmoil for the economy of both countries, particularly in the car industry. The international economic instability sparked by the oil crisis in 1973 and 1978 converged with the opening out of the economy, thereby curtailing the protectionism which Spanish and Portuguese manufacturers and assemblers had been privileged to.

The early 1970s saw major legislative changes which altered the rules of the game in the Spanish automobile sector. Firstly, there was a process of increasingly opening out subsequent to the signing, in 1970, of the Preferential Agreement with the European Economic Community (EEC). Amongst other things, the agreement lowered the tariffs which up until then had been levied on Spanish products, thereby favouring car exports towards Europe. Secondly, there was a slight liberalisation of the sector. In 1972, two decrees were approved to regulate the entry of international manufacturers, and which were specifically geared towards the arrival of *Ford*. The existing requirements for new carmakers were relaxed. In addition, the automobile industry was declared to be of special interest. The percentage of nationalisation was cut – from 90 % to

15 According to Biggart and Orrù (1997), the minimum volume should be 200,000 vehicles per year.

50 % – and a raft of tax breaks and subsidies was established for firms whose investments would enable a daily output of 500 vehicles. In December that year, *Ford* submitted its application to build a plant in Valencia with the capacity to produce 200,000 vehicles a year, and in 1976 the first vehicles rolled out of the factory. Three years later the UCD centre government approved a decree suited towards the intentions of *GM* to follow in the footsteps of *Ford*. The European subsidiary of *GM*, *Opel*, was granted authorisation to build a factory near Zaragoza, which started production in 1982. Together with the arrival of the North-Americans, the Japanese saw Spain as a big opportunity, given the prospect of the country's joining the EEC. *Nissan* and *Suzuki* introduced their products by acquiring Spanish firms who manufactured obsolete vehicles, such as *Motor Ibérica* (1979) and *Metalúrgica Santa Ana* (1982) (García-Ruiz, 2001).

Despite the economic crisis that hit Spain after 1974, and which saw a 25 % drop in the demand for vehicles between 1978 and 1981, production for the sector as a whole increased, and by 1986 (1.2 million) was twice that of 1972 (0.6 million).[16] This expansion was due to the arrival of *Ford* and *Opel* who, by the mid-1980s were together manufacturing over 500,000 vehicles a year, and thanks to exports proving easier as a result of the 1970 agreement. Exports went from representing 17 % of production in 1972, to over 64 % by 1985. Nevertheless, the arrival of North-American manufacturers at a time of stagflation, coupled with a decline in demand, had an impact on some of the traditional manufacturers. *SEAT* and *Citroën* cut production between 1975 and 1977, respectively, and in the mid-1980s (Castaño & Cortés, 1980; Castaño, 1986).[17] *SEAT*'s weight in the sector as a whole fell from 55 % in 1972 to 28 % in 1980, a year which saw it relinquish its number one position in automobile production to *FASA-Renault*. *SEAT*, which up until that point had been the leading Spanish manufacturer, went bankrupt, dragged down by the weight of its financial expenses. In 1980, *FIAT* and the Spanish banks pulled out of *SEAT*, and in 1982 the INI reached a commercial agreement with *Volkswagen* who, in 1986, took over the Spanish manufacturer.

If exports became crucial to Spanish manufacturers during the crisis, for the Portuguese they were even more so, given the small size of the country's domestic market, which was now shrinking. The political and social instability that followed the April 1974 revolution only served to compound the economic

---

16 According to the data gathered in Fernández de Sevilla (2013).

17 *SEAT* did not reach 1974 production until 1987. For its part, *Citroën* did not stabilise its 1976 production until 1987.

crisis. Industry experienced difficult years, which saw a gradual decline in production and in productivity as well as increases in nominal salaries (Sousa, 2005), with the automobile sector being one of the most severely affected. During that period, two thirds of the assemblers went bankrupt.[18] Of those backed by Portuguese capital only *SOMAVE* was able to weather the crisis and maintain its position as the country's leading vehicle assembler. With ups and downs, the number of registered vehicles and the production of cars fell slightly during the 1970s, and the levels of 1972 would not be matched again until the mid-1980s.[19]

The industrial policy implemented by the Portuguese government sought, on the one hand, to encourage reconversion and mergers between the companies that had been hardest hit, and on the other to drive up sales abroad and open up the country to overseas capital and technology. As did Spain, Portugal signed a commercial agreement with the EEC in the early 1970s. There was a commitment to gradually reduce the excise duties on vehicle imports until 1979, the year in which they were to disappear. In exchange, the tariffs levied on vehicle exports were cut.[20]

In 1977 a decree law (446/77 of 20 June) was passed aimed at once again boosting exports after the agreement signed with the EEC. To do this, the law allowed further increases in the imports of *CKD*, provided these were offset by a rise in exports, whether in terms of vehicles or parts manufactured at the assembly units or in the plants that emerged from their reconversion. By adopting this measure, the government sought to achieve its goals on imports set out in the commercial agreement signed with the EEC, whilst also aiming to boost exports – thereby partly compensating the balance of payments – and the reconversion of plants. Despite the greater facilities for exports, these still stood at a modest 13 % by 1978.

Faced with the need to reconvert the main car industry and its ancillary industry, and in view of the impending increased competition that would emerge from opening its economy to the European market, in 1976 the government decided to launch an international consultation that would eventually give rise to the Renault Project, heralding the era of domestic car production. In 1979 an agreement was reached between the Portuguese government and *Renault* to

18 ACAP, annual reports, 1974–1978.

19 ACAP, annual reports, 1972–1986.

20 In 1979, a few months before the deadline expired to remove tariffs, another law was passed extending the deadline until the mid-1980s.

set up a production unit in Setubal, under the name *Renault Portuguesa, SARL*. The aim was to produce 80,000 vehicles a year destined for the domestic market and for export, with a national incorporation rate of around 60 % by the late 1980s. Also envisaged were the installation of two subsidiaries in Cacia, one with mechanised production to build 220,000 engines and 80,000 gearboxes mainly intended for export, and an iron foundry to supply the plants. The project also foresaw reconverting the plant which *Renault* had had in Guarda since the mid-1960s in order to manufacture the commercial model *Traffic* (Schmidt & Almeida, 1987).

By the mid-1980s, after five years of activity, production of *Renault Portuguesa* vehicles was still some way off the target initially set. Nevertheless, and in spite of a dwindling market, with almost 40,000 vehicles produced in 1984 it became the leading vehicle manufacturer (45 % of total production) and exporter (48 %) in Portugal. Its models, which were of better quality than those on the market and which were also cheaper, became very popular among the Portuguese. The *Renault* project spurred the development of the ancillary industry, not only because it encompassed the creation of units dedicated to manufacturing parts, but also because it became a potential client for the industry. By the mid-1980s, it boasted nearly 70 local suppliers. Sales of parts and components had doubled since the first half of the decade and the overseas market came to represent over 36 % of the total, although it is true that much of the expansion was due to the *Renault Portuguesa* engine and gearbox subsidiary. The ancillary industry diversified its production, and for the first time companies appeared who manufactured electronic components and engine parts, which were of greater value than the traditional batteries and inner tubes. Apart from the technological boost for the ancillary industry – by providing local suppliers with technical advice[21] – the arrival of *Renault Portuguesa* also heralded a major step forward in worker training and skilling – with clear state aid through subsidies – and the creation of over 3,800 direct jobs.

Spain and Portugal's entry into the EEC in 1986 meant the disappearance of export incentives for both countries, the removal of excise duties and the gradual suppression of the nationalisation coefficient. Their car market became international, with high export rates which, by the end of the 1990s exceeded 80 % of production. There were also imports, which accounted for over 60 %

---

21 According to Monitor Company (1994), Portuguese vehicle manufacturers and assemblers maintained channels of communication with suppliers of parts to offer them technical advice.

of vehicle registrations in the case of Spain, and 90 % in Portugal. These high levels in both directions are explained by the fact that Spain and Portugal continued to manufacture low-end models, while levels of income rose and consumption patterns changed (García-Ruiz, 2001).

The reduction in costs and the increase in productivity demanded by the European market led Spanish manufacturers to adjust their workforces, to modernise their facilities and to implement organisation techniques learnt from Japanese manufacturers. *Ford* and *Opel* opened their factories with much higher levels of mechanisation than those found in companies that had already set up in Spain. In the case of *Opel*, mechanisation levels were even higher than those of the other factories in the group (Castaño, 1986).[22] *FASA-Renault*, *SEAT*, and *Citroën* soon followed suit. On the one hand, modernisation involved introducing revolutionary computer systems – CAD and CAM – as well as robot arms and programmable computers to deal with orders, and on the other, it meant implementing the new production organisation systems which western manufacturers had copied from the Japanese. These systems enabled resources to be combined more efficiently, thereby achieving greater productivity gains (Aláez et al., 2003). Nevertheless, this process was carried out gradually. By the mid-1980s, only *Opel* and *Ford* were using the just in time production system and few companies carried out controls on their suppliers (Castaño, 1986). This process became more intense as of the early 1990s and spread to the ancillary industry, although it was not implemented in the same way everywhere (Aláez et al., 2003).[23]

In Portugal, this process of modernisation and renovation in the car industry commenced in the late 1980s, thanks to the major overseas investment the country received. Some of the projects put forward during those years were accompanied by substantial public support from the EEC (ERDF funds). Projects included those undertaken by leading multinational car part and component firms who set up in the country after the 1990 announcement of the joint-venture (*AutoEuropa*) by *Ford* and *Volkswagen* to open up in Portugal. This project was authorised by the Portuguese government and the European authorities in 1991. An investment of over 2,200 million euros was anticipated, aimed at setting up a manufacturing plant at Palmela (Setubal peninsula) to produce 180,000 vehicles a year – with a 45 % national stake – that would

---

22 Since its opening, of all of Opel's plants in Europe, this has been one of the most productive.

23 These organisational techniques are currently in general use in the sector.

provide employment for 5,200 workers. The layout of the industrial site is a clear reflection of the organisational experiences of Japanese manufacturers. The assembly line was designed in accordance with the principles of JIT, where the parts reach the line following an ordered sequence. To achieve this, a large area was created close to the factory to house the supplier park. Consolidating the organisation model of *AutoEuropa* meant establishing a network of suppliers capable of ensuring high levels of efficiency, particularly in terms of quality, price and logistics (Palma, 1999; Vale, 2000). This network was formed by the companies located in the supplier park at Palmela, most of whom were backed by foreign capital, by other companies from the central and north regions – some of which were suppliers of *Renault Portuguesa* – and by multinationals located in the UK, Spain, and Germany. By the late 1990s, 31 % of *AutoEuropa's* suppliers were owned by national capital, with the rest belonging to multinational groups or others who had a stake in them.

After its establishment in 1995, *AutoEuropa* confirmed its position as the main vehicle manufacturer in Portugal, displacing *Renault Portuguesa* and *GM* (now *Opel Portugal*) who had been vying for leadership for years. National production rose from 125,000 vehicles in 1994 to 233,000 in 1996, thanks to the manufacture by *AutoEuropa* of over 119,000 automobiles (51 % of the total). This manufacturer's international focus was evident from the outset, with it being responsible for 54 % of Portuguese vehicle exports that year.

Barely two years after *AutoEuropa* commenced production, *Renault* sold its Portuguese subsidiary to the Portuguese state, and came to be known as *SODIA, S.A.* According to Guerra (1990), *Renault's* intention from the start was to operate in a market protected from international competition, which proved unthinkable after Portugal's entry into the EEC and the arrival of *AutoEuropa*.

4 Final considerations

The level of development reached by the automobile industry in Spain and Portugal has differed. Spain has emerged as the most successful of those European countries who were lagging behind in introducing the automobile industry. The country went from ranking thirteenth in car production in Europe in 1950 to ranking second – and indeed first in industrial vehicles – by 2019. A robust industry has gradually consolidated itself in the country with a clear focus overseas while at the same time a highly competitive supplier industry has emerged. Within this process, a key role has been played by industrial policy, in addition to restrictions on vehicle imports, and high nationalisation quotas. However, it has not proved possible to prevent all of the manufacturers and a good number of the suppliers from remaining in the hands of foreign capital, which to a certain extent means technological dependence on the outside.

In comparative terms, Portugal's success in developing this industry has clearly been modest, although it has made major strides compared to its initial situation. From merely incorporating the chassis into a few vehicles imported in the early 1950s, it moved on to assembling *CKD* during the 1960s before stepping up to actual production in the 1980s. Supply has been characterised by a wide range of brands and models which prevented serial production and the possibility of benefitting from scale economies. The industrial policy implemented during the *Estado Novo* did not prevent new models from being launched onto the market. In addition, it established very low nationalisation quotas compared to those of Spain, thereby hindering the development of the ancillary industry, which only began to take off after the arrival of *Renault Portuguesa* in the 1980s and which underwent a major transformation in the 1990s with *AutoEuropa*. Even though overseas capital controls the sector, there are important Portuguese multinationals which have adapted to a globalised and highly competitive environment.

5 Sources

Portuguese Institute for National Statistics (Statistical Yearbooks, Industrial Statistics).

GNIMFVA (National Guild of Industrials of Assembly and Manufacture of Motor Vehicles), annual reports.

ACAP, annual reports.

ANFAC National Association of Automobile and Truck Manufacturers, annual reports.

References

Aláez, R., Bilbao, J., Camino, V., & Longás, J. C. (2003). Los cambios en las relaciones interempresariales en la industria del automóvil: el caso español. En J. L. García (Ed.), *Sobre ruedas. Una historia crítica de la industria del automóvil en España* (pp. 191–212). Síntesis.

Alonso, P., & Ortúñez, P. P. (2019). La formación profesional industrial en Valladolid y su impacto en el desarrollo industrial de la ciudad (1880–1971). *Investigaciones Históricas*, 39, 473–516.

Barros, J., & Sousa, M. L. (2007). The myth of the Portuguese automobile: Dreams, projects and causes of failure. *Fifth Annual Conference on the History of Transport, Traffic and Mobility (T2M)*. Helmond, The Netherlands.

Biggart, N. W., & Guillén, M. F. (1999). Developing difference: Social organization and the rise of the auto industries of South Korea, Taiwan, Spain, and Argentina. *American Sociological Review*, 64, 722–747.

Biggart, N. W., & Orrú, M. (1997). Societal strategic advantage: Institutional structure and path dependence in the automotive and electronics industries of East Asia. In A. Bugru & B. Usdiken (Eds.), *State, market and organizational forms* (pp. 201–240). W. de Gruyter.

Castaño, C. (1986). Entorno internacional de la industria del automóvil. *Economía Industrial*, 252, 119–131.

Castaño, C., & Cortés, G. (1980). Evolución del sector del automóvil en España. *Información Comercial Española*, 563, 145–157.

Catalan, J. (2000). La creación de la ventaja comparativa en la industria automovilística española, 1898–1996. *Revista de Historia Industrial*, 18, 113–154.

Catalan, J. (2017). The life-cycle of the Barcelona automobile-industry cluster, 1889–2015. *Revista de Historia Industrial*, 66, 77–125.

Fernández de Sevilla, T. (2013). *El desarrollo de la industria del automóvil en España: el caso de FASA-Renault, 1951–1985*. Tesis Doctoral. Universidad de Barcelona.

García-Ruiz, J. L. (2001). La evolución de la industria automovilística española, 1946–1999: una perspectiva comparada. *Revista de Historia Industrial*, 19, 133–163.

Guerra, A. C. (1990). *Formas e determinantes do envolvimento externo das empresas: internacionalização da indústria automóvel e integração da indústria portuguesa na indústria automóvel mundial*. Tesis Doctoral, Universidad Técnica de Lisboa.

Lisboa, M. (2002). *A indústria portuguesa e os seus dirigentes*. Educa, Ciéncias Sociais.

Lourenço, M. (1978). *Sector automóvel, alguns dados*. Direcção Geral Do Comércio.

Monitor Company (1994). *Construir as vantagens competitivas de Portugal*. Monitor Company.

Ortiz-Villajos, J. M. (2010). Aproximación a la historia de la industria de equipos y componentes de automoción en España. *Investigaciones de Historia Económica*, 16, 135–172.

Palma, L. (1999). *A história do sector automóvel em Portugal (1895–1995)*. Documento de Trabajo (DT19–99). Ministério da Economia de Portugal.

Schmidt, A., & Almeida, J. C. (1987). *Fabricação automóvel e produção de componentes. Das trasnformações a nível mundial ao contexto portugués*. Banco de Fomento Nacional.

Simões, V. C. (2000). *Efeitos do Investimento Estrangeiro em Portugal: o caso da Industria Automóvel*. CISEP.

Sousa, M. L. (2005). *Uma perspectiva institucional do desenvolvimento: o caso da industria automóvel em Portugal (1960–1990)*. Tesis de Maestría. Universidad de Lisboa.

Sousa, M. L., & Diogo, M. P. (2012). Giving with one hand and taking away with the other: the automobile assembly industry in Portugal (1960–1988). *Revista de Historia Industrial*, 48, 155–181.

Vale, M. (2000). Imbricação de empresas trnasnacionais: uma análise do cluster automóvel em Portugal. *Finisterra*, 70, 57–86.

María Vázquez-Fariñas

12 Wine exporters in the city of Cádiz between the 19th and 20th centuries: *Lacave & Company*

Abstract Cádiz has historically been recognized by the importance of its businesses and its harbor: a relevant place for the trade between Europe, Africa and America for centuries. Sherry wines have always had a special position in that trade, particularly from the second half of the 18th century, when wine sales began to increase gradually. But it was during the 19th century when large winemaking houses appeared in the city: *Lacave & Company*, *Miguel M. Gómez S.A.* and *Abarzuza & Company*. This chapter focuses on the activity carried out by one of them, *Lacave & Company*, which offered a large variety of wines between the 19th and 20th centuries. Specifically, it analyzes the products portfolio, the main suppliers, the exports and the market areas. For this, the accounting information of the company has been used, which is kept in a private archive in the Wine Unit of the University of Cádiz.

1 Introduction

The wine business has traditionally been one of the most relevant economic activities in Andalusia, and more specifically in Cádiz, which acted as a bridge between the producers of the wine towns of *Marco del Jerez*[1] and the importers of wines from Europe, and it also was a producer and marketer city of wines from different regions (Vázquez-Fariñas & Maldonado, 2017). In this city was one of the main exporting companies of the 19th and 20th centuries: *Lacave & Company*, specialized in the production and sale of wines to Spain and abroad.

This company was created in 1871, after the dissolution of *Lacave & Echecopar*, which had been operating in Cádiz since 1830 (Vázquez-Fariñas, 2021b). In

1 The Sherry Wine Region, where sherry wines are produced. This area of wine production includes the towns of Jerez de la Frontera, El Puerto de Santa María, Sanlúcar de Barrameda, Chiclana de la Frontera, Chipiona, Puerto Real, Rota, Trebujena and Lebrija; the latter two are in the province of Seville and the rest are in the province of Cádiz.

1870, the partners (members of the families Lacave and Echecopar) decided to separate and dissolve the company to continue the businesses separately (Vázquez-Fariñas, 2018a, p. 84). From that point on, the Lacaves agreed to take on the businesses they had been developing until then, changing the company name to *Lacave & Company*. So, Pedro Lacave Mulé, Pedro-Luis Lacave Soulé and Juan-Pedro Lacave Soulé founded this company to dedicate themselves to the commission business and the export of wines. At the same time, they established a branch office in Seville under the same company name of *Lacave & Company*. Through it, the Lacave family was dedicated to the businesses of commissions, cork, cooperage and wine storage in the Andalusian capital. The growth of this new company, with offices in Cádiz and Seville, was constant throughout the following years, as they entered more and more markets and exported their products all over the world (Vázquez-Fariñas, 2017).

This company had many similarities with other wine companies of the time: search for quality and product diversification, managerial positions in the hands of the founding family and a clear strategic line of international vocation (Fuentes, Cabeza & Sánchez, 2020, p. 33).

Due to its relevance, this chapter analyzes in detail the characteristics of the wine business of this company, studying the types of wines manufactured and sold, the prices, the suppliers and the main materials that were used for the elaboration of their products, as well as the volume of their sales and the market areas in which they operated.

The deeds and accounting books of this company from Cádiz provide valuable information to reconstruct the business activity developed over the years. This chapter focuses on the last years of the 19th century and the first of the 20th century, according to information in the company's archive kept at the Esteban Boutelou Historical Studies Unit, at the University of Cádiz, and mainly on balance sheets, receipts and invoices ledgers, inventory ledgers and price lists. Specifically, the balance sheets collect information on the company's results, the composition of its assets and the operations with clients and suppliers, among other elements. The receipts and invoices ledgers contain copies of the invoices paid by *Lacave & Company* to its suppliers, and the inventory ledgers show a detailed list of all the tools, equipment, furniture, wines and other effects that the company had in its facilities. Finally, price lists offer the types of wines sold by the company and their market value. All in all, the analysis of these sources has revealed the characteristics of the wine business of this company and how it was developed.

2 The products portfolio: Main commercialized wines

The analysis of the different types of wines produced and sold by the company is essential to know the business strategies and the degree of growth achieved in the period under study. One of the main characteristics that defines the so-called sherry wines is their great variety, since there are many factors that influence them, such as the climate, the characteristics of the soil or the aging methods, among others. In addition, at the end of the 19th century, exporters fulfilled orders from samples, for which they mixed wines of different styles so that their wines could satisfy foreign demand, thus increasing the great variety in the wine market (González, 1970, p. 360). For all these reasons, it is very difficult to determine exactly all the types of wines produced by *Lacave & Company*, but the labels, inventory ledgers and price lists reflect that it came to sell more than one hundred different varieties of wine. Its different types were classified into three categories, White Card, Silver Card and Gold Card (*Carte Blanche*, *Carte Argent* and *Carte Or*), respectively, and each of them was divided into three subcategories marked with one, two or three stars, in order from lowest to highest quality. Like most of the exporters of the time, a large percentage of the wines produced by this company were mixtures of different types to adapt to the characteristics of the demand of the markets (Greiner, 1897, pp. 61–62). Thus, *Lacave & Company* had a wide products portfolio, among which were not only the typical sherry wines, but also others highly appreciated in those years, such as black *Málaga*, sweet *Dorado*, especially demanded in France, *Tintilla de Rota* and *Pajarete*, specialties of the company, as well as imitations of wines from other countries, such as Madeira and Porto (Vázquez-Fariñas, 2018b, p. 249). According to the information of the accounting books, they also sold wines from other regions as authentic, among which it is worth noting those of Malaga, Alicante, Bordeaux, Porto and Marsala.[2] It is probable that *Lacave & Company* used these wines both to sell them directly and to use them in their mixtures creating imitations.

As an example, at the beginning of the 20th century, the company offered the following wines in France[3]:

- Sherry pale (dry).
- Gold medium-dry sherry.
- *Amontillado* (very dry sherry).

---

2 Inventory ledgers, 1870–1927.

3 Price list for France, 1908.

- *Manzanilla* (very dry sherry).
- Marsala (dry).
- Madeira (medium-dry).
- Málaga black or white (very sweet).
- Porto red wine/Porto white wine (medium sweet/sweet).
- *Tintilla de Rota* (sweet).
- Alicante (sweet).
- *Malvoisie* (sweet).
- *Pajarete* (very sweet).
- Muscatel (very sweet).
- *Pedro Ximénez* (very sweet).
- *Lágrimas* (very sweet).
- Orange (very sweet).

Therefore, the company was dedicated to the sale of very different types of wines, since it not only made sherry wines, but also imitated those from other regions and sometimes was only dedicated to the commercialization of them, exercising mainly a distribution activity.

Among the best-selling products by *Lacave & Company* were liqueur wines, and specially its *Madera de Jerez* (Greiner, 1897, p. 63). Like other wineries in the province, since the second half of the 19th century they had been dedicated to the production, marketing and export of imitations of Madeira wines, given the increase in consumption and the popularity that this product had registered among the bourgeoisie in those years (Maldonado, 1998, pp. 141–162; Ramos, 1998, pp. 168–169). Furthermore, Maldonado Rosso (1998, p. 51) affirms that it is very likely that this company was one of the first to offer this type of wine on the markets, thus achieving an important advantage over its competitors. However, one of the main problems that these wines presented towards the end of the century was fraud, since the great foreign demand led some winemakers from Jerez to produce false Madeira (Gómez, 2003, pp. 43–59). Then, *Lacave & Company* took advantage of the increase in demand and popularity to introduce imitations of Madeira into its products portfolio. Two options were used in the labels of its wines to commercialize them, both the generic name of Madeira and that of *Madera de Jerez*. In any case, studies on the subject show that counterfeiting Madeira was a very beneficial activity for wine companies in the province of Cádiz, and especially for *Lacave & Company* (Maldonado, 1998, p. 154).

Another of the specialties of the company, due to its style and old age, was brandy from the oldest solera in its warehouses, which was sold under the brand *Fernando V.* Faced with the winemaking crisis of the late 19th century, exporters from *Marco del Jerez* were forced to look for different solutions, among which was the diversification of production. Then, pure wine spirituous liquors played a primary role, and more specifically, the so-called *Brandy de Jerez*, a Cognac-style drink that, in addition, would become the main factor for sectoral recovery and renewal in the region (Maldonado, 2019, pp. 9–10).

Likewise, the company created in those years other brands under which they sold their wines and which became world-famous, such as *León* and *Marqués de Fiel Pérez Calixto.*[4] The first of them owed its name to the emblem of the company, in which appeared a lion with the family coat of arms and the year the company was founded, 1810. The second of the brands, *Marqués de Fiel Pérez Calixto*, was used to identify the pale and sweet aged sherry, and owed its name to the marquisate that originally belonged to Mª del Carmen de la Rocha Pérez and was inherited by his son Pedro-Francisco Lacave de la Rocha in 1926, one of the capitalist partners of the company. The label of this sherry indicates that it was a wine destined for export, and more specifically, for sale in France, since the marquisate's crown appeared next to the name of the wine, the name of the city of Cádiz and the inscription "great fine wine from Spain", all written in French.

The importance of brands to distinguish the product was essential in those years, because, like other companies in the sector, the brand allowed them to retain loyal customers who were satisfied, since they could easily recognize what they consumed and buy it again, thus achieving a lasting relationship with its customers (Fuentes, 1995, p. 118). In addition, labels were also very important to identify the product. The use of them had become widespread back then, not only as an identifying element, but also as a fundamental distinctive to capture the attention of consumers (Fernández, 2019, p. 8.).

Considering all the above, it is reflected that *Lacave & Company* not only produced wines from the Jerez area, but also imitated and sold wines from other regions, which together with the use of the characteristic *criaderas* and *soleras* system of the region, made it a peculiar company and different from the typical wineries of *Marco del Jerez* in the first third of the 20th century (Vázquez-Fariñas, 2021a, p. 61).

Regarding the price of the wines, it should be noted that in those years it was set by the exporters, and it changed depending on the quality of the product and the cost of making it (Maldonado, 1999, p. 318). The price list for France

4 Copy of the incorporation deed of *Lacave & Company, limited partnership*, granted in Cádiz on February 18, 1927 in the presence of the Notary Luis Álvarez-Ossorio.

in 1908 is kept in the company's private archive, and shows the different types of wines that *Lacave & Company* sold on the French market. It gives an idea of the price level generally set for its foreign sales, although this was influenced by the tariffs and customs duties of each region. The Lacaves prepared their wines for exports in 16-liters barrels or in boxes of 12 bottles, and their prices varied not only depending on the type of wine, but also according to the aforementioned categories (White Card, Silver Card and Gold Card, and one, two or three stars).

The prices of their wines in the French market ranged from 32 to 128 francs for barrels, and from 28 to 87 francs in the case of boxes, although a large part of them corresponded to customs duties. Specifically, these taxes amounted to 16 francs per barrel and 12 francs for each case of 12 bottles, representing a considerable increase in prices on the foreign market. If the part corresponding to taxes and customs duties is deducted from the price, one of the strategies followed by *Lacave & Company* to increase its market share was to offer competitive prices in an increasingly globalized environment. From the last third of the 19th century, the so-called sherry wines sector had numerous exporters that vied to place their products in the main countries of Europe (Jeffs, 1994, p. 111). It is not only the relatively low price of their wines that is remarkable, but it is also important to emphasize that, in this increasingly competitive market, the Lacaves offered several types of wines and of different categories and styles, so they could cover larger market niches, satisfying the needs of consumers with very different tastes.

3 The suppliers of *Lacave & Company*

When studying the winemaking business of *Lacave & Company*, it is necessary to analyze its main suppliers of raw materials, tools and equipment, as well as their place of origin, since all this will allow knowing how they developed their winemaking activity.

Among the accounting books of the company, several titled "invoices and receipts" are kept, which include all the invoices that suppliers issued to *Lacave & Company* after receiving the effects in their warehouses in Cádiz between 1893 and 1898. This information has allowed to know the products that the partners acquired more regularly for their winemaking activity, and its origin. However, a complete study of all the company's suppliers would extend this chapter too much, therefore the most important will be pointed out.

The main products purchased for the normal development of the activity were: oil, alcohol, sugar, wheat, prunes, bitter almond shells, caramel, barley, cane honey, grape syrup, vinegar, bottles, casks, wineskins,[5] test tubes, cups and other effects for tests, small bottles for samples, capsules for bottles, labels, cases, metal seals, cork stoppers, straw covers, machinery and various tools, woods, steam machines, boilers, presses, filters, iron and wooden straps, and stills, among others.

Especially significant was the great variety of wines used by the company to make its own wines. At this time, they obtained most of the wines for transformation from other companies, since they only had some vineyard land in the Cádiz towns of Rota and Chiclana (Greiner, 1897, p. 64). Among the wines that the company bought in those years for its subsequent transformation and sale, it is worth mentioning: sweet wine, dry wine, red wine, white wine, Bordeaux, port wine, Rioja, cognac or brandy, muscatel, grape juice, *tintilla*, *manzanilla*, *amontillado* (medium-dry sherry), *Pedro Ximénez*, Grenache, black and red mistelle,[6] and old wine. They bought sweet wine from the growers of Alicante, Valencia, Cádiz (the capital and Chipiona) and Huelva (La Palma del Condado, Almonte and Moguer); white wine came mainly from the provinces of Cádiz (El Puerto de Santa María, Chipiona and Jerez), Huelva (Almonte and Bollullos del Condado) and Ciudad Real (Manzanares and Criptana); *Pedro Ximénez* from Málaga and El Puerto de Santa María (Cádiz); the grape juice was acquired in Valencia and Cádiz (Chipiona, Jerez, El Puerto de Santa María and Chiclana); *manzanilla* in Sanlúcar de Barrameda (Cádiz) and *amontillado* in Cádiz as well. Likewise, port wine and Bordeaux were brought from their respective producing regions; red wine from Ciudad Real, Logroño, Alicante and Valencia; Rioja from Bilbao; Grenache from Barcelona and the mistelles from Alicante, Cádiz and the Valencian town of Villena. Finally, they also bought cognac from the company *Riva & Rubio* in Jerez de la Frontera.

All in all, it can be said that the vast majority of wines and grape juices were purchased in nearby towns, mainly in other municipalities in the province of Cádiz and in the region of El Condado de Huelva. This reflects the importance that national suppliers had for the company, since they only went to the foreign market to buy wines from Bordeaux and Porto, mainly used for their imitations.

Moreover, among the main materials necessary for the normal functioning of the wine activity were the bottles, barrels and casks, and boxes to store the wines.

---

5 Wineskin: a bag that is made from the skin of an animal (such as a goat) and that is used for holding wine (Merriam-Webster Dictionary).

6 Mistelle: grape juice or slightly fermented white wine to which brandy has been added that is used in the production of other wines (Merriam-Webster Dictionary).

These products were acquired from companies located in Cádiz, Jerez, El Puerto de Santa María and Bollullos del Condado (Huelva), as well as from the German company *Actien Gesellschaft der Gerresheimer Glashüttenwerke*, which nowadays continues to operate and is dedicated to the manufacture of glass and plastic containers. To buy bottles and boxes for samples, they turned to companies in Barcelona, Paris and Le Havre, in France, where they also bought their postal boxes. Capsules for wine bottles were bought in Tolosa (Guipúzcoa), Málaga and Nuremberg (Germany). For the bottling of their wines, collars and labels were essential. The collars were brought from Paris (France) and the labels from Lyon and Paris, when they did not obtain them in Cádiz and Málaga. Finally, the metal stamps were purchased in Bordeaux and the cork stoppers in Puerto Real (Cádiz), although the main supplier of stoppers was the Sevillian house *Lacave & Company*, which was part of the family business network. Iron and wooden straps were also essential, which they bought from companies established in Cádiz, Antwerp (Belgium), Liverpool (England) and Seville, and more specifically, from the firm *Lacave & Company* established in the Andalusian capital, the main supplier of these products to the house of Cádiz.

In general terms, most of these materials came from Jerez, Cádiz and Seville, but they also brought products from various regions of France, England, Germany or Belgium. So, regarding the supply of raw materials other than the wines, it can be said that *Lacave & Company* did not only use the internal market, as they also worked with several foreign companies to obtain the best quality of their products.

4 Wine sales in the international market at the end of the 19th century

In order to know the position of the company in the wine market towards the end of the 19th century, its sales between 1870 and 1896 will be analyzed next. In general, its exports remained stable in the period considered, with some exceptions (Tab. 1). The decade of the seventies began with an increase in exports, which went from 15,215 hectoliters (hereinafter hl) in 1870 to 18,260 hl in 1872. After a few difficult years, by that time business has been reactivated in Cádiz and wine sales were one of the bases for the growth of the city. In 1873, *Lacave & Company*'s exports fell to 15,985 hl, probably due to the decrease in British demand at that time. In the following years, its sales remained stable around 20,500 hl per year. In 1887, its volume of transactions fell again slightly, thus following the same trend as other wines produced in Jerez and the like. The sector was then in crisis, due to the decrease in exports and prices, and the signing of the Spanish-British treaty of 1886, which heavily taxed sherry wines (Pan-Montojo, 1994, pp. 181–185). However, despite these difficulties, exporters from *Marco del Jerez* progressively increased their sales in the following years, thus confirming the fact that the crisis of the turn of the century did not affect them immediately.

Especially significant is the strong increase in the company's transactions in 1891, although Spanish exports of sherry wines also registered a great growth in general terms, probably due to the fact that the phylloxera and oïdium pests led to the diversion of demand from other areas to *Marco del Jerez* (Piqueras, 2005, pp. 117–120; Cárdenas, Carrera & Vitriago, 2015). In addition, the company not only made sherry wines, but was also engaged in the commercialization of other types of wines and imitations, as has been mentioned before. So, its extensive products portfolio also influenced these sales figures.

Thereafter, exports decreased and stabilized in the following years at around 19,000 hl per year, once again following the same trend as that registered by the wines of the area, whose sales abroad remained relatively stable, in around 230,000 hl (Lignon-Darmaillac, 2004, p. 473). In addition, since that date there had also been a progressive drop in the total volume of *Lacave & Company*'s stocks in its warehouses, which is consistent with the reduction in its sales abroad.

Tab. 1: *Lacave & Company* wine exports, 1870–1896 (hectoliters)

Year	Exports	Year	Exports
1870	15,215	**1884**	21,735
1871	16,320	**1885**	20,759
1872	18,260	**1886**	20,060
1873	15,985	**1887**	17,860
1874	17,720	**1888**	21,035
1875	19,630	**1889**	19,915
1876	20,917	**1890**	17,825
1877	21,040	**1891**	40,605
1878	20,890	**1892**	18,321
1879	20,430	**1893**	19,585
1880	21,135	**1894**	18,630
1881	20,820	**1895**	19,330
1882	20,365	**1896**	19,375
1883	21,430	**Total**	**545,192**

Source: author, based on Greiner 1897, p. 78.

In general terms, between 1870 and 1896, the company's exports totaled 545,192 hl of wines, a lower figure than that recorded, for example, by *González Byass*, with 688,296.63 hl in those years (Lignon-Darmaillac, 2004, pp. 466–468), and by *Jiménez & Lamothe*, a company specialized in Málaga and Manzanares wines, which exported 804,888 hl in the same period (Greiner, 1898, p. 31). However, the foreign sales of *Lacave & Company* then exceeded those of one of the most important wine houses in *Marco del Jerez* at that time, *Domecq*, whose exports amounted to 339,426.01 hl (Lignon-Darmaillac, 2004, pp. 466–468), which may be due, once again, to the wide products portfolio of the Lacaves' wineries.

The case of the Portuguese company *Companhia Geral da Agricultura das Vinhas do Alto Douro*, which between 1878 and 1890 maintained its position in the national market and increased its sales of port wines abroad, should also be noted. Between 1890 and 1896, this company registered a sharp decrease in its exports, since in 1891 it sold wines abroad for a value of 180,284.918 real, and in 1896 it fell to 75,758.915 real, thus entering the company in a phase of stagnation or recession that the Portuguese wine trade experienced in the last years of the 19th century (Sousa, 2006, pp. 340–344).

Furthermore, it is worth mentioning the Ricasoli family, dedicated to the wine business in Italian Tuscany, as their production and sales of wines fell sharply in the 1870s. Specifically, production fell from 2,436.46 hl in 1870 to 1,756.12 hl in 1879, and its sales in Florence decreased from 1,661.80 to 492 barrels between 1870 and 1877, a sign that Italian wines were also facing adverse circumstances at that time (Biagioli, 2000, pp. 514–516).

Taking all into consideration, it can be said that the variations in exports of *Lacave & Company* at the end of the 19th century were related to the socioeconomic situation of the time. However, despite the instability that characterized the Spanish wine sector in those years, in general terms the Cádiz house managed to maintain its sales abroad in a context of continuous fluctuations, unlike other large companies, which were more affected by the changes of the international market at the end of the 19th century.

5 National and international market areas

Over the years, *Lacave & Company* managed to become one of the main wine exporting companies in *Marco del Jerez*. Towards the last third of the 19th century, the socioeconomic situation of Cádiz made it difficult for businesses to develop, especially those related to the wine sector, due to the monetary crisis of 1864, the banking crisis of 1866, the fall in the price of wine and the decline in exports that took place since 1867 (González, 1970, pp. 165–166; Sánchez, 1970, pp. 90–92; Caro, 1990, pp. 188–190; Cózar, 2003, p. 142). However, the mercantile traffic of the port of Cádiz increased in the 1870s, making Europe the main destination for products that came from Cádiz, including wine and salt (Espigado, 1992, p. 168). In those years, Europe became the main market for *Lacave & Company*, as it sold wines in France, Sweden, the Netherlands, Switzerland, England, Scotland, Denmark, Finland, Belgium, Greece and Austria. Its wines were also sold in Russia, Turkey, Egypt, Algeria, the USA, Colombia, El Salvador, Mexico, Australia and the French Antilles (Vázquez-Fariñas, 2018b, p. 252), thus expanding its market to the five continents.

Their infrastructures allowed them to send products abroad easily. They had a private quay to ship their wines directly from their warehouses to the large ships anchored in the Bay of Cádiz, to later travel to the main consumption areas. One of its most relevant markets was France. Shipments to this country were made through regular steam services that left Cádiz bound for the French ports of Le Havre, Bordeaux and Saint-Nazaire on the Atlantic, and for Marseille in the Mediterranean. For this, the company had special agents who acted on behalf of the house and were responsible for the entry of the wines and the payment of customs duties. Once the goods arrived at these ports, the wines were dispatched from there to the different areas of the country through the railroad (Vázquez-Fariñas, 2020, p. 208).

The distribution network was one of the key pieces in the business development of the region's wineries (Jiménez, 2008–2009, p. 136). *Lacave & Company* used the agency system that had been so widespread in the wine sector throughout the 19th century, which allowed exporters to obtain large market shares. The agents made available to their clients the wines that the winemakers sent to them, while at the same time passing on to the Cádiz entrepreneurs the possible complaints, suggestions and opinions of consumers about their wines, so that they could adjust production and prices to the characteristics of the foreign market as much as possible (Maldonado, 1999, pp. 288–294). This system had been conceived around the first third of the century, when *Marco del Jerez* companies had to choose between creating their own network of agents, a rather slow process, or establishing agency contracts with foreign merchants who already had a consolidated network (Montañés, 2001). The Lacaves opted for this last option, working with a wide network of merchants spread all over the world, who acted as correspondents of the Cádiz house to place their products in the different markets.

At the beginning of the 20th century, in addition to agents or correspondents in the French ports of Le Havre, Marseille, Bordeaux and Saint-Nazaire, *Lacave & Company* had more than sixty agents spread across the main commercial squares in the world, including San Francisco, New York, Boston and Philadelphia (USA), Montreal (Canada), London (England), Bremen and Hamburg (Germany), Havana (Cuba), Manila (Philippines), Caracas (Venezuela), Mexico, Glasgow (Scotland), Dublin (Ireland), Oslo (Norway), Copenhagen (Denmark), Cairo (Greece), Algiers (Algeria), Vienna (Austria) and Tangier (Morocco), among others. In all cases, they were merchants with long commercial experience with whom the Lacaves signed agency agreements to sell their products. Some of them acted as general agents and were responsible for the distribution of all the wines made by *Lacave & Company* in their respective markets, and others focused on the sale of a specific type of wine (Vázquez-Fariñas, 2018b, pp. 253–254).

The information of the company's agent book shows that, in general terms, the minimum commission established for correspondents in the different destinations was 10 %, and it could reach 20 % for older wines. Freight charges were paid at destination, and transportation insurance was borne by the agents. In addition, the cost of the bottles, casks and containers of sherry was charged to the agents' accounts and paid off when they were received in Cádiz in perfect conditions. Possible losses were borne by the agents and lastly, *Lacave & Company* was responsible for the correspondence expenses in most cases.

In addition to the agents, the company had branch offices in Paris (France), Stockholm (Sweden), Marsala (Italy), Porto and Funchal (Portugal) to distribute its products more efficiently to different markets.[7] The long tradition of the Lacave family as ship consignees greatly facilitated them access to markets; the network of commercial relationships established during years allowed them to sell their wines in advantageous conditions (Vázquez-Fariñas, 2020, p. 213).

Regarding the domestic market, a significant improvement in peninsular transport had been observed since the mid-19th century, which was mostly notable for Cádiz, especially since the establishment of the railway in the province in 1854, which allowed a greater influx of goods from other locations (Pérez & Román, 2006, p. 5). The railway was essential for the development of the wine business, since 8 out of 10 tons transported through this mean of transport towards the end of the 19th century were sherry wines (Gómez, 1984,

7 The branches offices in Marsala, Porto and Funchal appear as *maisons d'achats* on company documents (Price list for France, 1908).

p. 98). In addition, it was a great boost for the commercial activity of *Lacave & Company*, since the railway ran through all its facilities and its warehouses were located next to one of the city's train stations.

It should be noted that the railway lines were designed to serve the port in many cases, which led to the introduction of many lines along the coast, promoting, in turn, the development of ports and cities (Pozueta, 2006, pp. 69–71). In addition, the first years of the 20th century were characterized by attempts to modernize the city of Cádiz, which led to the start of several projects of great importance, including the modernization of the port and the construction of various quays, so that ships of large tonnage could dock (Millán, 1993, p. 58). These improvements in port and communication infrastructures favored the increase in commercial transactions and offered the possibility of serving a greater number of markets. In addition, maritime transport was cheaper than land transport in those years (Cózar, 1998, p. 173). Thus, maritime transport played a very important role in the development of the *Lacave & Company* businesses.

In the national market, the Andalusian region was essential for the company, since it had agents in the cities of Huelva, Málaga and Seville. Especially significant is the fact that, despite the company's headquarters were in Cádiz, the Lacaves had agents in the city: Juan-Bautista Lacave, Juan-Bautista Barthecoy, José Vilchez Chell and Manuel Lallemand Lemos, among others.[8] They were all in charge of managing the businesses without any restriction, that is, they were authorized to carry out commercial traffic, sell all kinds of merchandise and represent the company in the acts that were necessary. In addition, the company also had agents in Jerez de la Frontera, the most important city in *Marco del Jerez*, who were in charge of all the businesses of the company in that town.[9] Furthermore, the Lacaves also had agents to sell their wines in Madrid, San Sebastián and Santa Cruz de Tenerife, important strategically located shopping regions that allowed them to cover much of the national market.

All in all, the importance of the correspondents has been proven, since the expansion of this network of agents throughout the world led to the proper development of *Lacave & Company's* businesses, both nationally and internationally.

8 Provincial Historical Archive of Cádiz (hereinafter PHAC). Notary of Ramón Mª Pardillo, 1873, file no. 609, pp. 884–886; Notary of José Navarro, 1889, file no. 4.715, pp. 1–3; Notary of Luis Álvarez-Ossorio, 1902, file no. 2.744, pp. 1.395–1.396.

9 PHAC. Notary of Ramón Mª Pardillo, 1873, file no. 608, pp. 324–326; 1875, file no. 627, pp. 2.505–2.507; Notary of Luis Álvarez-Ossorio, 1917, file no. 2.839, pp. 4.456–4.462.

6 Conclusions

Over the course of this chapter, we have seen that the Lacave family developed an important business in the wine sector between the 19th and 20th century. The Lacaves had founded *Lacave & Company* in Cádiz to dedicate themselves to the commission business and the export of wines and, towards the last third of the 19th century, the situation of the sector offered new opportunities to Spanish companies, which then increased their production and sales in the international market. Specifically, the Lacaves set up branches in Alicante, Stockholm, Oporto, Funchal and Marsala.

In addition, *Lacave & Company*, in the face of growing competition, and like many other companies, developed various alternatives to stay in the market, for example, the sale of bottled sherry in Spain and the production of new products such as cognac. So, this Cádiz company offered a wide portfolio of products in the period under study; not only did it make and sell sherry wines, but it also imitated those from other regions and, on occasions, dedicated itself solely to their marketing, thus exercising a mainly distribution activity. The company had in its products portfolio wines from Jerez, but also from Alicante, Málaga, Porto, Marsala, Bordeaux and Madeira, among others. Therefore, *Lacave & Company* was not only a typical company from *Marco del Jerez*, as it offered a highly diversified range of wines to different markets.

In the last years of the 19th century, economic decline was characteristic in the region. However, despite the economic difficulties, *Lacave & Company*'s exports were not substantially affected by this crisis and remained stable in the last years of the century, due to the strategies developed then. On the one hand, the company had increased and diversified its production and commercialization of wines, greatly expanding its products portfolio, but also its markets. On the other hand, the strategy consisting of buying their raw materials instead of planting the grapes themselves (at that time *Lacave & Company* only kept some lands in Rota and Chiclana), also helped them to avoid the devastating effects of the crisis of the last years of the 19th century.

The large network of agents spread throughout the world was also very important for the growth of the company. Over the years, *Lacave & Company* had managed to establish a network of trusted agents to sell its products, while also having branches offices in some of the most important commercial centers. With all this, they managed to sell their wines throughout the world.

All the business activity developed by *Lacave & Company* led it to become one of the most important houses in Cádiz at the beginning of the 20th century. Its remarkable development in the wine sector continued throughout that century, as the partners, always members of the Lacave family, entered more and more markets and exported their products all over the world, making the company a famous exporter of wines of great relevance with an important historical trajectory and tradition.

7 Sources

Lacave's Archive (Historical Wine Studies Unit of the University of Cádiz):

- Agents' book.
- Inventory ledgers, 1870–1927.
- Price list for France, 1908.
- Copy of the incorporation deed of *Lacave & Company*, limited partnership, granted in Cádiz on February 18, 1927 in the presence of the Notary Luis Álvarez-Ossorio.

Provincial Historical Archive of Cádiz:

- Notary no. 2: file no. 608, 609, 627.
- Notary no. 13: file no. 2.744, 2.839.
- Notary no. 19: file no. 4.715.

References

Biagioli, G. (2000). *Il modello del proprietario imprenditore nella toscana dell'ottocento: Bettino Ricasoli. Il patrimonio, le fattorie*. L'Officina dello storico, vol. 6. Florence: Leo S. Olschki.

Cárdenas del Rey, L., Carrera, A. & Vitriago Valdivielso, L. (2015). El comercio de cabotaje del vino de Jerez en el siglo XIX: un análisis cuantitativo. *Sociedad Española de Historia Agraria – Documentos de Trabajo*. doi: 10.13140/RG.2.1.1457.0325.

Caro Cancela, D. (1990). *Burguesía y jornaleros: Jerez de la Frontera en el sexenio democrático (1868–1874)*. Jerez de la Frontera (Cádiz): Caja de Ahorros de Jerez.

Cózar Navarro, M. C. (1998). *Ignacio Fernández de Castro y Cía. Una empresa naviera gaditana*. Cádiz: Servicio de publicaciones de la Universidad de Cádiz.

Cózar Navarro, M. C. (2003). El tejido empresarial en la ciudad de Cádiz. *Revista de Estudios Regionales*, 67, 139–166.

Espigado Tocino, G. (1992). El comercio gaditano a finales del siglo XIX: Análisis de un año de actividad portuaria. *Trocadero: Revista de Historia Moderna y Contemporánea*, 4, 157–195. doi: 10.25267/trocadero.1992.i4.10.

Fernández Portela, J. (2019). Las etiquetas de las botellas de vino: su valor como recurso comercial y como expresión del paisaje vitivinícola. *Boletín de la Asociación de Geógrafos Españoles*, 81. doi: 10.21138/bage.2759.

Fuentes García, F. J. (1995). Viñedo y comercio de vinos en Córdoba: Las bodegas Alvear en el siglo XIX. *Revista de Estudios Regionales*, 42, 87–129.

Fuentes García, F., Cabeza Ramírez, J., & Sánchez Cañizares, S. (2020). *Alvear. La empresa familiar decana de las exportadoras andaluzas*. Valencia: Tirant lo Blanch.

González Gordon, M. M. (1970). *Jerez-Xerez-Sherish Saris: noticias sobre el origen de esta ciudad, su historia y su vino*. Jerez de la Frontera (Cádiz): Fundación Manuel Mª González Ángel González Byass.

Greiner Gindroz, E. (dir.). (1897). Los vinos finos de España y la Casa Lacave y Compañía, Cádiz. *El Álbum Nacional, revista ilustrada. Serie de números dedicados a la industria y al fomento de la producción española*.

Greiner Gindroz, E. (dir.). (1898). La casa Jiménez y Lamothe (Málaga y Manzanares). Elaboración de vinos finos y de mesa y destilación de aguardientes puro vino. *El Álbum Nacional, revista ilustrada. Serie de números dedicados a la industria y al fomento de la producción española*.

Gómez Díaz-Franzón, A. (2003). Vinos de Oporto y Madeira. Antigua iconografía publicitaria emitida por bodegueros de Jerez. *Revista Douro: Estudos & Documentos*, 15, 43–59.

Gómez Mendoza, A. (1984). *Ferrocarril y mercado interior en España (1874–1913): Cereales, harinas y vinos*, vol. I. Madrid: Banco de España.

Jeffs, J. (1994). *El vino de Jerez*. Cádiz: Servicio de Publicaciones de la Universidad de Cádiz.

Jiménez Blanco, J. I. (2008–2009). Capital español, beneficios británicos. Una gran bodega jerezana del siglo XIX. *Revista de Historia de Jerez*, 14–15, 133–156.

Lignon-Darmaillac, S. (2004). *Les grandes maisons du vignoble de Jerez (1834–1992)*. Madrid: Casa de Velázquez.

Maldonado Rosso, J. (1998). Producción y comercialización de Madeiras en la provincia de Cádiz (siglos XIX y XX). In A. Vieira (Coord.), *Os vinhos licorosos e a História. Seminário internacional* (pp. 141–162). Funchal, Portugal: Centro de Estudos de História do Atlântico.

Maldonado Rosso, J. (1999). *La formación del capitalismo en el marco del Jerez: de la vitivinicultura tradicional a la agroindustria vinatera moderna (siglos XVIII y XIX)*. Madrid: Huerga y Fierro Editores.

Maldonado Rosso, J. (2019). Los tres grandes cambios de la vinatería andaluza. La modernización de la vitivinicultura contemporánea. *Andalucía en la historia*, 66, 8–13.

Millán Chivite, J. L. (1993). *Cádiz siglo XX: del Cádiz hundido al Cádiz que resurge (1898–1979)*. Madrid: Sílex.

Montañés Primicia, E. (September 2001). *Los sistemas de comercialización y la expansión exterior del Jerez. 1835–1885*. Paper presented at the simultaneous session La competitividad internacional de la empresa española, in the Congreso de la Asociación de Historia Económica, Zaragoza, Spain. Available at: https://www.aehe.es/wp-content/uploads/2001/10/montanes.pdf. Accessed 2019 May 24.

Pan-Montojo González, J. L. (1994). El vino y la política comercial en la Restauración. *Revista Agricultura y sociedad*, 72, 167–204.

Piqueras Habas, J. (2005). La filoxera en España y su difusión espacial: 1878–1926. *Cuadernos de geografía*, 77, 101–136.

Pérez Serrano, J. & Román Antequera, A. (September 2006). *Los proyectos del ferrocarril en la provincia de Cádiz en el siglo XIX*. Paper presented at the IV Congreso Historia Ferroviaria; 150 años de ferrocarril en Andalucía: un balance, Málaga, Spain.

Pozueta Echavarri, J. (2006). El urbanismo de las ciudades portuarias: influencia y herencia de los puertos en las ciudades españolas. In J. I. Fortea & J. E. Gelabert (Eds.), *La ciudad portuaria atlántica en la historia: siglos XVI-XIX* (pp. 45–84). Santander: Autoridad Portuaria de Santander and Servicio de Publicaciones de la Universidad de Cantabria.

Ramos Santana, A. (1998). Comercio y consumo de Madeira en Cádiz. In A. Vieira (Coord.), *Os vinhos licorosos e a História. Seminário internacional* (pp. 163–178). Funchal: Centro de Estudos de História do Atlântico.

Sánchez Albornoz, N. (1970). Cádiz, capital revolucionaria en la encrucijada económica. In C. E. Lida & I. M. Zavala (Selec.), *La Revolución de 1868: Historia, Pensamiento, Literatura* (pp. 80–108). New York: Las Américas Publishing Company.

Sousa, F. de (2006). *A Real Companhia Velha. Companhia Geral da Agricultura da Vinhas do Alto Douro (1756–2006)*. Porto: Centro de Estudos da População, Economia e Sociedade (CEPESE).

Vázquez-Farinas, M. (2017). *El negocio del vino en el Cádiz del siglo XIX: las Bodegas Lacave* (PhD diss.). University of Cádiz, Cádiz, Spain.

Vázquez-Fariñas, M. (2018a). La industria vinícola en el Cádiz decimonónico. Lacave y Echecopar: bodegueros y consignatarios marítimos. *Revista de Historia TST. Transportes, Servicios y Telecomunicaciones*, 37, 70–90.

Vázquez-Fariñas, M. (2018b). Los vinos de la casa gaditana Lacave y Compañía hacia finales del siglo XIX: ventas y áreas de mercado. In A. Ramos & L. Lozano (Eds.), *Tres siglos bebiendo Jerez. Comercio y consumo (XVIII–XX)* (pp. 241–265). Cádiz: Ediciones Suroeste.

Vázquez-Fariñas, M. (2020). *El negocio del vino en la ciudad de Cádiz. Historia empresarial de Lacave y Compañía, 1810–1927.* Madrid: Marcial Pons.

Vázquez-Fariñas, M. (2021a). Lacave & Echecopar: strategies and businesses in the second half of the nineteenth century. In J. M. Matés-Barco & L. Caruana (Eds.), *Entrepreneurship in Spain: A history* (pp. 55–70). New York: Routledge.

Vázquez-Fariñas, M. (2021b). Wine entrepreneurs in 19th century Cádiz: Pedro Lacave Miramont. In M. Vázquez-Fariñas, P. P. Ortúñez-Goicolea & M. Castro-Valdivia (Eds.), *Companies and entrepreneurs in the history of Spain. Centuries long evolution in business since the 15th century* (pp. 83–100). London: Palgrave.

Vázquez-Fariñas, M. & Maldonado Rosso, J. (2017). Cádiz, ciudad vinatera entre mediados de los siglos XIX y XX. *Revista de Estudios Regionales*, 109, 95–119.

Carlos Larrinaga

13 Hotel businessmen in Spain in times of change (1930–1959). The case of *Hoteles Unidos, S.A.* (HUSA)[1]

Abstract *Hoteles Unidos, S.A.* (HUSA) was the most important Spanish private hotel chain in the years before the tourism boom of the 1960s when Spain became a world power in tourism. It was promoted by the Gaspart family, hotel entrepreneurs from Barcelona who, in 1930, decided to set up this hotel chain, with establishments in different Spanish cities. Previously there had been other hotel chains, but more modest. Hence, this Chapter analyses the evolution of this company, the role of the different entrepreneurs who participated in it and the changing contexts in which it developed, namely Alfonso XIII's monarchy, the Second Republic, the Civil War and the first Franco regime, that is, very different scenarios in a relatively short period of time.

1 Introduction

Spain's hotel industry expanded considerably in the first third of the twentieth century, coinciding with several particularly important events. One of these was the development of modern tourism, that is, the conception of tourism as an industry in which many agents intervened (Norval, 1936). It also coincided with the birth of the first tourism system with different regional developments in Spain (Vallejo, 2018). It is true that Spain was not yet included among the so-called tourist countries, in other words, those that received foreign tourists and had a surplus in their tourism balance. It was, rather, a tourism country in the sense that tourism was already conceived as a social practice and economic activity. Finally, we should point out the relevance that the International Exhibition of Barcelona and the Ibero-American Exhibition of Seville, both held in 1929–1930, had for Spanish tourism.

Not only did the number of hotels increase, particularly tourist hotels, but also their quality. This was particularly important because one of the main

1 This study forms part of the research project HAR2017-82679-C2-1-P, financed by the Minister of Science and Innovation of the Government of Spain and the FEDER/ERDF Fund.

complaints of the travellers and tourists at the end of the nineteenth century and beginning of the twentieth century referred to the poor quality of the hotel establishments in Spain (Baedeker, 1898, 1900; Moreno, 2007, p. 49). Things changed a lot in the first third of the twentieth century and by the beginning of the 1930s, Spain had a tourist hotel sector that was comparable to those of other neighbouring countries (Elston, 1930). Not only had it developed a large luxury hotel industry (Larrinaga, 2019a), but there were also more modest hotels that catered for the growing number of tourists. In this sense, we must not forget that the elite tourism characteristic in Spain at the beginning of the twentieth century began to give way to a new kind of tourism in which society's middle classes participated. This was in the 1920s and 1930s.

Another phenomenon that we should take into account is the consolidation of the private hotel chains in the first third of the twentieth century (Larrinaga, 2018, pp. 698–700). The first hotels appeared in the 1890s but the phenomenon became more common in subsequent years. The tourist hotel industry of the first third of the twentieth century was predominated by individual initiatives with few limited companies. In the majority of cases, the owners of the hotels were also their directors. And in only a few cases the owner and management were separate. The modernisation of the hotel industry experienced in Spain after the First World War favoured the expansion of limited companies and the consolidation of the first hotel chains. On a European level, there was the precedent of the Compagnie Internationale des Grandes Hôtels Européens directed by the Belgian hotel entrepreneur Georges Marquet. His activity in Spain involved the incorporation of the Palace and Ritz Hotels in Madrid, the Continental in San Sebastián, the Hotel Real in Santander and Alfonso XIII in Seville into his business operations (Moreno, 2015, pp. 30–33). It was precisely in this context when, in 1930, *Hoteles Unidos, S.A.* (HUSA) was founded, the first large Spanish private hotel chain and precedent to the large expansion of Spanish hotel chains form the mid-twentieth century.

2 The founding of *Hoteles Unidos, S.A.* (HUSA)

In 1930, the brothers Antonio and Rafael Vilalta Jiménez (traders from Lérida), Ramón Ollé Badía (an industrialist from Tarragona), José Gaspart Bulbena (a trader from Barcelona), Ludovich Bouché. (a salaried worker from Madrid) and Eduard Ragasol Sarrá (a lawyer from Barcelona) constituted the company called *Hoteles Unidos, S.A.*, on 30 June 1930, with its business address in the Hotel Europa in Tarragona (Business Register of Madrid, Sheet 599). The objective of the new company was to exploit hotels and constitute a chain of hotels, spas, restaurants and other related businesses. To do this, an indefinite time limit was established with a social capital of four million pesetas, divided into 8,000 bearer shares of 500 pesetas each. Furthermore, the issue of 1,000 founder's shares at a value of 500 pesetas each was contemplated, giving their holders the right to a share of any profits.

Of this capital of four million pesetas, initially 4,350 shares were issued at a value of 2,175,000 pesetas. The rest remained as treasury stock for when it was needed. These shares were subscribed in the company's act of constitution according to two types of contributions. On the one hand the industrial contributions of each partner, namely: Antonio Vilalta: 761 shares worth 80,500 pesetas; Rafael Vilalta: 760 shares worth 380,000 pesetas; José Gaspart 1,521 worth 760,500 pesetas; and Ramón Ollé 808 worth 404,000 pesetas. And on the other hand, the cash contributions, namely: José Gaspart 300 shares worth 150,000 pesetas; Antonio Vilalta and Ramón Vilalta Salvadó, (half each), 134 worth 67.000 and Rafael Vilalta Jiménez 66 worth 33.000. In the company's act of constitution the first 760 founder's shares were also assigned, namely: 257 to José Gaspart, 124 to Antonio Vilalta, 123 to Rafael Vilalta, 81 to Ramón Ollé, 50 to Ludovich Bouché, 50 to Miguel Vidal Guardiola, 50 to Eduardo Ragasol and 25 to Antonio Muntañola.

The Board of Directors was formed as follows: Chairman, Antonio Vilalta: Vice-Chairman, Ramón Ollé; CEO, José Gaspart; board members, Rafael Vilalta and Ludovich Bouché; and Secretary, Eduardo Ragasol. Of these board members, we will focus on José Gaspart (HUSA, 2000, pp. 10–14), as he was the first entrepreneur to form a hotel dynasty which still has a presence in the industry today. He was born on 6 February 1885 in the spa town of Caldas de Montbuí (province of Barcelona) to a family of farmers. With no education and at a very young age he went to Barcelona to try his luck, and after working in several trades he became a waiter. This was his first contact with the hostelry. This was when he decided that this was the professional career that he would pursue and began to travel the world and learn languages. In fact, his first destination was Marseille where he also began to work in a bar. After this he went to England. There he was a butler for an English lord who was a keen traveller and took the young José Gaspart with him. On one of these trips they went to Cairo where he was able to work in some of the best hotels of the area. In this way he learnt French and English and also acquired a practical training that would be useful to him in his future professional career.

It is not known when he returned to Barcelona, but when he arrived he first began working in a bar and later as a concierge in the Palace Hotel, the former Hotel Ambos Mundos, established in 1893. This establishment, together with the Grand Hotel Continental and the Gran Hotel Colón represented a decisive step in the modernisation of the hotel industry of Barcelona (Rosselló & Valdívia, 2016, pp. 63–65) and investments also attracted local capital (Larrinaga & Vallejo, 2021). In short, José Gaspart found a position in one of the most important hotels in Barcelona. We could assume that his years of experience in the sector and his knowledge of languages worked in his favour. In this respect, we should not forget that, after the International Exhibition of 1888, Barcelona became a particularly relevant tourist city (Palou, 2012, chapters 1 and 2; Larrinaga &Vallejo, 2021). After his time at the Palace Hotel, he leased, on his own account, the Hotel España, also in Barcelona. This was his first big decision as a hotel entrepreneur. Moreover, encouraged by the good results obtained in the management of this establishment, in 1924, together with Joan Vilalta, he leased the Hotel Oriente, which would become the flagship of the HUSA group and a fundamental establishment for the Gaspart family in the following decades (Martínez Díaz, 1992, p. 52; HUSA, 2000, p. 16).

The International Exhibition held in Barcelona in 1929 and 1930 represented a huge opportunity for tourism in general and the hotel industry in particular. And, José Gaspart was not going to let it pass him by. The fiscal sources of the time reveal a considerable increase in the item referring to tourist hotels (Larrinaga & Vallejo, 2021). In the years prior to 1929 the hotel industry in Barcelona became consolidated. In fact, while the Guidebook of Hotels in Spain of 1916 cited only 26, the Official Guide to Hotels of the National Tourist Board of 1929 counted 45 establishments. The progress was substantial. From 1924, there was a considerable increase in the number of visitors to Barcelona, with 344,876 in 1929 and the following year 357,348 (Blasco, 2005, p. 375). Within this tourism boom, in 1927 José Gaspart ordered the construction of two more floors at the back of the Hotel Oriente in view of the expected increase in demand due to the Exhibition. Driven by his entrepreneurial spirit, he also leased several restaurants in the Montjuic exhibition ground. They must have been good years for Gaspart, as, with the profits earned through the management of the España and Oriente hotels and the exhibition restaurant businesses he founded the company *Hoteles Unidos, S.A.* (HUSA, 2000, p. 17).

Together with José Gaspart, we should mention the Vilalta brothers, with whom he collaborated for several years. Ramón Ollé, meanwhile, was the owner of Hotel Europa in Tarragona, where, as we have seen, the business address of HUSA was established (HUSA, 2000, 21). Finally, we should refer to the lawyer Eduardo Ragasol, born, like Gaspart, in Caldas de Montbuí, although a few years later in 1901. As a law graduate from the University of Barcelona, it is assumed that he was responsible for the company's legal matters. However, after 1930, his political participation in Acció Catalana was also prominent. This Catalan nationalist party became known as Acció Catalana Republicana in 1933 and Ragasol was elected as a member of parliament in the elections of February 1936. After the Civil War he went into exile (1939) and never returned to Spain (https://ca.wikipedia.org/wiki/Eduard_Ragasol_i_Sarr%C3%A0).

In short, the HUSA chain was born with only three establishments (the Hotel Europa in Tarragona and the Hotels España and Oriente in Barcelona), although subsequently, as we shall see, it expanded considerably in a very short space of time.

3 HUSA in the 1930s

It is traditionally believed that the idea of José Gaspart when founding HUSA was "to create the first Spanish hotel chain and then sell it to the Americans" (HUSA, 2000, p. 21). First, it was not the first hotel chain created in Spain. And second, going beyond this idea, which seems a little unrealistic, taking into account the state of the US economy due to the stock market crash of 1929, he was more likely to have had a more long-term business strategy. In fact, we should remember that the International Exhibition ended on 15 January 1930, when the international crisis had already erupted. The number of visitors to Barcelona in 1931 and 1932 decreased significantly (Blasco, 2005, p. 375), so it is possible that Gaspart sought a strategic alliance in order to withstand the difficult times ahead which would be even worse in Spain considering the political situation: a country transitioning from a dictatorship supported by the monarchy to a democracy with a republican constitution. On the whole, the early years of the 1930s were not good for tourism in Europe (Ogilvie, 1933).

It should be understood that the initiative taken by José Gaspart was based on business practices that had been implemented since the end of the nineteenth century. We should also remember that, within the context of this development of general capitalism, at the end of the nineteenth century and, fundamentally, in the first third of the twentieth century, large hotel chains began to emerge throughout much of Europe, such as the Ritz Development Company, the Compagnie International des Grands Hôtels Européens or the Compagnia Italiana Grandi Alberghi (CIGA).

Between 1931 and 1935, HUSA managed up to 14 hotels in Spain (HUSA, 2000, p. 29). In 1932, it was advertised as "the largest hotel organisation in Spain", with ten luxury hotels, 1,435 rooms and 935 individual bathrooms. It was geographically distributed in many of the Spanish cities that received the

Tab. 1: HUSA Business Results, 1930–1935

Years	Revenue	Losses	Profits
1930 (6 months)	1,088,838.85	8,828,00	
1931	3,642,573.96	66,349.98	
1932	5,313,400.10		261,645.47
1933	7,531,512.51		171,891.31
1934	7,047,216.41	180,775.29	
1935	7,552,798.83		126,960.39

Source: *Anuario Financiero de Bilbao*, 1936–1937, p. 1005.

most tourists: Barcelona, Tarragona, Alicante, Granada, Seville, Cadiz, Bilbao and San Sebastián (*Blanco y Negro*, 25 December 1932, p. 130).

These years of growth of the company saw some changes in its structure (BRM, Sheet 599). For example, from what can be derived from the modification of the company statutes of 1935, the presidency of the Board of Directors was assigned to the Barcelona-born industrialist Antonio Fabregat Cabré. Furthermore, new shares were subscribed and a steering committee was created as an intermediary body between the Board of Directors and the Management, formed by three members, namely: one from Management and two from the Board.

This was also the case of other hotels in Spain. In the early years of the Republic, HUSA experienced losses, albeit not very substantial (in 1930–1931), and was back "in the red" in 1934, a particularly conflictive year from a political point of view. However, it made a profit in 1932–1933 and 1935, suggesting that the 1930s were not as bad as could be expected and HUSA's hotel expansion strategy was successful despite this being a difficult period (see table 1). It also suggests the hotel business was viable with solid professional foundations (Larrinaga & Vallejo, 2021).

The Civil War (1936–1939) had a significant impact on the incipient tourism industry in Spain. Barcelona was, in fact, the last large city that remained in the hands of the Republican authorities, resisting the attack of Franco forces until it finally fell into their hands, practically finalising the conflict. We should note that the hotel establishments were particularly hard hit during these years, especially the large hotels as they had large spaces with high-quality facilities and good technical advances in terms of communication. Many of them were occupied by institutions, political parties or unions when they were not being used as hospitals or barracks. Therefore, in general terms, we can say that the hotels suffered damage during the years of the war. In the case of Barcelona, after the war, "the hotels and guest houses needed employees, cleaning, provisions, fuel and other requirements" (Bolín, 1967, p. 329), being in a rather miserable situation.

With respect to the hotels in the HUSA chain we can point out the following. The Hotel Oriente, for example, was seized by the anarchist union CNT (Fernández Casado, 2018, pp. 94–95), although it was closed in 1937 and damaged by a bomb at the end of the war (Martínez Díaz, 1992, p. 58). In these circumstances, José Gaspart decided to return to his village, Caldas de Montbui, believing that, he would be safer if he left Barcelona. However, this was not the case. Shortly after arriving he was arrested and sent to Montjuic castle where he was held prisoner for three months. He was liberated thanks to the intervention of a friend and he went first to France and then to Seville, controlled by the Franco authorities. Gaspart remained at the helm of Hotel Madrid in Seville until the end of the war, when he was able to return to Barcelona (HUSA, 2000, p. 31). The Hotel María Cristina in San Sebastián formed part of the HUSA chain. The war lasted for two months there, and in mid-September 1936 it was taken by Franco's troops. The María Cristina was partially occupied by the governing authorities of the Frente Popular as a hospital to treat wounded soldiers. Meanwhile, the presidential body of the first autonomous government of the Basque Country installed itself in the Hotel Carlton in Bilbao, which also formed part of the HUSA chain. In this case, Franco's army did not take control of the capital of Biscay until 19 June 1937 (Larrinaga, 2019b, p. 163). As a general rule, as the different cities fell into the hands of Franco's troops, the hotels were returned to their legitimate owners.

With respect to the second generation of the Gaspart family, before the Civil War broke out José sent his children to study abroad to learn languages and gain work experience in the hotel trade. Juan Gaspart Bonet went to Berlin and Felipe Gaspart Bonet to London. After two years the two brothers swapped destinations and did not return to Barcelona until the end of the war, a little before the Second World War broke out. After two years of military service, Juan Gaspart remained in Barcelona collaborating with his father José, while Felipe Gaspart moved to Andalusia to take over the HUSA business in the region, although over time he became independent and created his own hotel business (HUSA, 2000, p. 31).

4 The reconstruction of the company after the Civil War

After the war, the hotel company had to resume its activities and on 30 June 1939 an Extraordinary General Shareholders Meeting was held in order to establish a new modification of the statutes (BRM, Sheet 599). The first important change was to confirm the transfer of HUSA's business address to Seville (1937); specifically, to the Hotel Madrid where José Gaspart had moved to. The steering committee, created in the 1930s, disappeared and the management figure was reinforced. Ramón Vilalta Salvadó became the chairman of the company and José María Carbó Cassi became secretary. That said, in the Board of Director's meeting on 1 July 1939 José Gaspart was elected as the CEO of the company. The challenge was to improve the condition of the hotels in the chain which required the incorporation of new partners. Given the shortage of cash, part of the wages was paid with the company's shares (HUSA, 2000, p. 38). Meanwhile, on the initiative of the Gaspart family, HUSA diversified its businesses in Barcelona, opening in 1940 El Cortijo, an open summer venue that offered meals and shows with international stars, similar to those that existed in Europe and the United States. In the winter of the following year La Bodega de Calderón was opened with the same objective; meals and international shows. The idea was that when El Cortjo closed La Bodega would open for the rest of the year (HUSA, 2000, pp. 32 & 38).

In a meeting on 17 October 1941, the Board of Directors took the decision to move HUSA's business address to Barcelona. Specifically, in the Hotel Oriente, from where José Gaspart would run the business. But it was not easy and he was replaced "as his actions had not responded to the expectations and aspiration that the Board had placed in him". This was not the only replacement undertaken in 1943, as the Secretary, José María Carbó was replaced by Juan Carsi Giner. Moreover, Ramón Vilalta took over the position of CEO in addition to being the Chairman. Nevertheless, in a subsequent Extraordinary General Shareholders Meeting, it was decided to revoke these decisions (BRM, Sheet 599). It seems that there was a real power struggle between the Vilaltas and the Gasparts for the control of the company.

At the beginning of 1943 advertisements appeared in the press for the following hotels in the HUSA chain: Hotel Miramar in Málaga, Alhambra Palace in Granada, Madrid in Seville, Carlton in Bilbao, Victoria in Valencia, Europa in Tarragona, Terramar in Sitges and Oriente and España in Barcelona (*La Vanguardia*, 13 March 1943, p. 6). The Hostal de la Gavina was also part of the chain, located in S'Agaró in the Costa Brava. It was the best hotel establishment in the area and in a few years (second half of the 1940s) it became consolidated as a meeting point of the European bourgeoisie during the summer (HUSA, 2000, p. 46). A little later, on 23 March 1944, the Gaspart family created *La Industrial Hotelera, S.A.* (LIHSA) in order to manage the establishments in Catalonia, becoming the spearhead of its business activity in the following years (HUSA, 2000, p. 41). With a capital of three million pesetas, LIHSA exploited Hotel Oriente and Hotel España in Barcelona and Hotel Europe in Tarragona and several restaurants in Barcelona (*Anuario Financiero de Bilbao*, 1949–1950, p. 861). In this respect, the Gaspart family's response to the aforementioned power struggles can be seen in LIHSA. In fact, the presence of HUSA in Catalonia was made possible through LIHSA, an independent company from which the businesses of the Gaspart family expanded (HUSA, 2000, 41 & 81). Therefore, HUSA had separate accounts and balance sheets from LIHSA (*Anuario Financiero de Bilbao*, 1949–1950, p. 861). It may be assumed that there was an agreement between the two companies.

We should take into account that the early 1940s, coinciding with the Second World War and the Spanish post-war period, were the hardest of the Franco regime, due to the hardships suffered, the deterioration of the infrastructures and a very slow economic recovery. In fact, the GDP level of 1935 was not reached until 1951 (Carreras & Tafunell, 2004, p. 278). From a tourism point of view, the number of tourists in Spain, expressed in thousands, fell from 191 in 1934 to 18.9 in 1940, increased again to 30.8 in 1941, falling again to 30.6 in 1942, rising to 72.1 in 1943, decreasing to 34.3 in 1944 and standing at 39.2 in 1945 (Tena, 2005, p. 641). This spectacular fall in visitors brought with it a decrease in the number of hotel beds. In Barcelona, for example, in 1936 there were 3,542 beds, in 1939 there were 3,002 and in 1949 3,287. Moreover, in 1950, there were only 28 hotels in a city with more than a million inhabitants which had been an important tourist destination before the war (Palou, 2012, p. 264).

On 25 March 1944, HUSA held an Extraordinary Shareholders Meeting in which the decision was taken to reduce the social capital of the company from four to 2.5 million pesetas through the redemption of shares. With this measure the number of securities on the stock market fell, and the holders were reimbursed with the capital invested. However, in this meeting it was also decided to change the statutes, including the transfer of the business address to Madrid. In this respect, it does not seem like a coincidence that in a meeting on the same day, 25 March 1944, the Board of Directors agreed to name Jorge Marquet as CEO (BRM, Sheet 599). We should remember that he was the son of the afore-mentioned Georges Marquet who was then the Chairman of the Board of Directors of the company Madrid Palace Hotel, S.A. Coinciding with the thirtieth anniversary of the founding of the company, on the 7 October 1942 the Ministry of Labour awarded him the medal of merit at work due to his contribution to the hotel industry, and the opening of wide and extensive horizons. The success derived from his intelligence and hard work undoubtedly benefited not only the capital of Spain but also tourism and Spain in general (*Boletín Oficial del Estado* (Official Spanish Gazette), 14 October 1942).

From my point of view, the naming of Marquet as CEO was a significant strategic operation. This was achieved, first, not only due to Marquet's own business experience in the hotel trade, but also to his good relations with the authorities having adhered to the Franco regime from the outset. Second, HUSA did not have a presence in Madrid before or after the Civil War where the centre of Marquet's operations was based. Therefore, he could contribute to the development of HUSA without harming his own interests. Finally, with the transfer of the business address to Madrid and with the entrance of Marquet in the company, Barcelona and the Gaspart family seemed to have lost influence in HUSA's trajectory. It also seems as though the creation of LIHSA by the Gasparts was related to this operation. In any event, the situation for HUSA was not easy as, in the Ordinary Shareholders Meeting of 12 March 1945, the annual report and balance sheet of the company at 31 December 1944 were approved with losses of 412,619.74 pesetas. In 1946, the losses amounted to 73,213.57 pesetas (National Historical Archive, index nº 167, inscription 10,347). The Managing Director was then Juan Hammerel Minerai, appointed by Marquet on 31 July 1944 to direct all of the company's businesses. This naming was particularly important, because three years later Hammerel replaced Marquet as CEO of HUSA. Furthermore, on 2 January 1950, Baldomero Carbó Cassi was elected by the Board of Directors for the position of Managing Director.

Soon the first symptoms of the emergence of international tourism began to be seen in Spain. In 1949 its contribution to GDP was still modest, reaching only 0.38 %, a lower share than in the 1930s. However, the economic potential of tourism was starting to become evident. Since 1947 the income from tourism represented more than 7 % of exports and imports and almost half of the revenue of the services balance. The revenue earned from tourism financed between 31 % and 54 % of the trade deficit in the period 1947–1949. Therefore, at the beginning of the 1950s tourism represented an important offsetting item of the trade and current account imbalances. Between 1946 and 1948 when the Spanish economy found itself without means of payments, the economic decision-makers began to focus on sectors able to provide foreign currency in the short term and they realised that tourism was one of them (Vallejo, 2013, pp. 433–435). In thousands of tourists, the number of visitors grew from almost

137 in 1947 to 457 in 1950 (Tena, 2005, p. 641). This was undoubtedly an excellent opportunity for the businesses of HUSA.

5 The 1950s

Due to the breakout of the Cold War between the allies of the Second World War, General Franco's Spain was starting to come out of the political isolation to which it had been subjected at the end of the Second World War. In 1950, the UN removed the sanctions that it had imposed on Spain in 1946 and allowed the return of the ambassadors. In addition, between 1949 and 1950, the US government approved the first financial aid items for Spain through three financial entities, namely: the Chase Manhattan Bank, the National City Bank and the Export-Import Bank. However, this process would culminate with two especially important events: the signing of the concordat with the Holy See in 1953 and the Madrid Pacts of the same year with the United States, under which four American military bases would be installed on Spanish soil in exchange for economic and military aid. In 1955, Spain entered as a full member of the UN and from that year onwards, it was integrated into the various international financial organisations. This international context was highly favourable for attracting tourist flows to Spain which would benefit the different national agents, including hotel companies (see table 2).

Therefore, the acquisition from the Banco Vitalicio of the building located in the Gran Vía in Barcelona represented a milestone for the Gaspart family and LIHSA. At a time of great expansion of the tourism sector in Spain, for the first time the company decided to open a large hotel characterised by comfort

Tab. 2: Foreign tourism in Spain's balance of payments and GDP 1950–1960

	1950	1952	1954	1956	1958	1960
Tourists (thousands)	457.0	776.8	993.1	1,560.9	2,451.9	4,332.4
Revenue from tourism (billions of pesetas)	0.64	1.67	4.66	4.43	4.10	17.86
Tourism revenue / trade deficit (%)	104.9	44.6	86.4	27.3	26.1	
Tourism revenue / Exports (%)	11.6	13.5	30.1	26.9	15.3	39.8
Tourism revenue / GDP (%)	0.38	0.7	1.56	1.1	0.75	3.04

Source: Vallejo, 2013, p. 437.

and luxury. It took several years for the project to be developed and the hotel was opened in 1952. In 1949, the payment was made for 50 % of the purchase of the building; in 1950 the remaining 50 % was paid. In 1951 the construction work began and the following year the Hotel Avenida Palace opened its doors to the public, coinciding with a particularly relevant event for Barcelona, the 35th Eucharistic Congress held between 27th May and 1st June of that year (HUSA, 2000, pp. 49 & 53). It was the first large international celebration held in Barcelona during the dictatorship. As many thousands of visitors were expected, the City Council opened three tourist offices on 16 May of this year: in the Plaza de Cataluña, in the Francia station and in the Prat airport. This was a good indicator of what this event meant for the tourism of this city (Palou, 2012, pp. 281–282). With the Avenida Palace, the objective was to attract this international travelling, cosmopolitan and wealthy clientele, once the European economy had began its recovery from the ravages caused by the Second World War and when the tourist flows had reactivated with relative force (HUSA, 2000, p. 54).

Also in 1952, HUSA carried out a capital increase worth two and a half million pesetas through the issue of 5,000 shares at 500 pesetas each. In this way, the social capital increased to 5 million pesetas. With José Soto Reguera as Chairman, Juan Hammerel as CEO and Baldomero Carbó (named in 1950) as Managing Director, HUSA embarked on a new phase characterised by a progressive expansion of its hotel business, which was reflected in the increase in social capital which reached ten million pesetas in 1954 through a further 10,000 shares (BRM, Sheet 599). In fact, during these years HUSA expanded beyond the peninsula, extending its business to the Canary Islands, an increasingly important tourist destination within the international panorama. It should be noted that a little after the end of the Civil War and with the bankruptcy of the production model of the islands before the war, in 1941, the new Franco authorities created the *Mando Económico de Canarias*, an organisation led by the Captain General of the Canary Islands and whose responsibilities included the promotion of tourism. In fact, 17 % of its budget was allocated to the construction and purchase of hotels and inns. Of the total 180 million pesetas invested by the *Mando Económico de Canarias*, almost 14 million were allocated to the construction of two luxury hotels (the Mencey in Tenerife and the Santa Catalina in Las Palmas in Gran Canaria), to the purchase of the old Hotel Taoro (Tenerife), the construction of the Parador of Fuerteventura, the opening of the Parador of Cruz de Tejada (Gran Canaria) and the purchase of land on which to construct the Parador of Santa Cruz in La Palma. That said, the *Mando Económico* ceased its activities in 1946, and the Island Councils became the owners of these infrastructures and handed over their exploitation to the private sector. HUSA knew how to take advantage of this opportunity in order to penetrate the Canary Island market. At the beginning of the 1950s, as well as taking over the Mencey, Santa Catalina and Taoro Hotels (Macías & Pérez, 2011, pp. 204–205), it also began to exploit the Gran Hotel Parque of Las Palmas in Gran Canaria (*Anuario Financiero de Bilbao*, 1951–1952, p. 987). Moreover, shortly afterwards it incorporated two hotels in Tangiers, El Minzah and the Rif (Central Archive of the Ministry of Finance, index 653, inscription 3.455-B), and another in Casablanca (1954), El Mansour (Central Archive of the Ministry of Finance, index 653, inscription 3.509-B) As we can see, in a few years the company expanded spectacularly beyond the peninsula, seeking to tap into the tourism potential of the Canary Islands and Northern Africa.

In the mid-1950s, significant changes took place at the heart of the company. In the Extraordinary General Shareholders Meeting held on 30 April 1954, the provisional naming of Ernesto Anastasio as Chairman and José Soto Burgos as Board Member were ratified (BRM, Sheet 599). The Board of Directors during the second half of the 1950s was formed by Ernesto Anastasio Pascual as Chairman, José Luis Bas Rivas as Vice-Chairman, the entrepreneur Juan Claudio Güell Churruca and banker Emilio Botín Sanz de Sautuola López as CEOs, José Soto Burgos as Board Member and Joaquín Chapaprieta Ornstein as Secretary. Only a few changes were made at the end of the decade. After the death of Juan Claudio Güell in 1958, Emilio Botín was the only CEO and Alfonso Güell Martos and Emilio Botín Sanz de Sautuola García de los Ríos entered as Board Members (*Anuario Financiero de Bilbao*, several years).

The expansion of HUSA's businesses obliged the company to raise more financial resources and in 1957 the insurance company La Unión y el Fénix Español granted it a loan for fifteen years for an amount of 14 million pesetas with an annual interest rate of 8.25 %. The following year, however, there was an increase in social capital of another five million pesetas through the issue of 10,000 bearer shares worth 500 pesetas each. In this way, the company's capital increased to 15 million pesetas. At the same time as this increase, the Board of Directors was authorised by the Extraordinary General Meeting of 9 May 1958 to be able to increase this capital to 22.5 million pesetas over the following five years, which suggests that the future plans of the company included further expansion, taking advantage of the good tourism data in Spain (BRM, Sheet 599). By 1960, HUSA had incorporated two new establishments, namely the Hotel Fénix in Madrid and the Hotel Zahira in Córdoba (*Anuario Financiero de Bilbao*, 1960, p. 521). The incorporation of the Hotel Fénix was particularly important because it was the first hotel of the company in the Spanish capital.

In this respect, we should not forget that Madrid was a strategic location for any hotel chain. In this way, HUSA covered an important gap in its geographical development.

On the other hand, in 1959, HUSA took out a new loan for 3,640,000 pesetas from the Banco de Crédito Industrial to cover the investments that it needed to make to modernise the facilities of the Hotel Miramar of Málaga. The loan finalised on 30 June 1969 and the repayments were to be made in ten yearly amounts (1960–1969). The bank established an annual interest rate of 4 % and an annual commission of an eighth of the total amount (BRM, Sheet 599). Moreover, on 1 October 1959, Joaquín Chapaprieta was authorised by the Board of Directors to increase the capital to 17,500,000 pesetas. At the end of this year, HUSA had the following hotels: Carlton in Bilbao, Felipe II in El Escorial, Alhambra Palace in Granada, Miramar in Málaga, Madrid in Seville, Zahira in Córdoba, Mencey in Santa Cruz de Tenerife, Parque and Santa Catalina in Las Palmas, Taoro in Tenerife and Fénix in Madrid.

As for LIHSA, José Gaspart Bulbena remained at the helm of the company as CEO until his death on 17 August 1961, while his son Juan Gaspart Bonet was Chairman for all of these years. This company also expanded over the years which was manifested both in the successive capital increases (up to seven and a half million pesetas in the mid-1950s) and in the incorporation of new hotels. In 1951, it exploited the Hotel Victoria in Palma de Mallorca, although by the mid-1950s this establishment no longer formed part of LIHSA's hotel portfolio (*Anuario Financiero de Bilbao*, 1955–1956, p. 731). A few years later it acquired the Hostal Roger de Flor in Lloret de Mar, considered as the best establishment in the southern part of the Costa del Sol. As we have already seen, the company had been managing for some time, also in the Costa Brava, the Hostal La Gavina, through which it increased its commitment to quality beach tourism (HUSA, 2000, 69; *Anuario Financiero de Bilbao*, 1960, p. 522)

6 Conclusions

HUSA was not the first private hotel chain to be created in Spain, but it was the most important Spanish hotel chain during the historical period of this study. Established in Catalonia, a few years after the Spanish Civil War it transferred its headquarters to Madrid. New managers entered the company and were able to expand the company's business as the tourist flows increased and Spain became a relevant tourist destination. In parallel, the Catalan business remained in the hands of LIHSA, a company controlled by the Gaspart family, founders of HUSA in 1930, but who, in the mid-1940s, decided to create this company that was independent of HUSA although closely linked to it. In the same way as HUSA, LIHSA also benefited from the expansion of the hotel industry in Spain from the end of the 1940s.

7 Sources

Business Register of Madrid
Central Archive of the Ministry of Finance
National Historical Archive

References

Baedeker, K. (1898). *Spain and Portugal. Handbook for travellers.* Leipzig: Karl Baedeker Publisher.

Baedeker, K. (1900). *Espagne et Portugal. Manuel du voyageur.* Leipzig: Karl Baedeker Publisher.

Blasco, A. (2005). *Barcelona Atracción (1910–1936).* Universitat Pompeu Fabra, Barcelona, Spain. Drawn from: https://www.tdx.cat/bitstream/handle/10803/7465/tabp.pdf?sequence=1&isAllowed=y. Accessed on September 1, 2020.

Bolín, L. (1967). *España. Los años vitales.* Madrid: Espasa-Calpe.

Carreras, A. & Tafunell, X. (2004). *Historia económica de la España contemporánea.* Barcelona: Crítica.

Elston, R. (1930). *Cook's Traveller's handbook to Spain and Portugal.* London: Simpkins Marshall, Ltd.

Fernández Casado, A. (2018). *Hospitales de sangre o cuarteles.* Madrid: Editorial la Cátedra.

HUSA (2000). *Grupo HUSA, 70 años, 1930–2000.* Barcelona: HUSA.

Larrinaga, C. 2018. La hotelería turística y las primeras cadenas hoteleras en la España del primer tercio del siglo XX. In R. Vallejo & C. Larrinaga (Eds.), *Los orígenes del turismo moderno en España. El nacimiento de un país turístico, 1900–1939* (pp. 679–722). Madrid: Sílex.

Larrinaga, C. (2019a). La hotelería turística de lujo en España en el primer tercio del siglo XX. *Ayer* (114), 65–94.

Larrinaga, C. (2019b). El impacto de la Guerra Civil en el sector turístico. In M. Fernández-Paradas & C. Larrinaga (Eds.), *El impacto de la Guerra Civil española en el sector terciario* (pp. 153–172). Granada: Comares.

Larrinaga, C. & Vallejo, R. (2021). The origins and creation of the tourist hotel industry in Spain from the end of the 19th century to 1936. Barcelona as a case study. *Tourism Management.* https://www.sciencedirect.com/science/article/pii/S0261517720301291.

Macías, A. & Pérez, C. (2011). El turismo en la historia económica de Canarias. In C. Barciela & al. (Eds.), *La evolución de la industria turística en España e Italia* (pp. 179–231). Palma: Institut Balear d'Economia.

Martínez Díaz, F. (1992). *Hotel Oriente*. Barcelona: Labor.

Moreno, A. (2007). *Historia del turismo en España en el siglo XX*. Madrid: Síntesis.

Moreno, A. (2015). Madrid, 1912. El reto del turismo. *Cuadernos de Historia Contemporánea*, 37, 23–44.

Norval, A. J. (1936). *The tourist industry.* London: Sir Isaac Pitman & Sons.

Ogilvie, F. W. (1933). *The tourist movement.* London: P. S. King.

Palou, S. (2012). *Barcelona, destinació turística*. Bellcaire d'Empordà: Vitel.la.

Rosselló, M. & Valdívia, P. (2016). Els primers establiments hotelers. In S. Palou (Ed.), *Història del turisme a la ciutat de Barcelona* (pp. 48–67). Barcelona: Efadós & Ajuntament de Barcelona.

Tena, A, (2005). Sector exterior. In A. Carreras & X. Tafunell (Eds.), *Estadísticas históricas de España*, vol. 2 (pp. 573–644). Bilbao: Fundación BBVA.

Vallejo, R. (2018). La formación de un sistema turístico nacional con diferentes desarrollos regionales entre 1900 y 1939. In R. Vallejo, and C. Larrinaga (Eds.), *Los orígenes del turismo moderno en España. El nacimiento de un país turístico, 1900–1939* (pp. 67–170). Madrid: Sílex.

About the authors

Alonso Villa, Pablo is Associate Professor at the University of Valladolid. He holds a degree in Economics, a master's degree in Economics Research and a PhD in Economics from this University. He made a research stay at the Institute of Social Sciences of the University of Lisbon. He has published numerous articles in indexed journals and a book chapter. His research focuses on the industrial history of Castilla y León and especially in the metallurgical sector and its connections with the automobile industry.

https://orcid.org/0000-0001-5363-3600

Caruana de las Cagigas, Leonardo is Tenure at the University of Granada (Spain). His research is on insurance and reinsurance history. Has published *From Mutual to Multinational, Mapfre, 1933–2008* with G. Tortella and J. L. García Ruiz. About the internationalization of the Spanish Insurance the case of Mapfre in ICE with J. L. García Ruiz. Also, the *History of Spanish Insurance* with G. Tortella, A. Manzano, J. Pons and J. L. García Ruiz. About Corporate Forms has published in Oxford University Press. Recently has published with André Straus (eds.) *Highlights on Reinsurance History* (Peter Lang, 2017). Also did research on economic warfare with H. Rockoff and publish in the *Journal of Economic History* and in the *European Review of Economic History*.

http://orcid.org/0000-0003-4707-7323

Castro-Valdivia, Mariano teach Economic History at the University of Jaén. Degree from the University of Valencia. Doctor from the University of Jaen. Participant and coordinator of several teaching innovation projects at the Universidad de Jaén. He develops two lines of research. The first analyses the teaching of Economics at the Spanish University and the dissemination of classical economic thought, while the second studies the provision and management of public water, electricity and gas services, of which several works have been published.

https://orcid.org/0000-0002-9331-9955

Fernández-Paradas, Mercedes is a Doctor and Head Professor of Contemporary History at the University of Malaga. She specializes in Economic History and public services, especially business history, gas and electricity. She is principal researcher of the Research and Innovation Project of Excellence of the Government of Spain *La industria del gas en España: desarrollo y trayectorias regionales* (1842–2008). She has carried out several research stays, including at the London School of Economics and Political Science. She has won several awards, including the Extraordinary Doctorate Award in Philosophy and Arts for the History Department of the University of Malaga.

https://orcid.org/0000-0002-3049-0907

Lafuente del Cano, Jorge is Lecturer in Economic History at University of Valladolid. He holds a degree in History, a degree in Journalism and a PhD in History. He made a research stay in the University of Oxford and also in the University of Roma-La Sapienza. He is a member of "Studies on Economic History" Research Group and a member of "Studies on Recent History" Research Group as well. Dr. Lafuente has published two books and numerous articles on entrepreneurship, economic history of Spanish Transition to democracy, negotiations for Spain's entry into the European Economic Community and the figure of former Spanish prime minister, Leopoldo Calvo-Sotelo.

http://orcid.org/0000-0001-5850-8171

Larrinaga, Carlos is Associate Professor of Economic History at the University of Granada (Andalusia, Spain). His research is in the history of tourism, railways in the 19th century and the service sector. He is currently leading an interdisciplinary project on the history of tourism in Spain and Italy in the 20th century, funded by the Spanish Ministry of Science, Innovation and Universities and the European FEDER funds. He has undertaken research in several stays at Bordeaux University and at Aberystwyth University.

http://orcid.org/0000-0001-7053-5877

Martínez-López, Alberte is Professor of Economic History at the University of A Coruña (Spain). He has been a Visiting fellow in several European and American universities. His main recent research fields are utilities (gas, electricity, transport, water) and foreign investment in utilities. He has published several articles and books about these subjects in Spanish and international journals, for example "The gas companies in Spain, a long-run approach (1842–2018)", *Business History*, with Mercedes Fernández-Paradas and Jesús Mirás Araujo.

http://orcid.org/0000-0001-7267-386X

Matés-Barco, Juan Manuel is Professor of Economic History at the University of Jaen. Bachelor of the University of Zaragoza. Doctor from the University of Granada. He has made stays at the Università degli Studi di Firenze, at the European University Institute (Italy) and at the Université Michel de Montaigne Bordeaux 3. Member of the Group of Historical Studies on the Company. Researcher of the Permanent Seminar Water, Territory and Environment. It is part of the Editorial Board of the Journal *TST*. He is director of the Journal *Agua y Territorio*, co-edited by the School of Hispanic-American Studies of Seville-CSIC and the University of Jaen. His research is focused on the public water supply service and has published studies on the economy of contemporary Spain.

https://orcid.org/0000-0002-9302-4209

Mirás Araujo, Jesús is Associate Professor of Economic History at the University of A Coruña. His research deals with urban history, business history and public utilities (gas, electricity, water, transport). He has published in journals such as *Business History, Continuity and Change, Journal of Urban History, Urban History* . . .., and in publishers such as Routledge, Marcial Pons, Sílex, etc.

http://orcid.org/ 0000-0003-3049-1106

Muñoz Rubio, Miguel (PhD in History) has specialized in railway history, having researched widely on the Spanish railways. He was director of the Railway History Archive and the National Railway Museum and professor of Economic History for ten years at the Madrid Autonomous University. He has published more than fifty books and papers, and was founder and editor of the Journal *TST* between 2001–2009 and 2013–2015. He also was a member of the High Commission for Administrative Documentation Rating of the Spanish Government; vice chairman of the International Association for Railway History (IRHA); curator of several exhibitions; and secretary of the VIII International Congress of the International Committee for the Conservation of the Industrial Heritage (1992).

https://orcid.org/0000-0001-9726-910X

Núñez Romero-Balmas, Gregorio (PhD. in History) is Professor of History and Economic Institutions at the University of Granada. He has carried out various research stays at foreign universities and has been a visiting professor at the

European University Institute of Florence (Italy). His research has focused on the Spanish electricity industry and urban service companies. He has collaborated in various research projects and is currently working on the development of analysis on the Spanish business demography in the first third of the 20th century.

http://orcid.org/0000-0003-1793-5817

Ortúñez-Goicolea, Pedro Pablo (Ph.D., University of Valladolid, 1999) is Senior Lecturer in Economic History at the University of Valladolid (Spain). His research interests include the Spanish railway system and the public sector before nationalization of the railway; regulation and business history. He has published his research in books (on editorials of first quartile like Oxford University Press, Ariel, Pirámide, Comares) and specialized journals (indexed in JCR or Scopus) and has participated in conferences in these fields. He has undertaken research in several stays at the London School of Economics and at the École des Hautes Etudes en Sciences Sociales (Paris).

https://orcid.org/0000-0001-6730-6248

Rodríguez-Martín, Nuria is a Lecturer in Contemporary History at the Complutense University of Madrid (Spain). She earned her PhD. in History from the Complutense University in 2013, with a dissertation on the social changes in Madrid during the 20s and 30s, which received the Distinguished Doctoral Dissertation Award from the Spanish Association of Contemporary History. She is the author of *La capital de un sueño. Madrid en el primer tercio del siglo XX* (CEPC, 2015), awarded as Best Book in Art and Humanities at the 19th Spanish University Presses Prizes. Her research is concerned with the history of urban infrastructures and public services.

http://orcid.org/0000-0003-0179-7392

Vargas-Machuca Salido, María José (Degree in Economics and Business Administration) is Professor of the Department of Economics at the University of Jaen, where she teaches the subjects of Spanish Financial System and World Economy. It belongs to various research groups and teams related to her area of knowledge. Her research has focused on the history of the financial system, especially at the local level. She has published several articles in specialized journals on this topic. Her doctoral thesis deals with "La Caja Rural de Jaen. 60 years at the service of the province of Jaen."

http://orcid.org/0000-0002-9941-032X

Vázquez-Fariñas, María teach Economic (Department of Economics) at Jaen's University. Doctor in Social and Legal Sciences at Cadiz's University. She has been actively involved as a component of the Esteban Boutelou Historical Studies Research Group, and Lean Management of Production and Hyperconnected Universal Integrated Logistics Research Group, at Cadiz's University. Her lines of research focus on the Economic and Business History of Cadiz in the 19th century, the wine industry of the region and the development of commerce and the port of Cadiz between the mid-nineteenth and mid-20th centuries. She has published several works.

http://orcid.org/0000-0003-2387-0554

www.ingramcontent.com/pod-product-compliance
Ingram Content Group UK Ltd.
Pitfield, Milton Keynes, MK11 3LW, UK
UKHW041827100926
8556IPUK00002B/64

9 783631 843857